*Wordsworth's "Natural Methodism"*

RICHARD E. BRANTLEY *WORDSWORTH'S*

*"NATURAL*

*METHODISM"*

NEW HAVEN AND LONDON
YALE UNIVERSITY PRESS
1975

Library of Congress catalog card number: 74-20078
International standard book number: 0-300-01834-7

Designed by Sally Sullivan
and set in Baskerville type.
Printed in the United States of America by
Vail-Ballou Press, Inc., Binghamton, N.Y.

Published in Great Britain, Europe, and Africa by
Yale University Press, Ltd., London.
Distributed in Latin America by Kaiman & Polon,
Inc., New York City; in Australasia and Southeast
Asia by John Wiley & Sons Australasia Pty. Ltd.,
Sydney; in India by UBS Publishers' Distributors Pvt.,
Ltd., Delhi; in Japan by John Weatherhill, Inc., Tokyo.

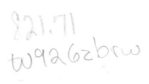

## For Diana

*We from to-day, my Friend, will date*
*The opening of the year.*

# CONTENTS

# PREFACE

At least since 1876, when Leslie Stephen's essay on "Wordsworth's Ethics" appeared in *Cornhill Magazine,* most studies of Wordsworth's thought—or of what Melvin Rader has called the "presiding ideas" underlying his poetry—have concentrated on the several and sometimes conflicting senses in which his poetry can be considered philosophic. Since 1922, with the appearance of Arthur Beatty's *William Wordsworth: His Doctrine and Art in their Historical Relations,* we have never doubted the poet's grasp of English Associationism nor his effective exploitation of empiricist language for poetic purposes. But within the confines of this scholarly "given" we have entertained widely differing points of view; we have argued, shifting the philosophic focus from ethics to metaphysics, that Wordsworth transcendentalized Locke and Hartley, and even that in his ontology he was at once materialist and transcendentalist. And we have also focused, perhaps most sharply, on epistemology and hence on Wordsworth as a kind of verbal alchemist who combined elements of tension, paradox, conflict, and "both/and" logic, to express in his poetry a precariously balanced formula: a rich but strange and tenuous coalescence of subject and object.

This near-century of philosophic inquiry has helped to counter the naïve assumption that Wordsworth's vision was so spontaneous as to be culturally uninformed; the distinguishing ideas of any major writer, and certainly one who so well knew the philosophic Coleridge, relate to (even when they do not derive from) the various traditional branches of philosophy. Throughout the following study I have acknowledged the philosophic mode of criticism—particularly the epistemological emphasis in many, if not most, twentieth-century studies of Wordsworth. But I have been primarily concerned to set a theological method of inquiry alongside the philosophic one, and indeed to emphasize that method.

For I have chosen not merely to effect a return to Stephen's emphasis on Wordsworth's ethics but even to change, or at least to challenge, the predominant interdisciplinary approach and to explore the historical senses in which Wordsworth can be called a definably moral and religious poet. These senses reveal an unproblematical (though not unprofound) figure whose complexity was more the result of deeply informed convictions than of the unresolved inner conflicts and the propensity for paradox characteristic of epistemological sophistication. And we can entertain, in advance of fuller correlations and reconciliations of the two approaches, a tentative conclusion: that the common ground of eighteenth-century British philosophy and late eighteenth- and early nineteenth-century British theology, insofar as these disciplines at an important moment in their historical development nourished Wordsworth's mind and poetry, is the perennially blossoming British reliance on observation and experience as the best means of knowing what is true scientifically and metaphysically, temporally and spiritually.

The poetry of Wordsworth is saturated with religious language, and though he indicated as much when he described *The Recluse* as an antechapel and his lesser works as smaller chapels and oratories, Wordsworthians have paid little more than lip service to the avowedly religious conception underlying his work. I have therefore had to establish what has not been sufficiently recognized: Wordsworth's close relation to Evangelical Anglicanism and Evangelical Nonconformism. In my exploration of the religious background to his life and thought, and in my application of this background to his poetry, I have been careful (sometimes at the risk of overstating the case) to suggest a new direction for Wordsworth scholarship and to gloss not only the religious vocabulary but whole structures of his described experience.

In establishing the extent of Wesleyan Methodism in his heritage and in tracing lines of specific influence, the introduction and chapter 1 counter the widely held view, stemming in part from *The Prelude,* that Wordsworth came to maturity innocent of all cultural impressions, disciplined and formed only through experiences of beauty and fear. Chapter 2 argues that the appropriate frame for understanding Wordsworth's spiritual journey is Evangelical rather than psychological, and that the imagery and structures of his poetry participate in, and draw significance from, biblical and more broadly Evangelical sources. Chapter 3 establishes the interpretive relevance to Wordsworth's poetry of the Methodist and Evangelical structure of New Birth leading, through a period of reciprocal covenant between spiritual pilgrim and Holy Spirit, to spiritual perfection. And chapter 4, which is primarily theoretical, examines the parallels between representative poems from all periods of Wordsworth's career and the Evangelical emphasis upon the emblematic and typological reading of the Book of Nature, an emphasis compatible with Thomas Burnet's famous fascination with the religious sublime, but including lowlier or more straightforwardly didactic elements.

My general argument—that the most distinctive features of Wordsworth's literary practice can best be understood in terms of his pervasive Evangelical idiom—goes contrary to a whole tradition of literary history which argues that his poetry and Romanticism generally are distinguished from earlier poetry by virtue of the originality and subjectivity of their language, form, and vision; and so my intention, in part, has been to temper the tendency to see Wordsworth in a secular and empiricist Germano-Coleridgean context, as a poet whose constant concern was either to fuse outer and inner worlds through the creative imagination and thus to carry on the dialectic of mind and nature, or to displace theological ideas into naturalistic and humanistic contexts.

Often the method has been to bring together similar kinds of evidence from all phases of Wordsworth's career in order to show the essential integrity of his lifetime of deep religious thought; the study of the Evangelical ideas underlying his poetry provides us with the basis for a synoptic criticism that sees him

steadily and sees him whole. An exhaustive explication of his
numerous works is beyond the scope of this work. Thus, while
it has been feasible to suggest terms of appreciation for many
unfamiliar poems and to offer fresh readings of familiar ones
such as "Lines Composed a Few Miles above Tintern Abbey,"
"Resolution and Independence," "Ode to Duty," and "The
Brothers," *The Prelude* and *The Excursion* receive the bulk of
critical attention; they are Wordsworth's most ambitious works
and the richest revelations of his Christian vision.

My debts are legion, and I am happy to acknowledge as many
as I can. Parts of this book were written with the aid of grants
from the University of Florida Humanities Council and the
American Philosophical Society during the summers of 1970
and 1972. Librarians at the British Museum and the University
of Florida have been invariably helpful; I would like especially
to thank J. Ray Jones of the University of Florida Graduate Re-
search Library. A portion of chapter 2, and scattered sentences
in chapter 4, have appeared in the Autumn 1974 issue of *Studies
in English Literature;* I wish to express my thanks for permission
to use that material here.

To all of my friends and colleagues—too numerous to be
named in this space—who have offered a great variety of pro-
fessional advice and moral support, I express my particular
thanks; I am fortunate that their generosity has contributed so
greatly to my efforts over the past six years. It is a pleasure to
acknowledge a profound debt to all my teachers, and I especially
want to mention four: at Wake Forest University John A. Carter
and Judson B. Allen introduced me to the historical method of
criticism and all its satisfactions; Edwin G. Wilson of Wake
Forest introduced me to the English Romantic poets and taught
me to read Wordworth's poetry and his biography; Carlos H.
Baker of Princeton University guided this study in its earliest
stages and first encouraged me to think that it might someday be
a book; and all four of these dedicated professors imparted their
friendship as well as their knowledge.

Among my many helpful colleagues at the University of Flor-
ida I gladly give my very deepest thanks to four in particular: to

Melvyn New for challenging and inspiring me with his strong example of discipline and fervor; to Aubrey L. Williams for believing in, and impelling me to express, an argument only dimly implicit in the manuscript he read; to T. Walter Herbert for sharing his knowledge of the Evangelical Movement and for rigorously appraising my work and correcting its errors; to Alistair M. Duckworth for sharing his knowledge of Romantic philosophy and literature and for reading and commenting on the final draft of this study; and to all four of these academic pilgrims for extending almost daily, on the heights and in the valleys, their interest and concern.

To my wife Diana I dedicate the book; she well knows, because she shared in, the rewards and punishments of writing it. And to my parents and their steadfast faith and support, I gratefully acknowledge my oldest indebtedness.

*Gainesville, Florida* R. E. B.
*August 1974*

# ABBREVIATIONS

EY      *The Letters of William and Dorothy Wordsworth: The Early Years, 1787–1805.* Ed. Ernest de Selincourt. 2d ed. rev. by Chester L. Shaver. Oxford: Clarendon Press, 1967.

*Lives*      *The Lives of Early Methodist Preachers.* Ed. Thomas Jackson. 2d ed. 3 vols. London: Mason, 1846.

LY      *The Letters of William and Dorothy Wordsworth: The Later Years.* Ed. Ernest de Selincourt. 3 vols. Oxford: Clarendon Press, 1939.

MY      *The Letters of William and Dorothy Wordsworth: The Middle Years.* Ed. Ernest de Selincourt. 2 vols. Oxford: Clarendon Press, 1937.

*Prelude*      William Wordsworth. *The Prelude: or, Growth of a Poet's Mind.* Ed. Ernest de Selincourt. 2d ed. rev. by Helen Darbishire. Oxford: Clarendon Press, 1959. Unless otherwise indicated, quotations are from the text of 1805–06.

PW      *The Poetical Works of William Wordsworth.* Ed. Ernest de Selincourt and Helen Darbishire. 5 vols. Oxford: Clarendon Press, 1940–49. 2d ed. of vols. 2 (1952) and 3 (1954) rev. by Helen Darbishire.

Sugden      *Wesley's Standard Sermons.* Ed. Edward H. Sugden. 2 vols. London: Epworth Press, 1921.

Watts    *The Works of the Reverend and Learned Isaac Watts,*
         *D. D. Containing, Besides His Sermons, and Essays on*
         *Miscellaneous Subjects, Several Additional Pieces, Se-*
         *lected from his Manuscripts by the Rev. Dr. Jennings,*
         *and the Rev. Dr. Doddridge, in 1753: to which are*
         *Prefixed, Memoirs of the Life of the Author, Compiled*
         *by the Rev. George Burder.* 6 vols. London: Barfield,
         1810–11.

Wesley   *The Works of the Rev. John Wesley, A. M.* Ed.
         Thomas Jackson. 14 vols. 3d ed., 1831; rpt. London:
         Wesleyan Methodist Book Room, 1872.

*WORDSWORTH AND*
*EVANGELICAL*
*ANGLICANISM*

This study presents biographical and poetical evidence for William Wordsworth's indebtedness to Evangelical Anglicanism, the most vital manifestation of the Christian mainstream in late eighteenth- and early nineteenth-century England.[1] As a young man Wordsworth imbibed the attitudes of Evangelical Anglicans (and indeed of Evangelical Nonconformists) toward such timely issues as political liberty, public education, church order, and practical charity; and his poetry, throughout his career, not only reflects his religious temperament in all its contemporaneity but, more importantly, preserves the Evangelical emphasis upon the twin Christian traditions of spiritual and natural theology.

I swim against a strong current of fashion, but I am not entirely alone. Lane Cooper, compiler of the Concordance to Wordsworth's poetry, and hence a Wordsworthian steeped in all characteristics of the poet's language, has declared that he was in "the main stream of European poetry, which in England, from the beginnings down, has been Christian." [2] Many students of the Romantic period, choosing to stress how it anticipates the twentieth century, argue that Wordsworth (like the other Romantics) helped to begin the modern religious skepticism; [3] and this viewpoint has often led us to overlook the theological con-

tent of the earlier poetry and to be triumphantly impatient with
it in the later (one scholar forbears to quote the "theological ef-
fusions" of *The Excursion* [1814] "in deference to the modern
reader").[4]

Readers hoping to understand Wordsworth as fully as possible
may profit from exploring the merits of Professor Cooper's
judgment. The appropriate method of investigation is reflected,
ironically enough, in Saul Bellow's character Herzog, whose
*Romanticism and Christianity* "showed by objective research
what Christianity was to Romanticism"; Herzog continued to
think, long after writing his book, that Romanticism had pre-
served the "religious teachings . . . of mankind, during the great-
est and most rapid of transformations."[5] The evidence, I think,
clearly shows that at least one of the great Romantics did guard
the vitality and did cherish the profundity of the most venerable
religious teachings, and that he did so at a skeptical time that
tried the souls of religious men and challenged the epistemologies
of thoughtful men who, like himself, sought spiritual nourish-
ment and reached for valid philosophical concepts. Moreover, the
evidence calls into question two of the most widespread modern
views: that Wordsworth attempted to substitute for Locke's de-
mythologized universe a nature-myth entirely of his own crea-
tion, and that he secularized inherited theological concepts.[6]

We shall focus, then, on a neglected subject: Wordsworth's
religious thought as it parallels that of his age and as it deeply
affects his writing—his themes, symbols, structure, tone, irony,
characterization, and narrative patterns. We cannot fully enter
into the spirit of his poems without realizing that he endeavored
to *re*mythologize his Christian heritage and that he thus partici-
pated, as did the Evangelicals, in the revival and not the seculari-
zation or rejection of Christian myth and morality (for which he
never found and seldom sought a substitute). We shall see that
the Evangelical element of his early milieu lies behind many of
the most distinctive features of his literary practice.

We shall observe, for example, how the Great Awakening with
its indulgence in confessional introspection, its aspiration to ex-
emplary conduct, its reliance on amazing grace, and its close
reading of God's Word and works in their spiritual sense, pro-

vides the strictest analogues for his fear of solipsism, his yearn-
ing for self-mastery, his high moral tone, his quest for guidance,
his experience of renewal, and his discernment of spiritual mean-
ing in the objects of nature. Aware of these historical glosses
upon his own idiom and point of view, we can acknowledge the
fundamentally religious vision of the poems themselves; and
seeing that they are not "secular"—that they uphold a morality
grounded in faith—we can begin to redefine the sense in which
he was indeed among the first "modern" poets; for we should
measure his modernity, and test its asserted secularity, in the
light of his deepest personal convictions and their immediate
theological context.

　　Soon after publication of *Lyrical Ballads* (1798), Wordsworth
sent a complimentary copy to the Evangelical Anglican reformer
William Wilberforce, with a lengthy covering letter in which he
praised Wilberforce's *A Practical View of the Prevailing Reli-
gious System of Professed Christians . . . Contrasted with Real
Christianity* (1798), and claimed to be "a Fellow-labourer with
you in the same Vineyard" (*EY*, pp. 684–85). Eleven years later,
as a "labourer" skilled in the complexities of English ecclesiology,
he reaffirmed his choice of vineyards and his admiration for its
workers: "with the Methodists on one side, and the Catholics on
the other, what is to become of the poor Church and people of
England, to both of which I am most tenderly attached?" (*MY*,
1 : 291).
　　Wordsworth felt a warm spiritual kinship with his fellow
Anglicans and their most famous Evangelical leader at the turn
of the century. Thus he indicated that he held to the established
point of view even as he recognized and reflected the new reli-
gious spirit (he affiliated with Evangelicalism without qualifying
his allegiance to Anglicanism): he shared the Anglican lack of
sympathy with the Methodist and Catholic civil positions (he
thought his vineyard rightfully occupied the vast middle ground);
and like the "first" Evangelical John Wesley, whose lifelong
loyalty to the Anglican Church helped keep his Methodist so-
cieties from leaving it until after his death in 1791, and undoubt-
edly like his contemporary Wilberforce, whose leadership in the

Great Awakening coexisted with his fidelity to the ritual and doctrine of an ancient Church, he feared threats to the Anglican position. His conservative ecclesiology was fully consistent with a spirit of vitality that originated at the center of English church organization.

His ecclesiological question concerning Methodists and Catholics appears in a letter to the Reverend Francis Wrangham, an Evangelical Anglican who patterned his theology after that of the Congregationalist Philip Doddridge, an early exemplar of the Evangelical spirit; [7] and the letter, addressing problems of church organization, examines several other religious topics and reflects in particular the Evangelical emphasis on an active, conscientious ministry (Wordsworth praises Wrangham's sense of his "appropriate duties as a parish priest"). Hence the context of the question suggests a sympathy, if not with the civil position of the two extremes, then with the moderate kind of Evangelical zeal to be found, not just in Anglicanism from about 1740 to 1840, but in eighteenth-century British Methodism (and Nonconformity) and nineteenth-century British Catholicism.

In 1842, near the end of Wordsworth's spiritual labor (and well after that of Wesley, Wilberforce, and Wrangham), Crabb Robinson described him as a "high churchman" who respected the new Oxford Movement not only for "inspiring the age with deeper reverence for antiquity and a more cordial conformity with ritual observances" but also for encouraging "a warmer piety." [8] The first phrase reflects the Anglican or even Catholic nature of his faith, while the second accords with Evangelical fervency; Wordsworth favored both tradition and personal zeal and thus retained two important marks of Evangelical Anglicanism. The faith he shared with Wilberforce and Wrangham predisposed him to sympathy with this nineteenth-century Anglo-Catholic renewal, the Oxford Movement, which, as G. R. Balleine and Horton Davies have shown, included Evangelical Anglicans among its allies. [9]

That movement, as they have also shown, was in fact the direct descendant of Wesley's revival; it is therefore possible to conjecture that the poet's lifelong blend of traditional faith and personal fervor, nourished by his early admiration for both Wilber-

force and Wrangham, and reaffirmed in his later endorsement of
the Oxford Movement, originated at or near the zealous but
learned source of the revival itself. We have no record that
Wordsworth heard Wesley, but five times during his boyhood
at Cockermouth (1770–78), and eighteen times during a thirty-
three-year period (1751–84), Wesley preached to the townspeople
there—upper as well as lower classes, indoors as well as in the
marketplace.[10] And in any case, we can begin our examination of
Wordsworth and the Evangelical Movement by focusing upon
the inescapable mind, personality, and influence in that movement
—a man whose deep private thought and lucid public theology
have considerable literary merit and therefore accord with, and
should therefore enhance, our study of how Evangelical theology
affected an important religious poet.

Wesley was peculiarly suited by birth to start the revival that
effectively retouched the various colorations of doctrine to be
found throughout the disparate kinds of English church organi-
zation.[11] Samuel Wesley, his father, was an Anglican vicar; his
mother Susanna was the daughter of the famous Presbyterian
divine, Samuel Annesley of London; and he was therefore in a
position to know at first hand about the English varieties of
doctrine and organization at the beginning of his century, a time
when the Anglicans and the Dissenters (Congregationalists, Bap-
tists, and Presbyterians) went their separate ways for the most
part, afraid of reopening the wounds of the seventeenth-century
civil war.

Nurtured in both traditions, Wesley venerated the Anglican
liturgy and sacraments, and at the same time responded to the
covenant organization of Nonconformist ecclesiology. As a true
son of the Puritans, he may well have considered himself—as
Susanna thought him—a "brand snatched from the burning" or
member of the Elect; yet he often expressed his Anglican fear of
the excesses of enthusiasm. Among the guiding lights of his
spiritual life were not only the seventeenth-century bishop Jeremy
Taylor, but also the eighteenth-century Congregationalist Isaac
Watts, whose hymns and theology Wesley helped to popularize.[12]

Thus he was equipped to reconcile potentially opposing tradi-
tions; Wesley was "unique," says Horton Davies, "in being the

bridge that crossed the chasm between . . . Anglicanism and Dissent" (*Worship and Theology in England,* p. 184). He seemed destined to remind England that her two religious heritages are not mutually exclusive, that the Calvinism appropriated by the Puritans and their Nonconformist descendants can also be found in Archbishop Cranmer's *Book of Common Prayer,* and, moreover, that the Augustinianism preserved in Anglican theology nurtured the thought of the well-educated Evangelical—Dissenter and Anglican alike.

The effects of his ministry were astonishing. Without agreeing completely with Davies that at the beginning of the century "both the Anglicans and the Nonconformists supinely accepted their inheritance, rather than entered into and possessed their heritages" (p. 19), we can say with confidence that both Dissent (including the radical Quakers) and Anglicanism (including the Highest Churchmen) had undergone considerable changes by the end of that century; and the greater Evangelical Movement, for which Wesley deserves much credit, effected the change. Evangelical Methodism might be said to have begun in 1738, when Wesley's heart was "strangely warmed" in Aldersgate Street, and Evangelical Anglicanism in 1742 or 1748, with the conversion of William Grimshaw or the appointment of William Romaine as Lecturer at St. Dunstan's in the West, London.[13] It has been estimated that when Wesley died, there were nearly one million adherents to Methodism (to say nothing of Evangelical Anglicans) in England and America, with more than half of these in England. Henry Bett's claim for the revival, therefore, does not seem extravagant: "All this had been accomplished in half a century. Never since the apostolic age had there been an evangelistic campaign so rapid, so continuous, so widespread, and so immense in its results." [14]

If Dissent had been somewhat complacent in the early years of the century compared with its zealous Puritan beginnings, the Evangelical spirit soon renewed that zeal. For example, Philip Doddridge, the Independent (or Congregational) minister, took to heart the lament of his Presbyterian friend John Barker, that among Dissenters "evangelical truth and duty are quite old fashioned things." [15] In 1742 Doddridge published the first of many editions of *The Rise and Progress of Religion in the Soul,* regarded by Davies as the prose analogue to Charles Wesley's hymns in its attempt to "meet the needs and psychological moods of Christians in many conditions and circumstances" (p. 202); and Doddridge's faith in religious education, a faith embodied in his school at Harborough, influenced Wesley's experiment at the Kingswood school.[16] A spirit of common endeavor grew as the century passed, until it included even the most radical sects. Wesley, for example, came to feel a kinship with the Quakers and rejoiced over the evangelistic labors of such Cambridge ministers as Robert Robinson, the popular Baptist preacher there during Wordsworth's matriculation.[17]

It is sometimes suggested that Evangelicalism, thus binding together differing religious persuasions, helped to mold the character of the British people, who gradually showed a new humanitarian spirit—or, more precisely, a practical charity—that bore no small part in doubling the population during the century.[18] An awareness of the sociological as well as religious importance of the phenomenon may have led T. B. Macaulay to be impatient with earlier historians of the eighteenth century for their failure to discuss the Evangelical revival.[19]

Its importance has never again been ignored. In the late nineteenth century, for example, W. E. H. Lecky observed that Wesley's conversion "meant more for Britain than all the victories of Pitt by land and sea," and more recently we have learned to accord Wesley the kind of praise sung by Augustine Birrell: "No single figure influenced so many minds, no single voice touched so many hearts, no other man did such a work for England." [20] And though historians took almost a hundred years to speak of the Great Awakening, its significance and the stature of its leaders were recognized from the beginning: the Deist Lord Bolingbroke called George Whitefield "the most extraordinary man in our times" out of genuine admiration for his piety; George III actively supported the burgeoning Sunday school movement; and Dr. Johnson, monarch of literary London, not only admired Wesley but espoused the kind of earnest faith that led his first modern editor, Birkbeck Hill, to conclude: "In his personal religion Johnson was, in the best sense, a Methodist." [21]

The next literary men to respond to the revival were the first-generation Romantics, whose formative years were passed during the period when Wesley was still active and Evangelical faith in the flush of increasing vigor. When we understand how widespread was the sense of a neoapostolic age, it is not surprising that Coleridge, sometime Unitarian and always the theologian, respected Wesley's leadership and even wrote in his copy of Robert Southey's *Life of Wesley* (a work in Wordsworth's library too) that Arminian Methodism "has been the occasion, and even the cause, of turning thousands from their evil deeds, and . . . has made . . . bad and mischievous men peaceable and profitable neighbors and citizens." [22]

On the basis of both favorable and hostile reaction to *The Excursion,* we can ask whether Wordsworth himself consciously permitted the Methodists in particular, as well as the Evangelicals in general, to affect his literary practice: Charles Lamb praised the "natural methodism" in the poem, and Francis, Lord Jeffrey, in his notorious review, explicitly denounced Wordsworth's "mystical verbiage of the Methodist pulpit." [23] Lord Jeffrey overstates his case for effect, and Lamb's phrase does not demonstrate any precise Methodist allegiances on Wordsworth's part. The phrase, however, was perhaps intended to suggest the poet's enthusiasm for nature—an enthusiasm to be found among many Evangelicals—or, more generally, his affinity for the larger movement. And the word *methodism* suggests the religious quality of his thoroughgoing reliance on one's own experience as a basis for knowing the good and the true. It seems reasonable to conclude, through an extension of Lane Cooper's metaphor, that Wordsworth heard, saw, and to some extent traveled the swift English currents of "main stream" Christianity.[24]

That Wordsworth might have been influenced by one of the most conspicuous developments of his day would seem an obvious possibility for his critics to consider. Yet apart from the hints of such early twentieth-century literary historians as Louis Cazamian, Oliver Elton, and William J. Courthope, students of literature

have not investigated the nature of his religious thought, though
they often perceive that he was, in some sense, a religious poet.[25]
Critics who think of the Evangelicals tend to assume, as did Lord
David Cecil, that they merely cast a regrettably "black, melodra-
matic silhouette" across the pages of history and had little effect
upon literature.[26] Abbie Findlay Potts has devoted much con-
sideration to Christian themes in Wordsworth, but only M. H.
Abrams and Geoffrey Hartman have suggested that the Evangeli-
cal Movement might have influenced the poet.[27]

Church historians and Anglican divines have made some asser-
tions about Wordsworth and the Evangelicals, but they confine
their observations to analogy without attempting to establish in-
fluence.[28] The most thorough studies by scholars of this kind are
F. C. Gill's *The Romantic Movement and Methodism* and T. B.
Shepherd's *Methodism and the Literature of the Eighteenth Cen-
tury,* and we owe a debt to both. Gill points out the parallel be-
tween Romanticism and the Methodist emphasis on emotion,
personality, and "the doctrine of familiar language" (pp. 160–63),
and he suggests that *Lyrical Ballads* resembles the hymns of
Methodism in a common "lyricism, sincerity, and spontaneity"
(p. 29). Shepherd adds the Evangelical and Romantic "love of
liberty, a deeper interest in man, a love of Nature, and simple,
domestic joys" (p. 266). These provocative insights remain tan-
talizing generalizations, the terms of which need definition. Mod-
ern churchmen see the relationship and gravitate to it, but per-
haps they would agree with A. W. Harrison that the "borderland
country between Romanticism and Religion may be attractive to
the adventurous traveller, but its maps are as vague as those of
Africa." [29]

We can undertake the journey if we are guided by an adequate
knowledge of both Wordsworth's poetry and Evangelical theol-
ogy. We must be aware of the historical significance of Evangeli-
calism outlined above, and of the ethical and doctrinal emphases
of Evangelical writers; for then we may establish wherein he
shared with them a quality of faith. The problem is not an easy
one. Indeed, Wordsworth himself seemed to know that he created
the difficulty while at the same time characterizing his work as
essentially religious. When in 1840 Henry Alford, the Dean of

Canterbury whose early training was in the Evangelical school,
sent him an essay on the religious aspects of his poems, he re-
sponded with obvious approval:

> I was particularly pleased with your distinction between
> religion in poetry and versified religion. For my own part,
> I have been averse to frequent mention of the mysteries of
> Christian faith; not from a want of a due sense of their mo-
> mentous nature, but the contrary. I felt it far too deeply to
> venture on handling the subject as many scruple not to do.
> I am far from blaming them, but let them not blame me, nor
> turn from my companionship on that account. Besides gen-
> eral reasons for diffidence in treating subjects of Holy Writ, I
> have some especial ones. I might err in points of faith, and I
> should not deem my mistakes less to be deprecated because
> they were expressed in metre.                [*LY,* 2 : 1006–07]

Such a sense of awe was valued among the leaders of the Ox-
ford Movement. On this subject Isaac Williams wrote two of the
most controversial *Tracts for the Times,* collectively entitled "On
Reserve in Communicating Religious Knowledge" (1838 and
1840). Concerning the first, which opposed the freedom with
which some descendants of earlier Evangelicals referred to the
deepest mysteries of religion, Crabb Robinson noted in his diary
(29 September 1839): "I have heard Wordsworth speak favor-
ably of this Tract." [30] Wordsworth's letter to Alford implies his
toleration for such latter-day Evangelical versifiers as James
Montgomery (cf. *LY,* 2 : 818), but his High Anglican or Catholic
side could not reflect their glibness. His faith, like the Oxford
Movement, was affected by the broader, higher, and more rev-
erential Evangelicalism of Wesley and Wilberforce.

It has been argued that original sin and justification by faith
are the characteristic Evangelical doctrines. [31] This combination
encourages both fear and love of God, and the spots of time in
*The Prelude* reflect the poet's corresponding dread of and devo-
tion to a God who chastens whom he loves. If, moreover, Horton
Davies is correct in suggesting that the Puritan and Nonconform-
ist cultus emphasizes revelation, while the Anglican encourages
aspiration (*Worship and Theology in England,* p. 32), both tradi-

tions are to be found in Wordsworth, whose rhapsodies of praise (in which, for example, he learns to commune with God by joining in "one song" of "transport" with all things of nature—*Prelude* II.429–31, 446) constitute a personal, heartfelt liturgy, and whose spots of time seem to be epiphanies or received moral insights resembling those recorded in Puritan and Methodist spiritual autobiography. Perhaps he could not so well have mixed these somewhat disparate experiences had not Wesley and others made it possible for the two great Christian heritages in England to unite, at least in spirit, during most of the eighteenth and nineteenth centuries.

Like Wesley, then, Wordsworth was syncretistic. His reverence for Anglican church order, acquired in all probability from the Evangelical Anglicans at Cambridge (see pp. 21–23), kept him well away from Wesleyan and Calvinist Methodists. We may suspect, however, that the poet who felt a calling to which he was bound "else sinning greatly," or who cherished the criterion of sincerity, or who welcomed opportunities to relieve the distress of poor souls like the Old Cumberland Beggar, would owe something to the three common emphases of both Methodist and Anglican Evangelicalism—conversion, experiential faith, and practical charity.[32] Wesley's emphasis on the doctrines of Christian perfection and justification by faith did not prevent him from being attracted to such Puritan-Calvinist concepts as covenant church organization and extemporaneous prayer and preaching; [33] and similarly, as we shall see, Wordsworth favored informal Evangelical preaching, reflected the sense of moral commitment demanded by the covenant, and strove in faith for spiritual perfection.

Through the Evangelicals, moreover, he absorbed some of the most venerable traditions of apostolic, European, and English Christianity. Leaders of the Great Awakening such as George Whitefield, John Newton, John Fletcher, and of course Wesley, were learned as well as active men who stressed the Third Person of the Trinity and taught the spiritual reading of the book of nature with a full command of the appropriate traditions of theology dating back through Saint Augustine to the New Testament. Wesley's *Christian Library* included popular editions of

Augustine, who taught natural theology, and Ignatius Loyola, who practiced spiritual communion.[34]

The Evangelicals may also have accepted the Pentecostal gift of the Spirit with greater seriousness than most of their theological predecessors, for they cherished the biblical fruits of the Spirit as the sustaining force of their daily lives. They also practiced the medieval method of reading the book of nature spiritually or figuratively. They observed nature carefully, however, before interpreting it, just as they understood the spirit of God's Word in part because they mastered its letter.

Wordsworth also reflects the spiritual vocabulary associated with the Holy Ghost, and he regards the objects of nature as divine symbols—types of things to come and emblems of moral truth. In sum, he built his literary world upon the foundation of spiritual and natural theology. One of the most vital Christian epochs in two thousand years nourished his affirmation of a faith remarkable for both its spontaneity and its traditional grounding in the external sources of religious truth: "I look abroad upon Nature, I think of the best part of our species, I lean upon my friends, and I meditate upon the Scriptures, especially the Gospel of St. John; and my creed rises up of itself with the ease of an exhalation, yet a fabric of adamant" (*LY*, 1 : 204–05).

## CHAPTER ONE

*WORDSWORTH'S*

*SPIRITUAL BIOGRAPHY*

Biographers have helped to create the assumption that Wordsworth was skeptical toward matters of faith and doctrine. In one of the first ambitious attempts to record his early life, *La Jeunesse de William Wordsworth* (1897), Emile Legouis supports his view that the poet was not religious with evidence which equally well supports the view that he was a professing Christian. Legouis asserts that Wordsworth broke with "all religious creeds" after his disillusionment with the French Revolution; he quotes from Coleridge's letter, written in May of 1798, stating that Wordsworth "loves and venerates Christ and Christianity," but subordinates this firsthand evidence by emphasizing Coleridge's pious addition, "I wish he did more." [1] Legouis concludes that "no road to fame and happiness remained open to him but that of poetry." And thus implying that the road led away from God, he projects the somewhat sentimental image of an irreligious poet interested primarily in the formal aspects of his art, an image flattering to modern theories about the moral neutrality of aesthetics.

Legouis was writing in the 1890s when *ars gratia artis* was the right poetic slogan; Wordsworth wrote much earlier. In a letter to Sir George Beaumont (January or February 1808), he suggested that he was capable of the characteristic didacticism of eighteenth-century literature: "I wish either to be considered as a Teacher, or as nothing" (*MY*, 1 : 170). And we shall see that he never cultivated the idea of "poetry" apart from clear moral purpose. Wordsworth's disillusionment with the French Revolution, moreover, did not cause him to lose his faith (except, perhaps, during the brief period of his flirtation with Godwin— see pp. 103, 190); he, rather, aspired to labor in the same vineyard with Wilberforce.

Subsequent biographers have also tended to slight the importance of his faith. George McLean Harper, for example, observes that Wordsworth did not "habitually think of nature as leading up to God; he thought of nature as having the Life of Life abiding in her." [2] George Wilbur Meyer ignores religious influences altogether, arguing that Wordsworth was the "victim of what modern psychologists would probably describe as maladjustment and emotional immaturity." [3] The work of these scholars is dated, but Harper's and Legouis's books have been reprinted (in 1960 and 1965, respectively). The most comprehensive study, Mary Moorman's *William Wordsworth: A Biography* (1957–65), specifically argues that he "was not attracted or convinced by the piety of the Evangelicals." [4]

A notable exception to the continued neglect of the evidence is *The Later Wordsworth* (1933) by Edith C. Batho, who shows that his religious views remain essentially the same throughout his career and that each of his professions of faith applies to most periods of his life. She has considerable fun at the expense of American scholars who, reared in a narrow orthodoxy, lose their faith and then find even the catholicity of Anglicanism an offense. Such modern readers, she observes, seize on Wordsworth's intellectual crisis during the French Revolution as evidence that he forsook a creed which, they assume, he could never have regained without being intellectually dishonest. She argues that he, like others reared as Anglicans, relied during periods of crisis on the external forms of a venerable faith; and she demonstrates that he decided against becoming an Anglican minister, not because he had lost his faith, but because he did not think himself good enough (pp. 261–64).

Her argument is weak, however, when she turns to the Evangelicals. When she says Wordsworth "was unaffected as a young man by Evangelicalism, and never learnt its language" (p. 279) she supposes that it constituted a departure from tradition and was somehow largely "original." She also assumes that High Church Anglicanism and Evangelicalism were mutually exclusive (pp. 279–80, 292); but the Evangelicals nevertheless could and did reflect the "medieval Christian thought" that she believes to be the exclusive property of the non-Evangelical Anglican.

This corrective notwithstanding, it is regrettable that the new direction indicated in *The Later Wordsworth* has been ignored. Let us now begin once more at the beginning of his life, paying attention, as Batho puts it, to "Wordsworth's religious background in childhood" (p. 235) and also in his young manhood, since we have more information about those years. To reveal an important but neglected dimension of his life, I shall emphasize the slighted facts of his religious background and refer to the poetry only when it is biographical and Evangelical in the narrowest sense. We shall see that his early milieu, his letters, and many details from his poetry reflect the ideas and attitudes of many participants in the Great Awakening—whether Evangelical Anglican, Nonconformist, or even Quaker. An awareness of the Christian influences in Wordsworth's formative years prepares us to examine the spiritual and natural theology underlying his poetry, but an initial biographical emphasis also affords us an added luxury in the study of poets and poetry for which Dr. Johnson felt no need to apologize: he liked biography best.[5]

Wesley's eighteen visits to Cockermouth—five during the 1750s, four during the 1760s, six in the 1770s, and three in the 1780s—suggest the wide extent of his ministry. In effect, he made England his regular parish—quite an ambitious undertaking before the days of good roads. Cornwall, Bristol, and the North responded to his preaching soon after his conversion in May of 1738 and considerably earlier than the populous London area.[6] Despite its remoteness, the North saw a good many emissaries of the Evangelical spirit—Methodist, Dissenting, and Quaker; preachers covered the Lake District especially well. Besides Cockermouth, Wesley himself often went to Kendal, Ambleside, Carlisle, and Whitehaven.[7] A master organizer, he also delegated preaching responsibilities in the area to some of his two hundred

or so itinerant ministers: Christopher Hopper and William
Black, for example, liked the district, and Black spent six months
at a time in Cumberland (*Lives,* 1 : 46; 3 : 139, 157, 159). Besides
the Methodists, the famous Dissenter Rowland Hill (whose "real
Christian experience" Wesley recognized) and the Quaker au-
thor John Woolman (whose argument against the slave trade
deeply affected Wesley) brought the Great Awakening to the
Lake Country.[8] Tangible results of the revival there may be
seen in the enrollment of 102 Methodists at Penrith and 309 at
Kendal in 1815, a year for which records survive.[9]

The young Wordsworth could not have remained unaware of
this far-reaching phenomenon, for Wesley made a favorable and
enduring impression on Cockermouth. As early as April of 1751,
his fame assured him "a large and serious congregation" there
(Wesley, 2 : 227), so that only two years later (15 April 1753)
he preached "to well nigh all the inhabitants of the town"
(2 : 285). By 1777, when Wordsworth was seven years old, such
sizable audiences were apparently commonplace; Wesley reported
on June 3 that "a large congregation" was "waiting in the castle-
yard" for his arrival (4 : 101). Earlier in his journal he reported
what typically happened: at Cockermouth in 1759 he wrote, "I
preached at the end of the market-house. High and low, rich and
poor, attended; and by far the greater part of the audience
seemed to be conscious that God was there" (2 : 481). Or again,
in 1757: "I hastened to Cockermouth. I began without delay,
and cried to a listening multitude, 'If any man thirst, let him
come unto me and drink.' The word had free course. Even the
gentry seemed desirous to drink of the 'living water' " (2 : 409).
Wordsworth might have been among similar multitudes during
the 1770s, and he could not have grown up in a town so often
visited by this renowned preacher without hearing about him.
In *The Prelude,* particularly in the spots of time, he expresses
the remembered mood of his childhood and recaptures its Evan-
gelical atmosphere (see chapter 2).

A similar atmosphere prevailed at Cambridge. His recollec-
tion that he was "not for that hour / Nor for that place" (*Pre-
lude* III.80–81) has suggested that Wordsworth gained very lit-
tle from the university (Legouis observes that it "was then in

the very last stage of intellectual languor" and that religious life was "in a state of spiritless stagnation," pp. 71, 73). But Ben Ross Schneider, Jr., in *Wordsworth's Cambridge Education,* has shown that his undergraduate years (1787–91), despite moments of homesickness, were an important formative period when, for example, he was first exposed to "political radicalism"; [10] and Charles Smyth has evoked the Evangelical atmosphere of the town in his *Simeon and Church Order: A Study of the Evangelical Revival in Cambridge.* Intellectual languor might have characterized the curriculum, but in the community at large the Great Awakening enjoyed what Davies has called a "second spring" (*Worship and Theology in England,* p. 216). Of all places in England, at the time of Wordsworth's matriculation, Cambridge afforded the greatest opportunity for absorbing the intellectual substance of the revival.

The evidence actually suggests that he there encountered the Evangelical spirit, both informally and formally. Several undergraduates whose lives were shaped by the revival were his friends: among his *"intimate* associates" at St. John's College he counted Thomas Middleton (later Bishop of Calcutta), and John Gisborne, who was there converted to Methodism.[11] One of his best friends from those days was William Mathews, the son of a London Methodist preacher; [12] Wordsworth regularly corresponded with him for five years after leaving Cambridge (1791–96). They planned to edit a "monthly miscellany" in which would appear not only discussions of painting, gardening, politics, and poetry, but also "essays on morals" (*EY,* p. 119). Wordsworth described the project in four letters written over a period of several months (May 1794 through January 1795). It should, he said, be "a vehicle of sound and exalted Morality." His grandiloquent prospectus included an echo of Isaiah (9 : 2): "I know that the multitude walk in darkness. I would put into each man's hand a lantern to guide him" (*EY,* pp. 119, 125).

Religious reading required by St. John's helped to inculcate such moral purpose; questions on *The Evidences of Christianity* (1758), by the Congregational herald of the revival, Philip Doddridge, comprised a part of the entrance examination that placed Wordsworth in the top half of his class.[13] His contemporary

Francis Wrangham, who attended Magdalene College and Trinity Hall (1786–90), noted in the "advertisement" to his 1820 edition of *The Evidences,* that it had been and still was "the subject of study and examination . . . in the University of Cambridge." [14] Wordsworth's twenty surviving letters to Wrangham, written over a twenty-four-year period (1795–1819) and often devoted to religious topics, show a continuing interest in the Christian training they shared at the university.

Besides offering moral instruction, the spiritual life in Cambridge encouraged the love of liberty—both civil and religious—and thus sounded a common theme of the Great Awakening. Robert Robinson, minister of the Particular Baptist Church in St. Andrew's Street, was well known, even in Scotland, Germany, and America, for his republican ideals; in his *Political Catechism* (1782), for example, he taught bold democratic principles: "When we speak of administration . . . we speak of what *is;* but when we speak of representation, we speak of what *ought to be.*" [15] John Wesley, of course, was bitterly hostile to secular republicanism; but many Evangelicals, including Wesley, exalted liberty as "a kind of Natural Instinct, antecedent to Art or Education," "the glory of *Britons* in particular," and saw no inconsistency between its spiritual and its temporal forms ("enthusiasm," David Hume observed, "is a friend to civil liberty").[16]

Five days before one of his visits to Cockermouth, Wesley noted the increase of population and trade in Cumberland and Westmoreland: "Such is the fruit of the entire civil and religious liberty which all England now enjoys!" (Wesley, 4 : 73). Wordsworth's enjoyment of at least the civil manifestation of this liberty was his birthright; if he was a typical Cumbrian, he was also a typical Briton, even when he first came down to Cambridge: "I was a Freeman; in the purest sense / Was free, and to majestic ends was strong" (*Prelude* III.89–90). And he was not an exception among undergraduates. Wrangham, described as a republican by the Evangelical don Isaac Milner, apparently espoused the "purest" forms of political "freedom"; he failed to get a divinity fellowship after "reports were circulated that he was a friend to the French Revolution, one who exulted in the murder of the king." [17]

The reports were undoubtedly exaggerated, for Wrangham's

Evangelicalism, inculcated at the university and strengthened in the town, would have helped him to distinguish between republicanism and civil liberty and eventually to favor the freedoms found under a limited monarchy and hence enjoyed for "majestic" ends. And similarly, Wordsworth's Cambridge education insured that religion in a vital Evangelical form would nurture his love of liberty and deepen his understanding of it. Robinson's sermons on liberty, delivered in simple language to the farmers and tradesmen of his congregation, attracted gownsmen as well, and Wordsworth's friend George Dyer was assistant minister of the Church and tutor in Robinson's household (six years after receiving his degree, Wordsworth called his presentation copy of Dyer's *Memoirs of Robert Robinson* [1796] "the best biography in the language").[18]

The preacher's love of political and religious freedom was a reason for the fifty-year-old Wordsworth's memory of his "beloved Cam" as a "collegiate shelter" where England's youth could enjoy "the air of liberty" (*PW*, 3 : 39); even before he went to France, where he experienced what Schneider has called a "confirmation" of his republicanism (*Wordsworth's Cambridge Education*, p. 151), he was therefore disposed from the religious point of view to respond to the slogan "Liberty, Equality, Fraternity." That same point of view would lead him to reject the secularism in French revolutionary ideals and to reaffirm the Evangelical and biblical belief that spiritual truth makes men free indeed (see pp. 102–10).

Cambridge University, with its history of religious toleration, was well suited to be the thriving center of the Evangelical Movement toward the end of the eighteenth century, and it may be helpful to review the most pertinent details of that history, in order more fully to understand the background and nature of Wordsworth's early allegiance to Evangelical Anglicanism. Under royal letters from James I in 1616, to be sure, anyone proceeding to a degree was required to subscribe to three articles, declaring the king to be Supreme Governor of the Church, and the *Book of Common Prayer* and the Thirty-nine Articles to be consistent with the Word of God.[19] Dissenters and Unitarians, however, could remain until they were asked to sign.

Oxford was considerably stricter, as it imposed religious tests on undergraduates at matriculation; in March of 1768 six Methodists were expelled from St. Edmund Hall, Oxford, as a warning.[20] Thenceforward, as Canon Smyth observes, "Cambridge was to be the University at which Evangelical clergy must receive their training" (*Simeon and Church Order,* p. 215). By 1820, the Reverend Richard Polwhele expressed deep concern that Cambridge was reported to "pour forth Evangelical students . . . copiously," and he therefore hoped that "the heads of the universities" would "check the slightest tendency in their youth to Evangelical irregularities."[21] By 1786, Magdalene College (where Wrangham first matriculated) had produced many fervent young men; Jesus, Peterhouse, Queens, and St. John's soon followed and even showed a liberal spirit toward Dissenters and Unitarians.[22] The Dissenter Robinson, who was sometimes attracted to Unitarianism, could not have enjoyed popularity in the less tolerant atmosphere at Oxford.

Cambridge harbored such a man as John Berridge of Everton, who began an itinerant ministry in 1759 and continued until his death in 1793.[23] A Calvinist in theology, Berridge stressed the doctrine of original sin and drove his message home by arousing his audiences to ecstatic displays of enthusiasm; Southey, in his *Life of Wesley,* remarked that "this man produced a more violent influenza of fanaticism than had ever followed upon either Whitefield's or Wesley's preachings."[24] And yet the Arminian Wesley, who learned to disparage the excesses of enthusiasm, found nothing alarming in Berridge's preaching. In his journal he recorded that Berridge preached in Cambridge on 21 May 1759 to "near ten thousand people . . . among whom were many gownsmen from Cambridge" and noted in particular that "the audience behaved with great decency" (Wesley, 2 : 487–88). Two months later Wesley visited Everton and satisfied himself that "love and joy," not "sorrow and fear," caused the cries from Berridge's congregation (2 : 508). In November of that year, he returned once more but was disappointed to find Berridge away, preaching "before the University of Cambridge" (2 : 518).

Berridge's effort to influence undergraduates and local ministers makes him an important figure in the Cambridge revival. He formed a friendship with Robinson, who began to itinerate through neighboring villages with Berridge's encouragement.[25] He also sent a note to Rowland Hill, then a freshman at St. John's, expressing a desire to meet him.[26] Undoubtedly flattered, Hill rode to Everton every Sunday, being careful to return in time for college chapel. Like Berridge and Robinson, Hill soon practiced an itinerant ministry. Though he preached in the streets of Cambridge even as an undergraduate, he was treated leniently by the authorities, and in later years, after he had been forced into Nonconformity, he was gratified to see the university become the center of Evangelical teaching.

The practice of itinerant ministries by early Evangelicals such as Berridge, Hill, and Wesley himself, threatened the order of the Anglican Church. At Cambridge, however, this issue was not disruptive, largely because of the infectious faith and personal diplomacy of Charles Simeon, Vicar of Holy Trinity, a figure third in importance only to Wesley and Whitefield among Evangelical leaders. Since Simeon made an effort to guide and befriend undergraduates,[27] it is possible that Wordsworth attended Holy Trinity. On a visit to Cambridge in 1800, at any rate, he went to hear Simeon preach,[28] and the story of Simeon's influence at Cambridge during the 1780s provides the background for his espousal of religious fervency within the confines of church order.

The issue of church order severely tested Simeon's peacemaking talents.[29] Berridge had tried to persuade Simeon to itinerate during his undergraduate years (1779–82), but the fatherly Henry Venn, a loyal Anglican, persuaded the young man not to do so. Without alienating Berridge, Simeon established a precedent against itinerant preaching by Evangelical Anglicans; he thereby made it easier for vicars tempted to itinerate—Walker of Truro and Adams of Wintingham, among others—to remain within the fold. At Holy Trinity during the 1780s, he instilled into the undergraduates "much moderation, obedience to superiors, and no breaking out to be teachers when they are mere novices." [30] Out of respect for his conviction about church order, Rowland Hill not only refrained from open-air preaching whenever he returned to Cambridge, but even "refused to preach in a dissenting place of worship at Cambridge, lest he should appear in any way to interfere with the course so wisely pursued by Mr Simeon." [31]

Simeon enjoyed such deference because he was himself a fervent Evangelical; in one imaginative stroke, for example, he compromised between rigid Anglican order and uncontrolled field preaching by introducing at Holy Trinity the Sunday evening service, which was widely adopted by Evangelical Anglicans (and finally, of course, by Nonconformists as well). His innovation drew much criticism, but Simeon never wavered after the admiring Wesley told him in December of 1784 to "take up the cross and persevere." [32] As Canon Smyth concludes, Simeon "taught the Evangelicals to believe in the Church of England and to steer clear, not only of the Scylla of academic latitudinarianism, but also of the Charybdis of that personal enthusiasm which walks disorderly in its indiscriminate and unthinking zeal" (*Simeon and Church Order*, p. 250).

The evidence suggests that Wordsworth built his faith on the Evangelical Anglican middle ground staked out by Simeon at Cambridge; from such a vantage point he embraced church order, strengthened his convictions, and thus avoided the two extremes defined by Canon Smyth. He rejected academic laxness of belief and shallowness of faith: "Latitudinarianism is the parhelion [mock sun] of liberty of conscience, and will ever successfully lay claim to a divided worship" (*PW*, 2 : 460). He showed his respect for church order by attending services even when led by the sottish Grasmere curate Edward Rowlandson.[33] And his attitude toward walking Evangelicals may be inferred from his letter to Wrangham of March 1796: "I have some thoughts of exploring the country westward of us . . . but in an humble evangelical way; to wit à pied" (*EY*, p. 168). This casual remark suggests his familiarity with itinerancy and hence the issue of church order. Simeon's resolution of the Cambridge controversy permitted his facetious attitude toward what had been a serious issue, and Wrangham, with his Cambridge background, would no doubt have caught his allusion and appreciated his humor.

Wordsworth's admiration for the later career of Robert Walker, well-known curate of Seathwaite from 1735 to 1802, exemplifies his approval of the kind of Evangelical Anglicanism made possible by Simeon's stabilizing influence. In a memoir, Wordsworth sensed in Walker the blend of fervent Anglicanism to which he himself had been introduced at the university: "[Walker] was indeed most zealously attached to the doctrine and frame of the Established Church. We have seen him congratulating himself that he had no dissenters in his cure of any denomination" (*PW*, 3 : 518).

Simeon would have been as gratified by Walker's evening services as by his devotion to the Church; Walker adopted the Cambridge practice because according to Wordsworth, he found "a more serious auditory" on Sunday evenings. Reading from the Bible was a typical feature of the Evangelical Anglican services,[34] and Wordsworth particularly praised "Wonderful" Walker's Sunday evening readings from the New Testament: "These lessons he read with impassioned emphasis, frequently drawing tears from his hearers, and leaving a lasting impression upon their minds."

Simeon's inauguration of Sunday evening worship betokened the general desire of Cambridge Evangelicals to combat what they deemed the spiritual emptiness of university services. Even before the decade of Simeon's greatest influence, Evangelical undergraduates sought to improve the quality of worship; in 1766 a religious society began regular meetings at St. John's College because Rowland Hill and others felt shackled by the "ecclesiastical trammels" of the university.[35] They saw that the forms of religion imposed by Cambridge authorities did not enhance the spiritual welfare of undergraduates, who sometimes made a mockery of enforced chapel attendance. After "running, laughing, staggering in," according to one report, they would hear the lesson read by a "drunken scholar either too blind to read or inclined to vomit"; on such occasions the assemblage would toss candles, mouth obscenities, or damn the Dean, while the Master slept in a corner or read *Fanny Hill*.[36]

Wordsworth and such Evangelical friends as William Mathews, Thomas Middleton, and John Gisborne undoubtedly inherited the attitudes introduced at St. John's in the previous generation by Rowland Hill's Society. Wordsworth's concern about the qual-

ity of worship in chapel services underlies his objection to the
frequent absence of those who were supposed to set a good ex-
ample for the younger students; "he would have suspended the
daily service in the college Chapels," wrote Christopher Words-
worth, "because some of the fellows betrayed their trust, and
neglected those services, and led self-indulgent or irreligious
lives." [37]

Wordsworth, then, was not opposed to the conducting of
services, but he saw no reason to require spiritually empty ones.
Like the members of Hill's Society, he detected the form without
the power, and so in *The Prelude* (III.407–59), he inveighed
against compulsory chapel by evoking Evangelical Anglican
ideals of worship; he employed language reminiscent of Simeon's
desire for the Church to conduct effective services. The "Presi-
dents and Deans" "brought disgrace / On the plain Steeples of
our English Church" by tolerating mere forms of worship, and
he besought them to forgo their "officious doings," give a "sea-
sonable rest" to chapel bells, and "spare the House of God" any
"Folly and False-seeming" (ll. 410–25). Toward the end of the
passage, he envisioned the building of an ideal "Sanctuary for
our Country's Youth," a kind of chapel royal filled with a spirit
"Primaeval in its purity and depth," a holy place in which the
congregation would sing songs, as Methodist and Congregational
Evangelicals did, and wear an Anglican "stamp of awe" (ll. 440–
47).

The winter season of Wordsworth's final year in Cambridge
coincided with the beginning of Dorothy Wordsworth's friend-
ship with William Wilberforce, who soon became a leading
figure at Clapham, the other important center of the revival; [38]
her association with Wilberforce influenced Wordsworth's ad-
miration for the author of *A Practical View*. Beginning in De-
cember 1789, when Dorothy was living with her uncle the Rev-
erend William Cookson at Forncett Parsonage, Wilberforce spent
four months there, renewing ties with his colleague in the min-
istry and fellow Johnian of the years 1776–79. In letters to Jane
Pollard (25 and 26 January 1790, 30 April 1790), Dorothy praised
him so warmly that her friend suspected her of setting her cap. [39]

Dorothy considered herself his pupil. Though his *Practical*

*View* did not appear until 1798, Wilberforce had been planning it for almost ten years and had written part of it before his visit to Forncett, where he reached the point of considering whether to publish in the near future.[40] He no doubt discussed the project with Dorothy, and for her spiritual benefit he recommended books written by other stewards of the Great Awakening, such as Philip Doddridge. To Jane Pollard, Dorothy gave an enthusiastic report on the rapid progress of her reading.[41]

Her correspondence with Jane Pollard serves to challenge the assumption that Dorothy's "religion consisted in loving flowers, birds, children, men and women, Coleridge, and above all William." [42] For his part, Wordsworth cherished his sister's intellectual gifts. He rejoined her at Forncett in December of 1790, and for many years thereafter they often engaged, as she put it, in "long, long conversations." [43] Insofar as these dealt with the subject of her reading, they helped to sustain and heighten her brother's awareness of Evangelicalism; Wordsworth's choice of religious literature reflected Dorothy's Evangelical taste. Upon reading *A Practical View,* he discovered a complete "bond of connection" between him and the author (*EY,* p. 685), and he took "great interest" and "much pleasure" (*EY,* p. 318; *MY,* 1 : 222, 250) in Francis Wrangham's *Thirteen Practical Sermons, founded on Doddridge's Rise and Progress of Religion in the Soul* (1800).

His admiration for Wrangham's sermons, with their acknowledgment of Nonconformist origins, implies the poet's concurrence in the unprecedented Evangelical interaction between Anglicanism and Dissent; it is a short step from the theological tenor of *Thirteen Practical Sermons* to that of *Rise and Progress,* which had gone through ten editions in the twenty-six years from 1745 through 1771 and had thus prepared the way for the first sermon in Wrangham's collection not simply to "deny any dread" of "the name of Enthusiast" but even to endorse "this warm and active spirit of Christianity." [44]

We do well to recognize the Puritan and Nonconformist character of Wordsworth's rigorous soul-searching and self-examination (see pp. 85–87), and we can share James Russell Lowell's recognition of a "Dr. Wattsiness" in his grave and moral po-

etry,[45] but we should remember that his implicit approval of
Isaac Watts's friend and fellow Independent Philip Doddridge
lies hid in his explicit praise of Wrangham. For Wordsworth
traveled the mainstream, and if he moved toward Dissent at all,
he did so through Evangelical Anglicanism (while Dissenters
pointed at "particular parts" of *A Practical View* and grudgingly
called it "legal," [46] he celebrated "one common truth" underly-
ing his own faith and Wilberforce's entire book [*EY*, p. 685]).

Wordsworth's taste in homiletical style and delivery further
indicates the Anglican context of his Evangelicalism; what he
heard was akin to what he read. In *The Prelude* he noted that
from certain London pulpits of the 1790s he acquired "awful
truths delivered . . . by tongues / Endowed with various power
to search the soul" (VII.547–48, 1850), and his metonymy sym-
bolizes the gift of kerygmatic expression, a power bestowed by
the Holy Ghost at Pentecost (Acts 2 : 3–4, 17, 38–47) and pos-
sessed in high degree by Evangelical Anglican preachers such as
John Newton, who often went to London to proclaim his mes-
sage.[47]

Such a powerful mode of Evangelical preaching departed from
late eighteenth-century imitations of latitudinarian style. In 1660
Robert South had reacted against the Latinate lectures of High
Church "metaphysicals" and the prophetic declamations of the
Puritans by fashioning the sermon of "genial discourse"; John
Tillotson, Isaac Barrow, and Benjamin Hoadly had also estab-
lished this "simple, elegant, candid, clear, and rational" style of
homiletics.[48] Toward the end of the eighteenth century, how-
ever, pulpit geniality began to break down because of laxness of
belief, dullness of style, and reliance on printed sermons. In
1760 Oliver Goldsmith complained about discourses that were
"eminently reasonable" but "unconscionably platitudinous" and
therefore "dry, methodical, and unaffecting." [49] In *The Task*
(1785), the Evangelical Anglican laureate William Cowper (who
found latitudinarian "reason" inadequate for the nourishment
of faith) revealed the apathy of ministers who could "huddle up
their work" in fifteen minutes and then preach by "reading what
they never wrote" (2 : 411–12).[50]

Evangelical practice, both Anglican and Methodist, was in

sharp contrast to such conduct. Berridge deeply affected his congregations; Wesley delivered his well-prepared sermons from memory and instructed his preachers to avoid "a dull, dry, formal manner." [51] Goldsmith recognized that "regular divines" had much to learn from the style of "methodists who go their circuits" and from Whitefield's "earnest manner of delivery." [52] Wesley taught his ministers to make their sermons plain in "every particular" and to reject such affectations as loud speaking or lolling with the elbows; [53] Cowper celebrated this conception by characterizing the proper sermon as "natural in gesture" and "plain in manner" and language (*The Task* 2 : 400–02). By contrast, the "insipid calmness" of delivery detected by Goldsmith further degenerated into the effeminate manner shown in Cowper's sketch of a decadent divine:

> What!—will a man play tricks, will he indulge
> A silly fond conceit of his fair form,
> And just proportion, fashionable mien,
> And pretty face, in presence of his God?
> Or will he seek to dazzle me with tropes,
> As with the di'mond on his lily hand,
> And play his brilliant parts before my eyes,
> When I am hungry for the bread of life?
> [*The Task* 2 : 419–26]

*The Prelude* contains a similar portrait. In London Wordsworth saw

> a comely Bachelor,
> Fresh from a toilette of two hours, ascend
> The Pulpit, with seraphic glance look up,
> And, in a tone elaborately low
> Beginning, lead his voice through many a maze,
> A minuet course, and winding up his mouth,
> From time to time into an orifice
> Most delicate, a lurking eyelet, small
> And only not invisible, again
> Open it out, diffusing thence a smile
> Of rapt irradiation exquisite.
> [VII.546–56]

This mincing Bachelor, whose ladylike "orifice" is comparable to the anatomical parts of Cowper's pretty preacher with lily hand, does not measure up to Wesley's ideal of unaffected men of God. Neither does he observe Evangelical principles of good preaching. His insipid smile, his un-Wesleyan vocal affectations, are unlikely to move and can only offend the worshiper. Instead of spending even fifteen minutes preparing his sermon, he has devoted two hours to primping. His message, therefore, can only miscarry; it is delivered through a mouth unfilled with the fruit of study. Perhaps a poor grasp of doctrine makes him rely on reading to the congregation bits and pieces of what he did not write:

> Meanwhile the Evangelists, Isaiah, Job,
> Moses, and he who penn'd the other day
> The Death of Abel, Shakespear, Doctor Young,
> And Ossian, (doubt not, 'tis the naked truth)
> Summon'd from streamy Morven, each and all
> Must in their turn lend ornament and flowers
> To entwine the Crook of eloquence . . .
>
> [ll. 557–63]

"The hungry sheep look up, and are not fed"; Wordsworth's "pretty Shepherd" does not offer the bread of life but "Leads up and down his captivated Flock" (ll. 564–65).

Evangelical standards of judgment, with which Wordsworth's satire is compatible, underlie the sermon criticism appearing in one of his letters to Sir George Beaumont (10 November 1806). He wrote that he and Sara Hutchinson had recently been "pleased with the singing" by the Anglican congregation at Coleorton (*MY*, 1 : 77), perhaps because this methodistical part of the service served spiritual needs; but nothing else had been satisfactory. The minister's "injudicious . . . discourse," delivered by reading what he may not have written, attracted only the most faithful: "I was sorry to see . . . few middle-aged men, or even women; the congregation consisted almost entirely of old persons." The experience reminded him of a similar situation at Keswick, where the Reverend Mr. Denton, whose theology was none the strongest, could think of no better sermon topic than "what a shocking thing it was to be a courtier." Thus Wordsworth lamented that ministerial discourse was often unaffecting, theologically shallow, and possibly derivative; like Goldsmith, he employed the latitudinarian term in its new pejorative sense.

His criteria of what was proper in sermons may be understood in the terms of Cowper's *Task*, which suggests that a minister's preaching becomes him only when it is clear and shows concern for the souls of his hearers. The "decent" preacher, Cowper wrote, knows that he is above all else "a messenger of grace to guilty men"; his sermons must therefore be "tender" toward sinners and "simple" in order to convert them (*The Task*, Book 2, ll. 399–401, 406–07). *The Excursion* reflects Cowper's attitudes and echoes his language. The Pastor, one of the "decent" ministers who weave "the spiritual fabric" of the English Church, expresses in "simple phrase" the "tender themes" of Christian immortality, so that his hearer, the wayward Solitary, might find the grace of consolation (*PW*, 5 : 186, 188, 215). Wordsworth's conclusion in the letter to Beaumont, that sermons should have "a bearing on the condition of the majority of the audience," helps to elucidate the passage from *Peter Bell* (1798) in which the voice of a fervent Methodist, "preaching to no heedless flock," calls the wicked Peter to repentance (*PW*, 2 : 376).

Wordsworth's solicitude for the souls of men, as indicated by his awareness of and apparent response to the kerygmatic character of Evangelical homiletics, is further evident in his criticism of the Unitarians: "Their religion allows no room for imagination and satisfies none of the cravings of the soul. I can feel more sympathy with the orthodox believer who needs a Redeemer and who, sensible of his own demerits, flies to him for refuge . . . than with the cold and rational notions of the Unitarians." [54] Wordsworth's judgment, expressed to the Unitarian Crabb Robinson in 1812, seems to combine the Arminian gratification of yearning ("Christ died for *all*"; Wesley, 10 : 360) and the Evangelical comprehension of depravity; he apparently thought that Unitarianism did not sufficiently liberate human aspirations or minister to those who, not amenable to reason, could still find solace if they hastened to Calvary and clung to the hope of salvation. Parenthetically he added that perhaps he did not want a redeemer for himself, but Coleridge's declaration of 1798, that Wordsworth loved Christ, lends at least some weight to the possibility that the poet stood in greater need of the Redeemer than he would be willing to express to a Unitarian who did not accept Christ's divinity.

Robinson did not begin as a Unitarian but as an Independent whose early faith was strengthened by the Great Awakening. At the age of fifteen he testified that Wesley's message, delivered in October of 1790 to a large gathering in "the great round meeting-house at Colchester," "went to the heart": "I looked upon him with a respect bordering upon enthusiasm." [55] Soon, however, the secular appeal of French revolutionary ideals nipped his budding faith and made him feel embarrassed about the Calvinism in which he had been nurtured. He found his home, not among the Wesleyan Arminians, but in a comfortable Unitarianism that echoed Locke and Newton more than the Bible.[56]

Such enfeeblement of faith, which was fairly common among sophisticated Dissenters, was anathema to the Evangelicals.[57] Wilberforce referred to Unitarianism as the "half-way house" on the journey from "orthodoxy to absolute infidelity" and accused its adherents of "seeking refuge" from the strictness of Christian precepts and doctrines.[58] In 1847 Robinson made light of Mrs. Wordsworth's orthodoxy: "The dear good woman fancies nothing to be *clear* but the 39 Articles—or rather the liturgy—God bless her." [59] Perhaps the doctrinal heterodoxy of Unitarianism fostered his air of condescension toward an Anglican declaration of faith.

Mary Wordsworth was so "clear" about her beliefs that she thought Robinson rather a "Muddletonian" in his, and Wordsworth undoubtedly concurred. Though he and Robinson shared an early awareness of the Evangelical Movement, they parted theological company during the 1790s—Wordsworth's faith stayed on course. In the Fenwick note to *The Excursion*, he expressed disappointment that the French Revolution helped cause another Dissenter, the Reverend Joseph Fawcett (the original of the brooding Solitary), to make the journey toward infidelity:

. . . his Christianity was probably never very deeply rooted; and, like many others in those times of like shewy talents, he had not strength of character to withstand the effects of the French Revolution, and of the wild and lax opinions which had done so much towards producing it, and far more in carrying it forward in its extremes.          [*PW*, 5 : 375]

His disdain for Fawcett, though expressed in his later years, suggests that Wordsworth's own belief, his "deeply rooted" and quasi-Evangelical faith, rescued him from despair during those trying revolutionary times (*The Prelude* makes the same suggestion—see pp. 106–10). At the time when he heard Fawcett preach in 1793, the Dissenter had been praised for avoiding "the cant of Methodism," [60] but Wordsworth himself might have observed that the faith of the Methodists would have helped Fawcett withstand the extremes of "wild and lax" opinion. By the time of the Fenwick note, in any case, he mirrored Wilberforce's animus against shallow convictions; he apparently expected Englishmen, disciplined in the strict precepts of native faith, to resist French excesses and superficiality.

The strength of Wordsworth's faith, as well as its essentially Evangelical character, can be seen in his spirit of practical charity, a spirit discernible among the poems and letters of his prime. The Evangelicals showed their concern for others not simply in their serious attention to the state of men's souls but in their care for the physical and emotional needs of the less fortunate; "prisoners, waifs and strays, the illiterate poor," Horton Davies observes, "in their thousands could rise up and call the Evangelicals blessed" (*Worship and Theology in England*, p. 222). Wesley defined charity in experiential terms, not as "ostentatious almsgiving," but as "the love of our neighbour," or "kind offices" toward those with whom a Christian comes in contact (Wesley, 7 : 47; cf. Luke 10 : 27). Wordsworth's emphasis, like that of Wesley and the other Evangelicals, was upon doing all the good he could (he did not, like Vaughan, tend to stop with philosophy nor, like Crashaw, with devotion).

In "The Old Cumberland Beggar" (1797; *PW*, 4 : 234–40), he shows that discrete "offices of charity," as opposed to collective almsgiving through tax-supported work-houses, nourish the lives of the doers and preserve the dignity of the indigent; and in the episode of the discharged soldier (*Prelude* IV.400–504), he emulates the Good Samaritan by finding shelter for a homeless stranger and thereby giving, as Christ did, a commonsense or "practical" answer to the Legalist's question, "Who is my neighbour?" (cf. Luke 10 : 25–37).

The kind woman in "The Old Cumberland Beggar" is a neighbor in both the physical and the Christian senses. The charitable Christian, said Wesley, must "seek no increase" of his goods, "deal [his] bread to the hungry," and be "ready to distribute to everyone, according to his necessity" (5 : 373, 376); Wordsworth's "neighbour" (l. 155), though "pressed herself / By her own wants," each week takes from "her store of meal" an "unsparing handful for the scrip / Of this old Mendicant" (ll. 156–59). Wesley believed that such charity profited the doer. "The blessing of him that was ready to perish through pining want" will assure the free giver, "rich in good works," of many "treasures in heaven" (Wesley, 5 : 376; cf. Matthew 6 : 19–20).

Each time the woman feeds the beggar, she returns from her door "with exhilarated heart, / Sits by her fire, and builds up her hope in heaven" (ll. 160–61). To suggest good works Wesley paraphrases the words of Christ ("I was sick, and ye visited me," "I was a stranger, and ye took me in," "I was an hungred, and ye gave me meat" [Wesley, 5 : 376–77; cf. Matthew 25 : 35–36]), and Wordsworth practiced these three forms of charity when he befriended the soldier:

> We gain'd the Cottage. At the door I knock'd,
> Calling aloud "my Friend, here is a Man
> By sickness overcome; beneath your roof
> This night let him find rest, and give him food,
> If food he need . . . ."
>
> [ll. 483–87]

In gratitude, the soldier suggests that Wordsworth has done God's work on earth: " 'My trust is in the God of Heaven, / And in the eye of him that passes me' " (ll. 494–95); and the poet seems to construe such a meaning in the utterance (he seeks his "distant home" with "quiet heart" [l. 504]).

Wordsworth's evident willingness to do God's practical work, moreover, included support of the fight against the slave trade, a battle led by such Evangelical Anglicans as Wilberforce, John Newton, and Thomas Clarkson.[61] *The Prelude* pronounces these crusaders a "strong levy of humanity," lauds their efforts against "the Traffickers in Negro blood," and asserts that their labors helped to "spread a novel heat / Of virtuous feeling" throughout England in the 1790s (X.205–06, 1805; 248–53, 1850). When Parliament abolished the slave trade in 1807, Wordsworth addressed his friend Clarkson in a sonnet commemorating the great charitable enterprise:

> And thou henceforth wilt have a good man's calm,
> A great man's happiness; thy zeal shall find
> Repose at length, firm friend of human kind!
>
> [*PW*, 3 : 126]

But Clarkson was in no mood to rest; he felt that religious advantage would attend political victory:

> there are yet blessings, which we have reason to consider as likely to follow from it. Among these we cannot overlook the great possibility that Africa, now freed from the vicious and barbarous effects of this traffic, may be in a better state to comprehend and receive the sublime truths of the Christian religion.[62]

The Evangelicals wanted to set slaves free not only from physical deprivation but from spiritual darkness. The work of lifting chains was finished, and Clarkson seemed prepared to apply Christ's promise of liberation from the bondage of sin: "And ye shall know the truth, and the truth shall set you free" (John 8 : 32–33).

With an emphasis on the Bible, of course, Evangelical Sunday schools taught many Englishmen to read, and this accomplishment constituted one of the most far-reaching manifestations of practical charity. What had been the secular effort of Robert

Raikes to teach prisoners how to read became an Evangelical experiment in education when John Wesley saw that schools outside prison walls might become "nurseries for Christians." [63] Beginning in 1783, Wesley called upon the readers of *The Arminian Magazine* to join Raikes's effort, and by 1795, 65,000 young scholars in 1,000 schools studied 100,000 spelling-books and began to read 5,000 Bibles and 24,000 Testaments.[64] During Wilberforce's Forncett visit of 1790, five years after the first Sunday school Society was founded, Dorothy Wordsworth conducted a class in which one girl "was able to read exceedingly well in the testament"; "the rest do not do quite so well, but . . . I have no reason to complain" (*EY*, p. 29). In 1811 Dorothy reported that she took Wordsworth's children John and Dora to Sunday school regularly and that she and Mary planned to resume teaching a class (*MY*, 1 : 452).

Her long-standing interest in the venture was matched by William's grasp of its significance for national education. In letters to Wrangham (5 June 1808 and 27 March 1811), he praised the distribution of Bibles and hoped that Sunday schools would continue to serve English youth until the establishment of state-supported instruction (*MY*, 1 : 226, 430). Since he feared that "a government which for twenty years resisted the abolition of the Slave Trade" (*MY*, 1 : 227) was unlikely to take up a second Evangelical cause in the foreseeable future, he advocated the immediate adoption of one of the pedagogical experiments of the Sunday school movement. In 1797 Joseph Lancaster, who had planned to teach God's Word to Jamaicans before the rise of Sunday schools inspired him to educate his own people, opened a school using the methods of the Reverend Andrew Bell, who first suggested that instructors distribute individual sand trays to facilitate the teaching of writing. Wordsworth told Wrangham in October of 1808 that Dr. Bell's *Experiment in Education* (1797) "entitles him to the fervent gratitude of all men . . . . [I] would . . . strenuously recommend [? the system] wherever it can be adopted" (*MY*, 1 : 246).

Isaac Watts had hoped that a mind "better furnished for such performances" would continue his effort to write spiritual verse

—someone convinced, as he was, that poetry should serve "religion and virtue" (preface to *Horae Lyricae* [1706]; Watts, 4 : 417). Two of his Evangelical descendants, Hannah More and James Montgomery, discovered such a mind in Wordsworth, in whom they recognized both native genius and religious conviction, and in whom they therefore saw the great Christian poet of the age.[65]

Wordsworth reciprocated their feeling of kinship. Toward the end of his career, he wrote to Montgomery and expressed the "firm belief that neither morality nor religion can have suffered from our writings" (30 November 1836; *LY,* 2 : 818); he felt, in other words, that his poetic faith had served what Watts called "religion and virtue." Moreover, according to the recollections of R. P. Graves, he came to believe that only the "vital movements" in Christian history were conducive to "religion in poetry" as opposed to "versified religion," and he implied that his own "expression of religious faith" had been enhanced by the vital movement of his day.[66] As early as 1800, after all, he had vowed to act, with "sincere convictions" though in the "less awful department" of poetry, upon the truths in *A Practical View* (*EY,* p. 685); and his poetry, testifying to his fulfillment of this vow, aspires to the purpose announced by Wilberforce: to spread "vital religion" by helping "to restore the prevalence of evangelical Christianity." [67]

Thirty-three years separate two of Wordsworth's most eloquent statements of purpose, yet they are similar in spirit, and together they constitute an elaboration of his blunt exclamation: "I wish either to be considered as a Teacher, or as nothing" (*MY,* 1 : 170). The first was written in May of 1807 to Lady Beaumont, who had been disturbed by the unfavorable reviews of his *Poems in Two Volumes* (1807):

Trouble not yourself upon their present reception; of what moment is that compared with what I trust is their destiny, to console the afflicted, to add sunshine to daylight by making the happy happier, to teach the young and the gracious of every age, to see, to think and feel, and therefore to become more actively and securely virtuous; that is their office,

which I trust they will faithfully perform long after we (that
is, all that is mortal of us) are mouldered in our graves.
                                                          [*MY*, 1 : 126]

The second was written in February of 1840 to the Evangelical
Henry Alford, whose essay on religion in his poems moved him
to respond:

> If they be from above, they will do their work in course of
> time; if not, they will perish as they ought. But scarcely a
> week passes in which I do not receive grateful acknowledg-
> ments of the good they have done to the minds of the several
> writers. They speak of the relief they have received from
> them under affliction and in grief, and of the calmness and
> elevation of spirit which the poems either give, or assist them
> in attaining. As these benefits are not without a traceable
> bearing upon the good of the immortal soul, the sooner, per-
> haps, they are pointed out and illustrated in a work like
> yours the better.                                    [*LY*, 2 : 1007]

Wordsworth's identity as a poet, then, derives from a religious
ideal of service, an ideal imbued with a zealous didacticism un-
like anything to be found in the work of other major Romantics
(perhaps because, as Wilberforce believed, "the literati" of the
time had read David Hume and were "sceptically disposed" [*A
Practical View*, pp. x, 266]). For his part, Wordsworth seemed to
want those who loved him best to continue Dean Alford's inves-
tigations, which point out and illustrate the Christian elements
that place his poetry within the mainstream of European litera-
ture, and show his mission to be evangelical in the historical and
timeless sense of the term: he sought to minister to the good of
the soul and thus to improve the spiritual welfare of his readers.

CHAPTER TWO *WORDSWORTH'S*
*SPIRITUAL*
*AUTOBIOGRAPHY*

In a letter to Sir George Beaumont (1 May 1805), Wordsworth announced that only "Two Books more" remained to be written of "the Poem on my own life"; he felt "sure of succeeding" and thought he had done his best thus far (*EY*, pp. 586–87). Exhilarated self-confidence, however, did not blind him to the probability that his autobiographical poem of "not much less than 9,000 lines,—not hundred but thousand lines long" would seem vainglorious. He acknowledged the "alarming length" and knew it was "a thing unprecedented in Literary history that a man should talk so much about himself," but he declared that he had never meant to vaunt himself: "It is not self-conceit . . . that has induced me to do this, but real humility." Some of *The Prelude*'s opening lines affirm that he did not write from a sense of pride:

> . . . it is shaken off,
> As by miraculous gift 'tis shaken off,
> That burthen of my own unnatural self.
>
> [I.21–23]

The letter to Beaumont reaffirmed the humbleness of spirit in which Wordsworth had begun the work. The letter, to be sure, may protest too much; but his satisfaction with what he had

written and his expectation of imminent success could signify
exaltation rather than arrogance or egotism. And real if exalted
humility may indeed underlie his self-examination in *The Pre-
lude.*

Self-consciousness tempered by the claim of humility is also
to be found among the spiritual autobiographies of Methodist
ministers. These personal narratives, patterned in part after the
adventures of Christian in John Bunyan's *Pilgrim's Progress*
(1678) and Bunyan's own Puritan experience in *Grace Abound-
ing* (1666), formed a popular feature of *The Arminian Magazine*
(later named *The Methodist*) from 1778, when Wesley first en-
couraged written testimonies, through the first two decades of
the nineteenth century; [1] the best were collected by Thomas
Jackson in *The Lives of Early Methodist Preachers* (1837).
These ministers attempted not only to explore the eccentricities
and recesses of the mind, as Southey pointed out in *The Life of
Wesley*,[2] but also to place a Puritan emphasis on the growth of
what Wordsworth might have called "real humility," and to ex-
press the Arminian joy of salvation.

The central event of their lives was conversion, that point at
which they felt the sinful burden of self fall away and new life
begin. The spiritual rebirth of John Pritchard, for example, en-
abled him to put off the old man of corruption and put on the
new man of righteousness and holiness (cf. Ephesians 4 : 22–24):
"In private the Lord poured his blessing upon me. . . . I looked
into my heart . . . and blessed the lineaments of God's image,
the transcript of his laws, the harmony of his gifts and graces"
(*Lives*, 3 : 454–55). Pritchard's introspection reflects gratitude for
God's redemptive act; therefore his tone, consistent with Chris-
tian humility, is more exuberant than proud or self-sufficient.
And Wordsworth, had he read this account, might have con-
cluded that the apparent restoration of Pritchard's innocence,
like his own proclaimed recovery of the natural self, was not
the sign of empty boasting but the miraculous gift of grace.

We can surmise that Wordsworth was familiar with the Meth-
odist lives, for on 6 February 1797, during the period of his closest
association with Coleridge, Coleridge wrote a letter to Thomas
Poole in which he expressed admiration for the sincerity and

power of contemporary spiritual autobiography, whether Methodist or Quaker:

> I could inform even the dullest author how he might write an interesting book—let him relate the events of his own Life with honesty, not disguising the feelings that accompanied them.—I never yet read even a Methodist's 'Experience' . . . without receiving instruction and amusement: & I should almost despair of that Man, who could peruse the Life of John Woolman without an amelioration of Heart.[3]

His further discussion of the subject, in this letter and in four additional ones to Poole (5 March 1797 to 19 February 1798), shows Coleridge's awareness of both the Puritan and the Wesleyan foundations of these autobiographies. As an example of the genre he mentioned Daniel Defoe's *Robinson Crusoe* (1719), which was indebted, as G. A. Starr and J. Paul Hunter have shown, to the emphasis on self-conquest and introspective moralizing in *Grace Abounding, Pilgrim's Progress,* and similar Puritan writings.[4] And his praise of his brother George, whose "moral character" approached "every way nearer to Perfection" than that of "any man I ever yet knew" (*CL*, 1 : 311), suggests that Coleridge was acquainted with the doctrine of Christian perfection so dear to Wesley, a doctrine that complemented the optimistic Arminian belief in possible redemption for all.[5]

The Evangelical blend of self-mastery and consciousness of redemption (a mixture understood by Coleridge and undoubtedly exemplified by John Pritchard) lies behind Wordsworth's paradoxical traits of humility and self-esteem, as shown, for example, in *Prelude* I and the letter to Beaumont. The poet admired "the splendour" of *Pilgrim's Progress,* which he believed to be "one of those productions whose merits were at first unacknowledged in the highest quarters"; [6] and he could therefore have been pleased by the survival of Christian's example in the lives of humble Methodist preachers, who ministered to the "lowest" quarters of English society. Perhaps he had also read the autobiographical *Grace Abounding,* with its profound self-examination. His own determined soul-searching—"I through myself /

Make rigorous inquisition" (*Prelude* I.158–59)—was due to his sober conviction, as expressed in the "Essay, Supplementary to the Preface" of 1815, that Christianity—"the religion of humility" —demands self-discipline (*PW*, 2 : 412), and no doubt helped to form his increasingly grave and serious countenance, which on 31 January 1802 moved Dorothy to remark that he could "sit for the picture of John Bunyan any day." [7]

At the same period of his life, however, Wordsworth also professed great happiness in his faith, which was for him "an elevation, and a sanctity" (*Prelude* X.427–28); and he later asserted the essential harmony of both aspects of religious experience. In "The Primrose of the Rock" (1831), he wrote of faith that descends to those with "humbleness of heart" and then "elevates the just," raising their souls to exaltation (*PW*, 2 : 304); and in the 1815 "Essay," he implied the purpose of his own career by arguing that poets in general should attempt to strip away men's pride and vanity by "establishing that dominion over the spirits of readers by which they are to be humbled and humanised, in order that they may be purified and exalted" (*PW*, 2 : 426).

The letters to Poole outlined Coleridge's plan to write his autobiography. "To me," he said, "the task will be a useful one"; his "reflections on the past" would reveal the origins and favor the increase of such wisdom and virtue as he now possessed (*CL*, 1 : 302). An examination of his plan as it relates to the typical sequence in the Methodist lives points a direct way into the poem on Wordsworth's life; for Wordsworth was undoubtedly familiar, if not with the lives themselves, then with his close friend's interest in spiritual autobiography. And we shall see, in any case, that the chronological sequence in *The Prelude* (as distinct from its passage-by-passage, book-by-book arrangement) broadly parallels Methodist patterns of spiritual event.

The Methodists, in recording their progress toward spiritual maturity, began with memories of childhood error leading to repentance; [8] and these lessons in humility took full effect during their early adolescence, when some compelling religious event convinced them of their sinful pride and marked an important step in their spiritual progress (such attainment of moral accountability effectively ended their boyhood). Like the fifteen-year-old Crabb Robinson, who was ripe for Wesley's message and long remembered its impact (see pp. 29–30), these youths who responded to the appeals of religion during the years of nascent accountability later construed their response to be a momentous structural point in the story of their early lives. During his later boyhood, for example, Benjamin Rhodes, one of the preachers, wandered in the woods overnight after committing an unspecified sin and then obeyed his father's firm but loving call to "deep repentance" (*Lives,* 3 : 414). He felt that he never again lapsed into boyish willfulness; his youthful experience, unlike that of Robinson (who later lost his faith), prefigured the asserted Christian purity and faithfulness, and the undoubtable religious exaltation, of his adulthood.

Rhodes's attainment of humility resembles the precocious Coleridge's experience at the age of ten, on the threshold of moral accountability. Coleridge remembered threatening his brother Frank with a knife, hiding in the woods all night, and then returning, like the repentant Prodigal Son (cf. Luke 15 : 11–32), to his stern but forgiving father, from whom he "expected a flogging" but whose tears of love were "streaming down his face" and whose perfect Christian example, reinforcing that of George, inspired him to turn to God in youth and to undertake spiritual introspection in adulthood (*CL,* 1 : 310, 353–54). He thus seemed familiar with the two main periods of Christian life as recognized by the followers of Wesley, who believed that humility exalted by the Arminian joys attending both conversion and subsequent renewals of the spirit, was the fruit of strict puritanical upbringing such as he and his ministers had known.[9] Coleridge's yearning for perfection and its joys made him pause to remember his early life; "what I am," he declared, "depends on what I have been" (*CL,* 1 : 302).

Wordsworth's famous axiom, "the child is father of the man" (*PW,* 4 : 279), is nearer in spirit to Coleridge's and the Methodists' sense of growth or progression than, say, to modern views concerning the psychological stages of life.[10] During the year following Coleridge's letters to Poole, when Wordsworth was a young man of twenty-eight, he began setting down the childhood memories or "spots of time" that were later included in *The Pre-*

*lude,*[11] and he was influenced, in part, by his friend's desire to trace the development of spiritual maturity from youth to young manhood. His autobiographical account of adult life (the persona's "conversion" and quest for perfection), and his "Evangelical" ideals of joy and humility as found throughout his works, are considered in chapter 3; at present, in the light of Evangelical views on the early development of spiritual maturity, I shall suggest interpretations of eight passages from *The Prelude,* passages recounting Wordsworth's boyhood progress from pride to humility and thence to new heights of religious experience.

In the first of these, we shall consider John Wesley's doctrine of grace and prescriptions for child-rearing, and some of James Montgomery's introspective verse, as Evangelical documents exemplifying the spiritual context of the lines in which Wordsworth recalls his 1783 Christmas vacation from Hawkshead Grammar-school (XI.345–97). This important spot of time, celebrating the persona's attainment of moral accountability, contains explicitly Evangelical language. The theological diction of the passage, in which the thirteen-year-old wrongs his father and then humbly submits to God (even as the near-adolescents Coleridge and Rhodes offended the fathers of their flesh and then bowed in penitence before God the Father), furnishes compelling evidence of the way Wordsworth looked upon six earlier spots of time—the episodes of stealing the boat, plundering the bird-traps, and skating on Esthwaite's Lake in Book I; the lines on the boy of Winander and the incident of the drowned man in Book V; and the episode of the moldering gibbet-mast in Book XI.

Wordsworth remembered these events in the way Coleridge, Robinson, and Rhodes remembered boyhood episodes; he remembered them as Bunyan remembered fearful encounters with God; he remembered them as the Methodists remembered childhood error leading to repentance; he narrates them according to the conventions, the patterns of event and crisis, which most conspicuously characterize the autobiographies that Wesley and the Evangelicals prized, praised, and elicited from men whose experience appeared apt to prompt others to wonder at God's redemptive power.

*The Prelude* suggests that the young Wordsworth's awareness of divine guidance and admonition checked his childish wrongdoing, made him aware of the mortality and hence the finitude of man, and led him to bow before God, and thus to attain complete humility at last, in the culminating epiphany of his boyhood. The eighth and final passage to be considered, the poet's memory of crossing the Alps in 1790 (VI.488–572), shows the intense religious experience of a "purified and exalted" young adult who looked forward to a spiritual life filled with the lowly joys of service to man and worship of God, partly because he had been "humbled and humanised" during childhood and at the age of accountability.

The main implication of this chapter (and the one to follow) is that Wordsworth's preoccupation with self is better understood as resembling Evangelical expressions of exalted humility than as Keats understood it. To Keats, the "proud" poet's philosophy appeared "the whims of an Egotist," and another phrase of Keats's coinage—"the wordsworthian or egotistical sublime"—has come to be associated with solipsistic introversion among poets.[12] A contemporary who knew Wordsworth better than Keats did, William Hazlitt, seemed to recognize the paradoxical nature of his mind, as well as his essentially religious spirit, when he observed that the poetry is "distinguished by a proud humility."[13] Perhaps so, for Wordsworth described the "spots of time" in our existence as helping us to retain a vivifying or renovating virtue that "enables us to mount / When high, more high, and lifts us up when fallen" (*Prelude* XI.258–60, 267–68; XII.210, 1850).

In the Christmas vacation episode, Wordsworth remembers himself as a restless and impatient youth who has scaled a crag near Hawkshead in order to discern the approach of the servant sent to bring him and his brothers home. He omits details about the servant's arrival and the vacation itself and simply announces the death of his father during the very holiday so eagerly anticipated. To him this death "appear'd / A chastisement," and he tells us that he repented of his boyish emotion:

> With trite reflections of morality,
> Yet in the deepest passion, I bow'd low
> To God, who thus corrected my desires . . . .
> [XI.373–75]

In annotating the passage David Perkins detects its substantially Christian content:

> A sensitive boy schooled in a Christian household of the nineteenth century might conceivably take the death of his father as a punishment for his own impatience, or more generally for forgetting—despite the dreary, grim, and threatening aspects of the natural world—that earthly life is a time of sorrow and probation.[14]

But the "Christian household" of Wordsworth's youth belonged to the eighteenth century, not the nineteenth; the passage becomes less difficult for ears attuned to Evangelical and Wesleyan terminology. The passage as a whole reflects a biblical doctrine of particular significance to Wesley and the Great Awakening: God hastens man's spiritual maturity through chastisement of pride. At the heart of this spot of time is a lesson in Christian humility, and when the passage is so understood we are less likely to be repelled by the puzzling proposition that the persona has done something for which the death of his father is a "chastisement" (it seems grotesque that God would kill a father to punish a child's impatience). Evangelical commonplaces also explain in what sense his reflections can be "trite" yet deeply religious.

The passage echoes the diction of Evangelical writers, who drew from a common fund of words to describe specific experiences in generic terms. In a hymn entitled "Religion," James Montgomery, whose poetry Wordsworth came to admire (see pp. 10, 35), associates "pride" with "guilty passions"; and in "The Peak Mountains" (1812) he identifies some emotions denoting pride.[15] Like Wordsworth he is "restless" before ascending a mountain, and his frame is "fever'd"—these are symptoms of a kind of discontented "pride, the strength of manhood's prime" (2 : 139–41). Though Wordsworth, for his part, never ostensibly identifies his attitudes at Hawkshead as pride, he describes himself as "feverish, and tired, and restless" (l. 347) and thereby indicates the same kind of discontent: two of these emotional states resemble those same "guilty passions" that Montgomery associates with pride; and elsewhere in *The Prelude,* the poet does associate pride with being feverish and tired.

In Book II he recalls his childhood habit of prolonging summer games beyond nightfall, going to bed "feverish" and "weary" (l. 18). These adjectives seem only a realistic description of an emotional state, just as the same (or synonymous) labels, to the modern reader, seem literally—and perhaps exclusively—to describe the schoolboy's mood; yet Wordsworth follows this description in Book II with a seemingly unrelated conclusion: each young person, he abruptly argues, "needs a warning voice to tame the pride / . . . of virtue's self-esteem" (ll. 25–26). His high tone comes unexpectedly for any reader unfamiliar with Evangelical code-words for pride, but in fact his earlier diction has prepared us for the moral comment. Such comment, then, is implicit or even primary in the Christmas episode, for Wordsworth's terminology, with its overtones of religious meaning, suggests that the schoolboy is as much discontented in spirit as restless in mood, as much prideful in nature as "naturally" boyish.

The boy, besides being feverish, tired, and restless, is "impatient" (l. 348) and full of the "anxiety of hope" (l. 372); other lines from *The Prelude* again shed light on the meaning here. His mother, in direct contrast to him, avoids "feverish" dread (V.277), rejects unnatural "hopes" (l. 279), and never asks with "impatience" more than the "timely produce" of any season (ll. 281–82). Her contentedness with the present amounts to an admirable humility, free of such guilty or discontented passions:

> . . . [she] rather lov'd
> The hours for what they are than from regards
> Glanced on their promises in restless pride.
>
> [ll. 282–84]

Adjectives denoting pride, while they do not apply to the mother, do characterize the schoolboy. In his restless if typically boyish impatience for the season to begin, he does not accept the timely produce of the present moment but feverishly wants to overleap the time remaining before the full enjoyment of his vacation; he wishes away some of his own life and, in a sense, some of his father's as well. On a day "Stormy, and rough, and wild"—a time when nature appears threatening—the impatient youth seems never to think of man's mortality, though the father's death is

imminent even as the son stands on the "Eminence" of the crag
(the horses that bear him "home," supposedly to holiday festiv-
ities, may bear his father's body "home" to the grave [ll. 349,
351–57]).

After his father's death, God assumes the paternal role of re-
proving the restless boy. The passage recalls the twelfth chapter
of Hebrews, a chapter comparing the disciplinary function of the
earthly father with the firm paternal guidance of God:

> My son, despise not thou the chastening of the Lord, nor
> faint when thou art rebuked of him: For whom the Lord
> loveth he chasteneth, and scourgeth every son whom he re-
> ceiveth. If ye endure chastening, God dealeth with you as
> with sons; for what son is he whom the father chasteneth
> not? But if ye be without *chastisement,* whereof all are par-
> takers, then are ye bastards, and not sons. Furthermore we
> have had fathers of our flesh which *corrected* us, and we
> gave them reverence: shall we not much rather be in subjec-
> tion unto the Father of spirits, and live?        [5–9; my italics]

Wordsworth employs biblical diction in describing God's pater-
nal punishment: after the boy's uneasy sense of "chastisement"
(l. 370), God "corrected" his guilty passions (l. 375). Though the
prideful offense calls for stern measures, the chastisement is
remedial. The God in Wordsworth's passage, like the stern
"Father of spirits" in Hebrews, administers a fatherly correction
both necessary and desirable; for the boy, in need of "chastise-
ment" from an earthly father, finally achieves legitimate sonship
under the paternal love of a chastening God; and the poet pays
to the Father of spirits the reverence formerly due to the father of
his flesh. He thus commemorates his spiritual coming of age.

The attainment of maturity, indeed, is the specifically Evangeli-
cal theme of Wordsworth's passage, reflecting Wesley's formula-
tion of current views on rearing children.[16] Referring to the same
passage in Hebrews (Wesley, 7 : 99), Wesley advises parents to
punish often and severely in order to conquer the natural pride
of their children, and his description of the disciplinary process
resembles that of Wordsworth. Like Montgomery, he associates
"pride" with "passions" (7 : 94), and, like Wordsworth, he calls

these guilty passions "desires" (7 : 89). He enjoins parents to administer "timely correction" of childish desires (7 : 103), and he implies a broader faith that God Himself will "correct . . . inordinate passions" (9 : 318).

This necessary chastisement effects a mature humility admired by both the poet and the preacher. After feeling God's punishment, the headstrong young Wordsworth finally "bow'd low / To God" (ll. 374–75); without punishment, warned Wesley, the strong-willed child will never "bow to God" (7 : 92). Wesley quotes from William Law (with whom Wordsworth was familiar)[17] in order to indicate the beneficial results of strong corrective measures: firm paternal control, wrote Law, will teach the child a spirit of "humility . . . and devotion" (7 : 88). The mature and now humble Wordsworth also acquires a spirit of devotion: life's journey remains difficult, but he is strengthened by "devoutest" habits (l. 397). Nurtured in admonition, this true child of God grows into manhood and becomes, like Christian, "a Pilgrim gone / In quest of highest truth" (ll. 392–93).

Wesley's theology helps to clarify other dimensions of the passage as well. Aware of personal guilt, the persona bows before God "With trite reflections of morality, / Yet in the deepest passion" (ll. 373–74), and these lines are puzzling, not only because passion and trite reflection seem mutually exclusive to the twentieth-century reader, but also because the boy's passion—his restless impatience—had presumably been corrected. Wesley, for his part, saw no inconsistency between a certain kind of reflection and a certain kind of passion. Concerning moral reflections, he believed that a man is disposed to "sober reflections" on the error of his ways whenever God corrects him (9 : 318). Perhaps Wordsworth's reflections spring from a similar cause. They are "trite" insofar as the lesson is an elementary one: pride is a vice, humility a virtue (there is hardly a more commonplace precept of Christian morality). The boy, however, thoroughly learns his lesson in humility for the first time. Because of God's direct teaching, he can grasp the simple truth with deep personal conviction, and his "deepest passion" is probably not the surface passion of pride, but rather one of zeal and certainty.

According to Wesley, depth of passion implies humility. Those

still burdened by "the pride of their unbroken heart" can feel
"no deep repentance, or thorough conviction," can experience
"no deep work in their heart" (5 : 470). The "passions" of "zeal"
or "fervent love," on the other hand, are consistent with humil-
ity, because this high degree of Christian love is "not puffed up"
(7 : 59; cf. 1 Corinthians 13 : 4). An emotional faith without
pride is therefore natural. For Wesley, the "turbulent" passions
of pride—"fretfulness, discontent, impatience"—make true zeal
impossible (7 : 59, 63). Wordsworth's "deepest passion," then,
seems to be one of fervent love; it occurs only when God puts his
impatient and restless discontent to flight. His new passion has
the depth of a properly humble religious zeal, and for him a
deep conviction reaffirms the validity of a basic moral truth.

The passage, indeed, emphasizes his "deep" response. The
ambiguous word *trite*, though not entirely pejorative, is primarily
so: superficial thoughts about morality, or even careful and sober
considerations of it, are less important than *passion* (from *patere*,
to suffer) when passion is, as in Gethsemane and at the Crucifix-
ion, an agony associated with total submission to God; and
Wordsworth's moral reflections are trivial in comparison to his
"passion," his new willingness to endure the threats of nature
and the chastisements of God. His former impatience, his stub-
born unwillingness to suffer or bear, could hardly yield to the
topoi of morality but does yield to loving reproof. The Evangeli-
cals, especially the Calvinists among them, reiterated that moral-
ity was, as good deeds were, mere "filthy rags"; [18] and Words-
worth's experience, like theirs, suggests that man can do little
without external aid and agency. With such aid, however, he
keeps his moral "rags" and also puts on the New Man, who sub-
mits to a control far higher than the laws of morality.

Wordsworth's encounter with God recalls, moreover, Wesley's
doctrine of free grace (9 : 373 ff.)—one cannot compel God to
save but must wait patiently, trusting in him to work his will.
By corollary, one is patient with the vicissitudes of life, accepting
every moment as the gift of God, not trying to press forward with
hectic calculation of how the present can insure the future one
desires. This doctrine might almost be said to explain the struc-
turing principle of the passage at hand, in which God's act of

grace at the center (ll. 364–75) is anticipated in the first part and acknowledged toward the end.

At the top of the crag the impatient youth looks toward the future, "straining [his] eyes intensely" to catch a glimpse of the servant (l. 362); he has yet to learn to accept the timing of events according to the will of God. But certain nearby objects foreshadow the remedial grace to come. The sheep on the boy's "right hand" (l. 359) seems a muted echo of Christ's invitation to the "sheep on his right hand": "Come ye blessed of my father, inherit the kingdom prepared for you from the foundation of the world" (Matthew 25 : 33–34). The "whistling hawthorn" (l. 360) or "blasted tree" on his "left" (l. 378) recalls the doomed and accursed goats on Christ's "left" hand (25 : 33) and thus may reinforce theologically the threatening aspect of the "stormy" day. The boy, in a sense, is suspended between promise and damnation but finds a makeshift refuge: he is "half-shelter'd by a naked wall" (l. 358) and thereby symbolically set apart until God corrects his desires and, in the words of a hymn by Wesley's Nonconformist friend Isaac Watts, gives full "shelter from the stormy blast."

After receiving God's loving chastisement, the spiritually mature Wordsworth often remembers details from this episode— including the "single sheep," the "blasted tree," and the "old stone wall" (ll. 378–79)—and "thence . . . drink[s] / As at a fountain" (ll. 384–85). His simile is a common image of grace, as Alexander Cruden's eighteenth-century Concordance suggests: not only does the fountain for "sin and uncleanness" in the Book of Zechariah (13 : 1) serve as a type for Christ the "matchless healing and purging Fountain" but, more generally and more importantly for this passage, symbolizes "all spiritual graces and refreshments communicated by the Spirit." [19] Wordsworth is spiritually refreshed by the memory of his encounter with God; his adolescent experience of grace, therefore, is extended to the present moment. Indeed, it seems reasonable to conjecture that he regarded other spots of time, with their "efficacious spirit" (XI.269), as fountains of grace sustaining him on the pilgrimage of life.

It is also possible, of course, that he employs Evangelical dic-

tion casually, to lend authority to his narrative; but this par-
ticular passage, in which God's presence is central, suggests that
a theology both traditional and vital survived in and helped to
shape his new kind of verse. The theme of spiritual maturity,
for instance, can also be found in other spots of time. The spir-
itual progress realized in the Christmas episode—the final spot in
*The Prelude*—is notably anticipated in six earlier memorable
moments, during which the boy's humbling but purifying aware-
ness of mortality and fear of God (or of some power external to
the self) strengthen his moral faculty. Sometimes the language of
these passages is less explicitly theological, but the general se-
quence maintains a spiritual emphasis leading to the lines dis-
cussed above.

In the famous boating episode (I.372–427) the young Words-
worth, finding a "Skiff" "within a rocky Cave" just off Ullswater,
loosens the tether and embarks, rowing "lustily" and with his
"best skill" (ll. 374–75, 380–82, 397, 401). Fixing his view on a
"craggy ridge" (ll. 397–98), he gauges his position, sets his course,
and thus gives evidence of that skill. The act of taking the boat
falls short of good conduct, but the misdeed is unpremeditated
and seems a manifestation of exuberant self-assurance. The older
Wordsworth, however, does recognize the questionable propriety:
"it was," he writes, "an act of stealth" (l. 388). Moreover, he sug-
gests that he acted "proudly" (l. 396), and this somewhat am-
biguous adverb, besides denoting the self-confidence with which
he maneuvered the boat, may connote the cause of his peccadillo.

An unexpected occurrence, announced in the central lines, in-
terrupts the boy's adventure:

> . . . from behind that craggy Steep, till then
> The bound of the horizon, a huge Cliff,
> As if with voluntary power instinct,
> Uprear'd its head.
>
> [ll. 405–08]

His first reaction is to hasten further out, in the hope of escaping
the sight. The "stately" pace with which he began, dipping his
oars "in cadence," now becomes somewhat desperate: "I struck,

and struck again" (ll. 386–87, 408). His speed makes the cliff appear to stride after him even faster than before, "with purpose of its own / And measured motion like a living thing" (ll. 383–84, 1850). The cliff, which at first is hidden by the closer steep, suddenly becomes visible as the boat moves from shore and then, as the boat moves faster, appears to grow larger and come closer. The boy's knowledge of boating gives him a certain wisdom in the ways of nature but apparently does not provide an explanation of this "spectacle" (l. 418), this optic phenomenon; perhaps he had never rowed far enough from land to observe the illusion. He now tries another way of eluding the menace: with "trembling hands" he reverses course and returns the "bark" to its "mooring-place" (ll. 412–15). The cliff disappears.

This adventure serves to enhance the boy's spiritual growth; he not only learns the limitations of his skill (and hence the folly of undue self-assurance), but also feels the awakening of conscience. With his means of guidance overshadowed (the cliff supplants the "craggy ridge"), and nothing now to lead him except the few stars in a "grey sky" (l. 400), he wisely abandons the forbidding journey. The cliff's appearance, besides introducing a disturbing variable into his experiment, supplies the instrumentality of his moral development. His exuberant "pleasure" was already "troubled," perhaps because an accusing "voice / Of mountain-echoes" had begun to speak even as he pushed from shore (ll. 389–90); but further out the cliff warns him unmistakably and seems to change troubled pleasure into salutary fear. The beginning of true wisdom supersedes mere skill. The boy rectifies his error, and the experience as a whole seems at once to tell him what he cannot do and to teach him what he should not do.

His emergent sense of "unknown modes of being" is "dim and undetermin'd" at this point (ll. 419–20), but the Ullswater incident exercises a lasting effect upon him. For days thereafter, his brain "work'd" ceaselessly (l. 419), trying to grasp the event's significance. Like Bunyan, whose boyhood nights were troubled by the "fearful dreams" and "dreadful visions" sent by a jealous God,[20] he is now disturbed, both waking and sleeping, by the memory of chastisement:

> . . . huge and mighty forms, that do not live
> Like living men, moved slowly through the mind
> By day, and were a trouble to my dreams.
>
> [ll. 398–400, 1850]

The reader may understand the natural explanation of the cliff's appearance; in these lines, however, he can share the boy's apprehension of another mode of being.

The God-fearing Methodist preachers recounted childhood experiences resembling the young Wordsworth's. Richard Rodda, for example, recalled an early error in terms more obviously theological but hardly more religious: "One time in particular, I was in such trouble that I thought God was frowning over me, and that hell moved from beneath to meet me" (*Lives*, 2 : 118). For the poet also, admonishment from a looming presence creates a kind of hell within, or at least disturbs the inward voice of conscience, as though the cliff were a moral warning, a warning comparable to the ones felt and heeded by the Evangelicals. The religious quality of his fear is further shown by the apocalyptic idiom of his reaction to his encounter with the unknown form. Like John on Patmos, prophesying "no more sea" at the latter day (Revelation 21 : 1), he sometimes envisioned destruction for the things of this world:

> No familiar shapes
> Remained, no pleasant images of trees,
> Of sea or sky, no colours of green fields.
>
> [ll. 395–97, 1850]

Referring to no supervenient mode of being, and focusing only upon the total absence of this-worldly phenomena, Wordsworth nevertheless manages, through a deliberate and effective indeterminacy of expression, to evoke the nearness and suggest the molding powers of some transcendent influence or some divine will. His language, to be sure, drives at what must remain ineffable, but he seeks to establish the reality of an active spiritual realm beyond the ken of sensuous perception, and his experience teaches him that neither he nor mankind in general can act as though the world were autonomous and not subject to the stroke of a higher moral law and the intervention of a condescending Spirit.

Wordsworth's attitudes in another passage from Book I, in which he remembers setting traps for woodcocks ("my shoulder all with springes hung, / I was a fell destroyer" [ll. 317–18]), compare with the tone of similar boyhood incidents in spiritual autobiography. Neither he nor the Evangelical writers attempt to glorify or justify their youthful deeds; they seek instead to dramatize the spiritual sense in which the period of childhood merits examination and remembrance. The persona's "joy" in destruction sent him compulsively "hurrying on, / Still hurrying, hurrying onward" from snare to snare (ll. 313, 320–21). So too, with "diabolical pleasure," the young Christopher Hopper killed birds of the wild *(Lives,* 1 : 5), and John Woolman recalled being "pleased" with the exploit of killing a mother robin and all her young ones.[21]

Despite their strange delight—or perhaps because of it, however—neither Wordsworth nor the autobiographers acted with impunity. A vague sense of horror attends his accessory practice of robbing other traps and plundering nests of "The Mother Bird" (l. 339); in time these variations of his sport, morally questionable if not diabolical, nullify the joy of it. The wind's "strange utterance" begins to disturb him, and the sky, which seems no longer "a sky / Of earth," lours overhead (ll. 348–50). "Low breathings" heard among "solitary hills,"

> sounds
> Of undistinguishable motion, steps
> Almost as silent as the turf they trod

—all seem to be "coming after" the boy (ll. 329–32). His awareness of being pursued suggests a fear of retribution reminiscent of Evangelical dread. A "few minutes" after Woolman's exploit, he was "seized" with the "horror" of being judged; and Hopper, "half dead with fear," felt "great terror" because he thought his deeds portended punishment from God.

Wordsworth and Woolman, whose records reveal both the awakening of conscience and a sound moral judgment, construe their fearful experiences as harbingers of spiritual maturity.

Woolman's youthful "cruelties" "troubled" him, but his mature recollection seems to disturb him even more, for "having in a sportive way, killed an innocent creature." Wordsworth felt, while setting the traps, that he was a "trouble" to nature's peace (l. 323); setting down his recollection, he pronounces his deeds "mean" and "inglorious" (ll. 339–40). Woolman implies that the "painful considerations" and "horror" in his experience began to transform the "contrary disposition" of youth into the "tender-hearted" Christian's habitual goodness. And Wordsworth suggests that his experience, filled with "terrors" and "regrets," began to temper his boyish "lassitudes" and "vexations" and thereby helped to assure adulthood's calm existence; the "end" (or effect) of his waywardness, therefore, was "not ignoble" (ll. 340–41, 356–60). For Woolman, killing the robins was "a thing remarkable," not because his act was inherently memorable, and certainly not because it was praiseworthy, but because it effected moral growth; and Wordsworth memorializes his behavior not to suggest that the free or natural spirit of childhood carries over into his spontaneous verse but to illustrate the dependence of "worthy" selfhood (l. 361) upon the early chastening of guilty passion.

The lassitudes and vexations underlying the boy's questionable practices seem identical with his weariness and feverishness in the Christmas episode, and his "strong desire," which prevails and overpowers his "better reason" (ll. 325–26), may also signify the passions of natural pride. Despite the beginnings of chastisement and the stirrings of conscience, the restless passion of the senses still predominates at this point, and the entire passage emphasizes the resulting mortal condition (as though to imply that "the wages of sin is death" [Romans 6 : 23]). During the winter season, when "frost and breath of frosty wind" snaps the "last autumnal crocus" (ll. 312–13), the boy undertakes destruction of natural life and thus personifies winter's deathly spirit.

But this young agent of death is shown to be mortal himself. "Scudding" like a bird (l. 319), he is associated with the woodcocks endangered by death, and he is soon hunted, in turn, by the undistinguishable force coming after him. His fear for his own life is in contrast to the naïve joy with which he began his trapping and seems more in accord with the reality of his weak moral position. After plundering nests he is "suspended," as in the Christmas episode, by the windy "blast" (l. 345); but in this instance, despite being exalted to some extent by nature in the spring, or by some extranatural force ("the sky seemed not a sky / Of earth, and with what motion moved the clouds!"), he finds no shelter, and indeed seems chastened once again: "Ill sustain'd" by "knots of grass" and "half-inch fissures," he hangs over a "perilous ridge," his survival in doubt (ll. 342–47); and the passage concludes in uncertainty, with the boy as yet rescued by no act of grace.

In the Esthwaite skating scene (I.452–89), it is again "the frosty season" (l. 452). The sun "was set," but the young Wordsworth at play does not heed the "summons" (ll. 453–55). Neither the warning light in the cottage windows, calling him inside, nor the tolling of the village clock, "clear and loud" as an ominous knell, can subdue the rapture of the youth, "proud and exulting, like an untired horse, / That cares not for its home" (ll. 457–60); he skates with his companions, absorbed in the game, "imitative of the chace / And woodland pleasures" (ll. 462–63). Soon, however, he is set apart from his friends, with their "din," "tumult," and "uproar" (ll. 466, 470, 474). Racing in the crowd, with the "shadowy banks on either side" sweeping "through the darkness," he decides to stop short as though to see whether the landscape will stop with him (ll. 480–84). He learns that it does not: "yet still the solitary Cliffs / Wheeled by me" (ll. 484–85).

The lingering effects of his own dizzying motion create the illusion of moving banks; and the illusion, as opposed to signifying the solipsism of an exclusively mental reality, seems well grounded in the noumenal and spiritual realms that underlie and validate phenomena. (The nature of perception, largely because of empiricist and skeptical philosophy from Locke through Hume and Drummond, was an important theme for Wordsworth, who poetically achieved a coalescing or interpenetration of subject and object [in his resistance to solipsism he drew upon philosophical as well as spiritual contexts]; and the disciplines of epistemology and theology served him equally well—they were allies in his effort to show how language leads outside the self and affirms a reality beyond.) [22]

In any case, the illusion instructs him, for he now recognizes, through an experimentation resembling that of the stolen boat episode, the unpredictability of nature: he realizes that earth's "diurnal round" continues with "visible motion" (1. 486) whether he is active or not, and his exuberant pride therefore changes to contemplative awe. In a mood far different from his initial coltishness, the boy now simply stands and watches till all is "tranquil as a dreamless sleep" (1. 489). In effect, then, he at last obeys the original summons to rest and thereby dimly anticipates some late hour of life's winter season, calling him to the dreamless sleep of death. Thus Wordsworth suggests once more that his increasing consciousness of mortality encouraged and reinforced humility; his sober and solitary moment chastens his rapture and gives him a salutary perspective. Somewhat like the youthful Woolman, who left his undiscerning companions to receive "gracious visitations," the boy becomes spiritually receptive when he leaves the "tumultuous throng" (1. 476).

Abbie Findlay Potts has pointed out similarities between Bunyan's style and the diction of Wordsworth's lines on the boy of Winander (V.389–422); she suggests, for example, that the calls exchanged between the boy and the owls,

> with quivering peals
> And long halloos, and screams, and echoes loud
> Redoubled and redoubled,
>
> [ll. 401–03]

are reminiscent of Christian's passage through the Valley of the Shadow of Death, where he hears the "continual howling and yelling . . . the doleful voices . . . and dreadful noises" of a "company of Fiends." [23] But there is more similarity of theme than of language: Christian must descend to the lowlands of death, and the boy of Winander, like the young Wordsworth in other spots of time, makes the humbling discovery of mortality.

The boy learns that whenever he cries to the "silent owls" they answer him, "responsive to his call" (ll. 398, 401); but soon he discovers that they may fail to answer—the experiment is not invariably repeatable. Sometimes, despite his efforts, "pauses of

deep silence mock'd his skill," and these unexpected pauses bring
sudden illumination:

> . . . in that silence, while he hung
> Listening, a gentle shock of mild surprize
> Has carried far into his heart the voice
> Of mountain torrents . . . .
>
> [ll. 406–09]

An unspectacular but nonetheless pivotal epiphany liberates him
from accustomed patterns of behavior and enlarges his general
awareness. Like the young Wordsworth skating on Esthwaite, the
boy seems to acquire a sense of detachment. And as Wordsworth,
after stealing the boat, finds his presumptive skill useless against
unknown modes of being, so the boy of Winander can rely on
finite skill no longer; the narrator suggests, indeed, that he ac-
knowledges an "uncertain Heaven, receiv'd / Into the bosom of
the steady Lake" (ll. 412–13). A dimly perceived spirit-realm, at
once transcending and indwelling, appears to administer the
gentle but timely shock.

The next verse-paragraph announces his untimely death: "This
Boy was taken from his mates, and died / In childhood, ere he
was full ten years old" (ll. 414–15); these lines, coming after what
seems only a simple descriptive passage, are themselves somewhat
surprising and may administer a gentle shock to the reader. Per-
haps the boy's gentle shock was also an intimation of mortality.
The sudden silence of the owls—traditionally omens of death—
casts the shadow of death; and at twilight when day is dying, the
boy himself nears his end despite apparent vitality. He could
gain consolation, however, from hearing the immortal "voice /
Of mountain torrents."

The tone of the passage is subdued but not somber, suggesting
that the boy, like Christian, comes through the valley of death.
He blows his clarion calls "as through an instrument" (ll. 397–
98), and this metaphor of joyful harmony, insofar as it exempli-
fies the Romantics' employment of the aural imagery of music to
herald, or at least to connote, a sure shift from the temporal to
the spiritual plane of being,[24] evokes the sounding of the last

trump (when the dead shall be raised—cf. 1 Corinthians 15 : 52);
and this possible metaphor of resurrection not only prefigures
death but tends to transfigure its finality, thereby muting the
shock of mortality and tempering surprise with assurance. Ritual-
istic remembrance, rather than despair, seems to characterize the
poet's regular visits to the churchyard on summer evenings, when
he stood "mute—looking at the grave in which he lies" (l. 422).
Indeed, the lines conclude in a hopeful tone, with Hawkshead's
"Village Church" listening

> to the gladsome sounds
> That, from the rural School ascending, play
> Beneath her and about her.
>
> [ll. 429–31]

Death does not banish joy from the congregation of the living.

The episode of the drowned man (V.450–81), like the passage
on the boy of Winander, recalls the language of *Pilgrim's Prog-
ress*. The "heap of garments" left on the "opposite Shore" of
Esthwaite (ll. 460–61) offers evidence of the drowning but also,
on a figurative level, recalls the "mortal garments" left at the
River of Death by Bunyan's pilgrims when they crossed over into
the heavenly Jerusalem.[25] Such language, therefore, contributes
metaphorically to the hopeful tone of the passage as a whole,
lending a shape of faith to the stark theme of death. Bunyan's
Christian, moreover, joins "a company" before entering the
Valley of the Shadow (Wharey, p. 68); and Wordsworth depicts
"a Company" sounding the mysteries of death, searching for the
body "with grappling irons, and long poles" (ll. 468–69). Both
Bunyan and Wordsworth thereby suggest the advantage of com-
panionship and fellowship in the face of unfathomable mortality:
companions can affirm the strong and enduring bonds of life
even as they join forces, in their spirit of mutual hope, to in-
quire whether death destroys life utterly.

This episode, however, also like the Winander passage, re-
sembles *Pilgrim's Progress* in theme more than language. In itself,
the metaphorical similarity leads only so far, but it does represent
and indicate a suggestive similarity of atmosphere: Christian's
fortitude in adversity, his fundamental and sustaining assurance

of immortality, broadly parallels the young Wordsworth's emerg-
ing and unshakable faith. The dead man is "a spectre shape / Of
terror" when at last his "ghastly face" appears, but for the boy
an "ideal grace" mitigates the terror, preventing him, for the first
time, from suffering apocalyptic or mortal fears (he feels "no
vulgar fear" because his "inner eye had seen / Such sights before"
[ll. 473–76]). His previous encounters with mortality have given
Wordsworth self-perspective and reduced death's terrors, so that
he does not fretfully seek to perpetuate his temporal existence
but seems receptive, like the boy of Winander, to the promise of
resurrection: the dead man "rose" out of the water (l. 472) and
apparently does not so much convey an impression of advanced
decay or utter annihilation as he calls to mind the sacrament of
baptism, thus denoting no death but that of the corrupt Old
Man, and indeed prefiguring the vital time when Christians,
held back and doomed by death no longer, shall be changed.

The episode of the moldering gibbet-mast (XI.279–345) returns
to the emphasis on strict training and shows, for the penultimate
time in *The Prelude,* the chastening of natural pride. In this
spot of time, immediately preceding the Christmas episode, the
boy mounts his horse and rides toward the hills with "proud
hopes," though his hand could scarcely "hold a bridle" (ll. 281–
82). An unspecified "mischance" separates him from the servant
James—his "encourager," "guide," and "comrade" (ll. 284–86)—
and initiates a painful lesson in humility. No longer so exuber-
ant, he dismounts and descends alone and fearful, "stumbling"
onward to "a bottom, where in former times / A murderer had
been hung in iron chains" (ll. 286–90). The "moulder'd" gibbet-
mast is not sufficient to tell him what occurred; only when he
reads the murderer's name, carved on the turf by "some unknown
hand" (ll. 291–94), does he recognize the place as one of ultimate
shame and retribution. His descent from proud hopes to abject
fear is completed.

Certain elements of this narrative closely resemble an anecdote
in Elizabeth Sherwood's *The Fairchild Family* (1848), called
"the last great Puritan work for children" (Sangster, *Pity My
Simplicity,* pp. 56–57). Because of a quarrel over a doll, Mrs.
Fairchild takes her young ones to see the execution of a man

who murdered his brother; she thereby hopes to teach them that
the wages of sin is death. They were confronted by "a gibbet, on
which the body of a man hung in chains . . . but the face of the
corpse was so shocking, that the children could not look upon
it." [26] The young Wordsworth's encounter with the gibbet-mast
is less ghastly than the event described by Mrs. Sherwood (though
by the time of the drowned man incident, two years later, he is
able, unlike the Fairchild children at this point, to stare death
full in the face). Like Mrs. Sherwood, however, Wordsworth
seems to know the effectiveness of gibbets in taming the high
spirits of youth: Mrs. Fairchild's children never quarrel again,
and the boy indulges "proud hopes" no more.

His fearful experience, in fact, establishes a humble sense of
dependence; he reascends the "bare Common" to search for his
"lost Guide" (ll. 303, 312). He finds instead a "Girl who bore a
Pitcher on her head" (l. 306). Her "garments vex'd and *toss'd,"*
she seems "with difficult steps to force her way / Against the
blowing *wind,"* while preserving the *pitcher* intact (ll. 307–08,
315; my italics); and Wordsworth's language, reflecting Bunyan's
in *Grace Abounding,* suggests that the girl represents steadfast
faith. Using similar imagery and diction, Bunyan tells of a time
in his youth when faith proved weak and unable to withstand
such adverse conditions: "Thus by the strange and unusual as-
saults of the tempter, was my soul like a broken *vessel,* driven
as with the *winds,* and *tossed* sometimes headlong into despair"
(my italics).[27] Bunyan and Wordsworth, moreover, seem to echo
Paul's exhortation to the Ephesians, that they "henceforth be no
more children, *tossed* to and fro, and carried about with every
*wind* of doctrine" (Ephesians 4 : 14; my italics).

The girl's determined resistance to the wind is undoubtedly
meant to suggest a spiritual maturity beyond her years; toward
the end of the passage, she is named not "Girl" but "Woman"
(l. 315). (Her difficult but steadfast progression from girl to
woman suggests that she preserves her spiritual integrity in the
midst of experience, and her intact pitcher, in terms of a long
line of traditional vessel imagery [see, for example, 1 Peter 3 : 7],
may be intended to symbolize her successful defense of her
feminine worth and frangibility against all threats, and indeed

against all odds.) [28] And toward the end of *The Prelude,* the concept of "struggling with storms" remains Wordsworth's way of visualizing faithfulness or "reverence for duty" (XIV.298–99, 1850). The boy, after aimlessly "stumbling on" in fear (l. 288), is confronted by one who purposefully forces her way, and one whose persistence exemplifies a better means of negotiating the rough road of life. The vision is especially timely for him, since he has just faced the gibbet-mast and seen the result of straying from the narrow path; he now finds a guide to lead him back to it.

Just before this passage, Wordsworth declares that such "spots of time"—his own and those in the lives of all—retain a renovating or vivifying virtue in the midst of "false opinion and contentious thought, / Or aught of heavier or more deadly weight" (ll. 258–62; 210, 1850). Implicitly, then, they offer strength in times of moral weakness or religious doubt (if need be, for example, the poet can recall the struggling girl, his symbol of steadfast faith). Moreover, such experiences humble and humanize the child in order to purify and exalt the man; at the end of the passage, Wordsworth suggests that his "remembrances" (l. 325) at once tempered his pride and self-assurance and heightened his joy and self-esteem. He humbly acknowledges that from time to time he still feels "lost" (l. 330), as though without a spiritual guide; but "divine radiance" prevails in the "blessed time" of his maturity. On the one hand his spirits seem uplifted by the "mystery of Man," whose honors proceed "from what a depth" (ll. 329–30); but he also preserves the humbled awareness of death so deeply inculcated throughout his early years: "I see by glimpses now; when age comes on, / May scarcely see at all" (ll. 338–39). And toward the end of *The Prelude,* immediately following the Christmas episode, he attributes this mature synthesis of exaltation and humility to his particular upbringing. "Not in vain," he writes, was he

> taught to reverence a Power
> That is the visible quality and shape
> And image of right reason; that matures
> Her processes by steadfast laws; gives birth

To no impatient or fallacious hopes,
No heat of passion or excessive zeal,
No vain conceits; provokes to no quick turns
Of self-applauding intellect; but trains
To meekness, and exalts by humble faith.
[XIII.19–28, 1850] [29]

In a familiar passage (VI.494–572), Wordsworth commemorates his crossing of the Alps during the Long Vacation of 1790, when he and Robert Jones were on their walking tour through France and Switzerland. After traveling "a length of hours" from the Vallais toward Italy, they and their guides take the "noon's repast" at "an Inn / Among the mountains" (ll. 495–500). The guides do not tarry; they leave their charges lingering idly "at the Board" (l. 501). The guides wish to pursue the journey and seem conscientious in their role, but the young men, strangely unconcerned about making time or covering ground, do not choose to avail themselves of the services they have engaged.

And they are now alone. They resume their journey and begin descending in accordance with the "downward" trend of the "beaten road" (ll. 501–02; 568, 1850). The way seems plain enough, even without their guides; but suddenly the path disappears "at a rivulet's edge" (l. 503). The trail's downward trend would indicate its reappearance farther downstream, but the travelers are distracted by the "conspicuous invitation" from another route:

The only track now visible was one
Upon the farther side, right opposite,
And up a lofty Mountain.
[ll. 505–07; 572, 1850]

"After a little scruple" (l. 507), as though aware of possibly leaving the right road, they take the new path nevertheless; and their apparent expectation of a scenic route—"we had hopes that pointed to the clouds" (l. 587, 1850)—makes them forget their goal of crossing the Alps. Inevitably they suffer "anxiety" and "doubts," for they do not overtake their "Comrades gone before" (ll. 509–12), and they are to some extent rebuked when a be-mused if not scornful peasant tells them they have already *"cross'd the Alps"* (l. 524), presumably at some lower altitude on the downward route. From him they learn

> That to the place which had perplex'd us first
> We must descend, and there should find the road
> Which in the stony channel of the Stream
> Lay a few steps, and then along its Banks;
> And further, that thenceforward all our course
> Was downwards, with the current of that Stream.
>
> [ll. 513–19, 524]

Wordsworth temporarily suspends the narrative in the second verse-paragraph and retrospectively analyzes his mistake. He now knows that, instead of realizing the aspirations "that pointed to the clouds," he was merely "lost as in a cloud" (l. 529); the ap-parent promise of the ascending path proved illusory. He now recognizes, moreover, that instead of proceeding toward his Italian destination, he was in fact "halted" in his progress by the false lure of the mountain path (l. 530). Finally, he suggests that he was at fault for losing the way; back at the rivulet, he made no "struggle to break through" (l. 530), no attempt to per-ceive the road beneath the stream or to locate the place of its re-appearance. A single obstacle proved too much for his sense of direction.

The details of this story have spiritual significance, and indeed seem based on the traditional Christian metaphor of life as a journey. Like Bunyan's Christian, Wordsworth travels with "Comrades" and is led by "Guides." Sometimes he loses the way, and sometimes the way is "all plain to sight" (ll. 497, 511; 567, 584, 1850). His destination, unlike that of Christian, is temporal; but like Christian and like Bunyan he makes spiritual discoveries along the way and as he writes. The second paragraph, besides ex-amining what literally occurred, reveals a few of these discoveries. For example, the poet implies that just as the true road is not found without a "struggle," so the discernment of spiritual direc-tion, the expectation of "something evermore about to be," of something indeterminate and perhaps therefore rarefied or even otherworldly, is not made without disciplined "effort" (ll. 541–42). He recalls, moreover, that the power of his imagination "came / Athwart" him (ll. 528–29), not only counteracting any further tendency to stray from direct and beaten paths but also opposing any further commission of moral or spiritual error. For Wordsworth discovers, finally, that true "Greatness" lies not in conquering literal heights or in seeking other kinds of temporal glory but in developing receptivity to spiritual "visitings / Of awful promise that have shewn to us / The invisible world" (ll. 525–29, 533–36). "Our home / Is with infinitude," he declares, but "only there" and not at any finite place however "lofty"; and "our destiny" is indeed "with hope"—not with the "hopes" attached to temporal promise but with the "hope that can never die" (ll. 538–40). The soul has its glory and needs no vainglory to attest its prowess, no spoils or trophies of mountains climbed (ll. 544–45; 609, 1850).

The third paragraph resumes the narrative, with the spiritual sense apparent. The persona is now content to hurry "downwards" (l. 551), following a route previously scorned. The road is difficult, has a "narrow" chasm and gloomy "strait" reminiscent of the strait and narrow way to salvation (Matthew 7 : 14); but the persona, in a humble state of mind, willingly journeys "several hours / At a slow step" (ll. 553–56; 622, 1850); and when he is ravished by the unexpected beauty of the lower route, with its woods, waterfalls, rocks, crags, streams, and clouds, his dogged and quasi-moralistic perseverance is rewarded and even yields momentarily to a purely aesthetic enjoyment. But only momentarily, for on the figurative level his soul is exalted on this low road of humility where every object both lofty and mean

> Were all like workings of one mind, the features
> Of the same face, blossoms upon one tree,
> Characters of the great Apocalypse,
> The types and symbols of Eternity,
> Of first and last, and midst, and without end.
>
> [ll. 568–72]

This elevated passage takes its origin from an essentially unspectacular experience (man may feel the force of unknown modes of being, or of an uncertain heaven, in such lowland settings as Ullswater or Esthwaite's Lake). In the Patmos apocalypse, Christ encompasses Alpha and Omega (Revelation 1 : 8); and Wordsworth in his latter-day revelation comprehends the eternal First and Last in part because he knows earth's middle realm as well as her mountain heights.

Like the Christmas episode, the experience of crossing the Alps marks a coming of age; *The Prelude* suggests by such passages that early admonition has taken effect and that the man is spiritually mature. The extravagant "hopes" that led Wordsworth up the Alpine path may be a recurrence of the "proud hopes" with which, as a boy on horseback, he climbs the Lake Country hills; but as a young man of twenty, seven years after his attainment to humility one sad Christmastide, he finds that his "Imagination" (or "reason in her most exalted mood"—cf. *Prelude* XIII.170) is strong enough, without the threat of retribution or the intervention of God, to chasten lofty passion for high places and hence to assume the divine prerogative of correcting desire, to comprehend spiritual truth as autonomous and objectified and hence to escape solipsism (or what he and Coleridge regarded as "the abyss of Idealism").[30] His childhood spots of time augur his humility and exaltation among the Alps, his training prepares him to perceive the infinite in the mundane. "Oh! sorrow for the Youth," exclaims Wordsworth, "who could have seen" the "sanctified abodes" of Alpine valleys and heights

> Unchasten'd, unsubdu'd, unaw'd, unrais'd
> To patriarchal dignity of mind,
> And pure simplicity of wish and will. . . .
>
> [*Prelude* VI.441–45]

CHAPTER THREE  *WORDSWORTH'S*

*THEOLOGY OF THE*

*SPIRIT*


## The Theological Background

In a letter to Catherine Clarkson (December 1814), Wordsworth reported the following conversation with his "sweet little boy" John:

> "How did God make me? Where is God? How does he speak? He never spoke to *me*." I told him that God was a spirit,— that he was not like his flesh, which he could touch; but more like his thoughts, in his mind, which he could not touch. The wind was tossing in the fir trees and the sky and light were dancing about in their dark branches, as seen through the window. Noting these fluctuations, he exclaimed eagerly, "There's a bit of him, I see it there!"
>
> [*MY*, 2 : 618–19]

The poet's way of telling about God, in addition to being on a level the child could understand, indicates the persistence of an "Evangelical" temperament formed in youth; for the intimate and sustaining presence of God the Holy Spirit was the most distinguishing characteristic of religious life among the Evangelicals; and this poet-father, forty-four years of age, seems concerned to instruct John as his own "Father" instructed him: in the things of the spirit and the ways of the Spirit (see chapter 2).

His poems, in any case, consistently show Wordworth's continued belief in the spiritual character of both God and mind; and his untouchable (hence insubstantial and spiritual) "thoughts," as expressed in those poems throughout his career, apprehend and are indeed akin to the breathlike, empyreal, and luminescent manifestations of a spiritual Nature whose dark and material branches, touchable like the flesh, can yet appear to be no less animated and various, no less derived, no less inspirited and inspired, than human thought (see chapter 4). And we shall see, upon reviewing spiritual doctrines of the Evangelicals, how closely his vision accorded with theirs and therefore how richly he benefited, directly or indirectly, from their indisputable spiritual knowledge and their cohesive and consistent assertions of spiritual experience; for their thoughts, like his, arose from their lives and affected their actions; and their thoughts, like his, were grounded in the view that God is a Spirit whose image is Man.

Wordsworth's library contained two works by Isaac Taylor,[1] who recognized the antecedents of the Evangelical revival; in *Four Lectures on Spiritual Christianity* (1841), for example, he observes that "grave puritanism" contributed to "the evangelic principle" of the "recent religious impulse."[2] We need go back only to the prolific Nonconformist theologian Isaac Watts, whose spiritual roots were Puritan, to find expression of those seminal convictions that helped to establish the importance of the Holy Spirit among the Evangelicals. He concurs with the increasing testimony of his day, that the Spirit is "not utterly withdrawn from men," and cites a phenomenon of 22 October 1704 attested by John Howe:

> I then experienced an inexpressibly pleasant melting of heart, tears gushing out of mine eyes for joy that God should shed abroad his love abundantly through the hearts of men; and that for this very purpose mine own heart should be so signally possessed of and by his Blessed Spirit. [Watts, 1 : 714]

He also quotes from Dr. Owen's *Treatise of Communion with God* (1713), describing how the Spirit "worketh joy":

He doth it immediately by himself, without the considera-
tion of any other acts or works of his, or the interpositions of
any reasonings, or deductions, and conclusions. This does
not arise from our reflex considerations of the love of God,
but rather gives occasion thereunto. He so sheds abroad the
love of God in our hearts, and fills them with gladness by an
immediate act and operation. Of this joy there is no account
to be given, but that the Spirit worketh it when and how
he will: He secretly infuseth and distils it into the soul, pre-
vailing against all fears and sorrows, filling it with gladness,
exultations, and sometimes with unspeakable raptures of the
mind.                                                        [1 : 715]

In "The Witness of the Spirit," a famous sermon preached on
4 April 1767, John Wesley took up his Nonconformist friend's
earlier interest in the operations of the Holy Ghost; he described
the Spirit's witness as "an inward impression on the souls of
believers, whereby the Spirit of God directly testifies to their
spirit, that they are children of God" (cf. Romans 8 : 16) and,
significantly, elevated this belief to a position of prime impor-
tance for his followers:

It more nearly concerns the Methodists, so called, clearly to
understand, explain, and defend this doctrine; because it is
one grand part of the testimony which God has given them
to bear to all mankind. It is by his peculiar blessing upon
them in searching the Scriptures, confirmed by the experience
of His children, that this great evangelical truth has been
recovered, which had been for many years wellnigh lost and
forgotten.                                        [Sugden, 2 : 343–44]

Toward the end of the century, Wesley's beloved and saintly
friend John Fletcher taught that a special "Dispensation" of the
Holy Spirit "is now in force" and that Evangelical pastors should
defend this conviction "against all Opposers"; [3] and Wrangham,
Clarkson, and Wilberforce, the Evangelical Anglicans admired
by Wordsworth, would undoubtedly have pleased Fletcher in
their homage to the Third Person of the Trinity [4]—homage ex-

emplifying the ascendant theological emphasis in eighteenth-century England.

In *The Life of Wesley,* Southey discusses the typical stages in adult spiritual life and thereby gives details of that emphasis; Wesley, he writes,

> points out the exact analogy there is between natural and spiritual things. A child is born of a woman in a moment, or, at least, in a very short time. Afterwards, he gradually and slowly grows, till he attains to the stature of a man. In like manner a person is born of God in a short time, if not in a moment; but it is by slow degrees that he afterwards grows up to the measure of the full stature of Christ. The same relation, therefore, which there is between our natural birth and our growth, there is also between our New Birth and our Sanctification.[5]

The Evangelicals' experience of conversion, repeatedly characterized by Wesley and Whitefield as a regeneration by the Holy Ghost,[6] was only the first stage of their adult development in Christian maturity (even after their strict upbringing followed by conversion, they did not cease to be "children" of God in need of further guidance); "conversion," Horton Davies observes, "was the beginning and was accompanied by the inner assurance of God's love . . . the end was Christian Perfection, the growth in Scriptural holiness, or, as Whitefield would have preferred to term it, Sanctification" (*Worship and Theology in England,* p. 154). The long years between the New Birth and Perfection were characterized by a reciprocal, covenant relationship between the Evangelical pilgrim and the Holy Spirit, a relationship where sometimes the pilgrim took the initiative by choosing the Spirit through an act of will (as Matthew Henry's *Baptismal Covenant* [1713] illustrates: "I take God the Holy Ghost to be my Sanctifier, Teacher, Guide, and Comforter")[7] and sometimes the Spirit, when the wayfarer was not strong enough for such resolution, or even when he was, took the initiative through the Ordinary or the Extraordinary witness[8] and bestowed spiritual gifts that sustained him in his progress toward perfection and its rewards.

These gifts, also called "graces" or "fruits of the Spirit," are enumerated in Acts, Romans, Galatians, Ephesians, and 2 Timothy; and Watts cites all five texts in one of his discourses on grace (Watts, 1 : 536–37). Alluding to Pentecost where God "shed forth" His Spirit (Acts 2 : 33 ff.), he mentions "speaking in tongues," performing "wonders and signs," "healing the sick," and "prophesying" as gifts of the Spirit, and construes prophecy to mean not only "the foretelling of things to come" but, more simply, "a power to speak by inspiration," "the gift of utterance," or "freedom of speech." He defines the other gifts as "all those christian virtues or principles of holiness which are wrought in the hearts of men—by the influence of the Holy Ghost," and he lists them all: love, joy, peace, long-suffering, gentleness, goodness, faith, meekness, temperance (Galatians 5 : 22–23); patience, hope (Romans 5 : 4); power, a sound mind (2 Timothy 1 : 7); righteousness, and truth (Ephesians 5 : 9). According to Ephesians, moreover, such fruits inspire thanksgiving through psalms, hymns, and spiritual songs (5 : 19–20); and Watts, the first in a long line of eighteenth-century hymnwriters, includes "gratitude" and "the gift of singing psalms" in the canon of spiritual graces.

The presence of these in the Evangelical's life signified his prior communion with the Holy Ghost. "The true witness of the Spirit," said Wesley, "is known by its fruit . . . not indeed preceding, but following it"; or again, the Spirit's "testimony must precede the fruit which springs from it" (Sugden, 2 : 357–58); and his emphasis on the fruits of the Spirit as the sign of His grace provides an appropriate gloss on Wordsworth's declaration to Sir George Beaumont on 28 May 1825: "Theologians may puzzle their heads about dogmas as they will, the religion of gratitude cannot mislead us. Of that we are sure, and gratitude is the handmaid to hope, and hope the harbinger of faith" (*LY*, 1 : 204–05). His suspicion of dogma is consistent with the experiential nature of a belief that was grounded in such graces as gratitude, hope, and faith; his thanksgiving signifies, if not prior communion with the Holy Ghost, then some deep religious feeling, and one so strong as to bode the influx of additional grace.

The Spirit's witness was of two kinds, Extraordinary and Ordinary. Because of the Methodists' claim to "Extraordinary communications from God," Bishop Edmund Gibson arraigned them as "Enthusiasts" in his "Pastoral Charge" of 1 August 1739; and in 1744 the Reverend Thomas Church attacked Wesley himself, branding the leader's enthusiasm "a false pretension of an Extraordinary divine assistance" (Sugden, 2 : 84–85). Wesley, though he conceded the occurrence of too many false claims to inspiration, defended the possibility of a "genuine" Extraordinary witness, to be "known by its fruits" (Sugden, 2 : 85); and in this stand he seconded Watts, who had already warned against invariably ridiculing the "immediate and powerful," "short and sudden" nature of the Spirit's "peculiar" or "uncommon" operation:

> It is certain . . . that wise, and judicious, and holy men, have had very Extraordinary impressions of this kind made on their souls, so that they were almost constrained to believe that they were divine; and the effects of these impressions have been holy and glorious: We should set a guard therefore on our hearts and our tongues, lest we cast a reproach and scandal on such sacred appearances, which the Spirit of God will hereafter acknowledge to have been his own work.
>
> [Watts, 1 : 720]

Both Watts and Wesley cite two texts that identify for their purposes the sure marks of the Extraordinary witness, both of which are found among the fruits of the Spirit (Sugden, 2 : 87; Watts, 1 : 712). In the first (1 Peter 1 : 8), the believer rejoices "with *joy* unspeakable, and full of glory" (my italics); such joy, given by the Spirit, raises the heart "to holy raptures" and "the voice to shouting," so that "the person exults or leaps for great gladness of heart" (Watts, 1 : 711; 2 : 597). Ecstatic behavior, then, could accompany the Extraordinary witness, but another and a more important result of this unusual kind of visitation is announced in the second text: "the *love* of God is shed abroad in our hearts by the Holy Ghost which is given unto us" (Romans 5 : 5; my italics).

On the basis of this verse, Watts, Wesley, and Fletcher toward the end of the century (Fletcher, 7 : 329–30) distinguish between the merely "enthusiastic" believer who might "speak with the tongues of men and of angels" but lack "charity" (cf. 1 Corin-

thians 13 : 1) and the believer whose Christian love testifies to
the genuine Extraordinary witness of the Holy Ghost. E. H.
Sugden speculates that the effect of Wesley's defense against
charges of enthusiasm, by deemphasizing ecstaticism and claiming
the Extraordinary witness with its spiritual fruits of joy and love,
was to establish an honorific sense for the hitherto pejorative
term *enthusiasm*. He also suggests that Wesley was to have an
ally in this verbal rehabilitation: "With the spiritual revival, of
which Wesley on the religious, and Wordsworth on the literary
side, were the leaders, the word recovered from the blight that
had fallen on it" (Sugden, 2 : 86 n.); and we shall see the truth of
his suggestion as we examine poems reflecting the language em-
ployed by Evangelicals in their effort to express what they felt
to be an Extraordinary experience of grace.

"Unspeakable joy," of course, is only one among the more in-
tense of the fifteen spiritual graces, and the passage announcing
God's Extraordinary "love" shed abroad in the heart first men-
tions three equally important if more "ordinary" fruits of the
Spirit: "peace" with God, "patience" in tribulation, and "hope"
of the glory of God (Romans 5 : 1–3). Indeed, the Extraordinary
witness differs from the Ordinary not in kind but in degree; it is,
says Watts, a "very uncommon and powerful confirmation of the
Ordinary and rational witness" (Watts, 1 : 711); and sometimes
an encounter Extraordinary in the beginning becomes Ordinary
and "more durable" at the end (Watts, 1: 719).

In fact the genuine Extraordinary phase never wanes "with-
out awakening the exercise of such graces as are indeed the sure
marks and evidences of the children of God: Where the Spirit
comes, it will bring some of its own fruits with it in a sensible
manner" (Watts, 1 : 718). Watts implies that men cannot long
stand the "unspeakable joy" of direct communion and observes
that souls overwhelmed with more "revelation and pleasure"
than "feeble nature" is "able to bear" must cry out, "It is enough,
Lord; or, it is too much for a state of flesh and blood; Lord,
either withhold thy comforts, or enlarge the vessel; for I cannot
bear these joys."

The Ordinary witness is more concordant with human nature
and with human needs; it "maintains the soul in such a degree
of peace, comfort, and well-grounded hope, as carries the chris-

tian onward through the difficulties and duties of life, though without such raptures of inward joy." (This particular cluster of graces is reminiscent of John 14, where Christ holds out hope of heaven, promises that God will send "the Comforter, which is the Holy Ghost," and offers a gift of His own: "Peace I leave with you, my peace I give unto you" [verses 2, 26–27]). The beginning of a spiritual encounter was often short and immediate, bringing great joy and a sudden influx of God's love; but the milder graces that were left behind testified to a continuing and Ordinary witness as part of a single and cohesive experience; for the Evangelicals cherished the glowing coal of spiritual life as much as the Extraordinary kindling into fire.

Rarely, in fact, do they suggest that the Extraordinary witness is necessary; the commonplace manifestation more than suffices for daily sustenance. Watts contends that the coveted sense of being a child of God—the "Spirit of Adoption" enabling men to "say unto God, *Abba, Father*" (cf. Romans 8 : 15–16)—does not depend on "the Extraordinary witnessing of that good Spirit" (Watts, 1 : 720). For the most part, indeed, the Spirit works "connaturally and sweetly with our own spirits" so that His operations "are not to be easily distinguished by ourselves or others, from the rational motions of our own hearts, influenced by moral arguments" (Watts, 3 : 179). And Wesley, like Watts, lays the final stress on Ordinary fruits such as "righteousness and peace" (Sugden, 2 : 85–86), graces accessible and far from merely "enthusiastic."

Among the leaders of the revival, and many if not most of their followers, such emphasis on the Ordinary witness effectively checked excessive displays of ecstaticism; God speaks more often, said Fletcher, in a "still, small voice" than in "the wind, earthquake or fire" (Fletcher, 6 : 200; cf. 1 Kings 19 : 11–12). And Isaac Taylor, with whom Wordsworth was familiar, believed that moral action, though dependent on both kinds of spiritual experience, is most often a consequence of the Ordinary witness: the "indwelling influence" of the Holy Spirit brings with it not a continually heightened spiritual consciousness but "a settled and affectionate sense of security, or peace in believing, which becomes the spring of holy tempers, and virtuous conduct." [9]

Virtuous conduct, of course, was not wholly the result of the

Spirit's Extraordinary and Ordinary witnesses; for the Puritan-Evangelical, as indicated in Henry's *Baptismal Covenant,* period-ically sought out God's Spirit as Sanctifier and thus cooperated in his own spiritual growth. Among the non-Calvinist Evangelicals and their Puritan forebears, as congregations and as individuals, such exercise of will uneasily coexisted with the doctrine of un-purchasable grace and amounted to a recognition of responsi-bility in communing with God; for more than two centuries these godly men and women reciprocated the Spirit's gifts by making covenants with God and among themselves to obey moral law. Historically, of course, covenant-making was at the heart of Puritan and Nonconformist ecclesiology.[10]

After Puritan divines were ejected from the Church of England in 1662 and became Nonconformist, all the Nonconformists be-gan to adopt the Congregationalist conception of a "gathered Church," as opposed to the national or parish concept of church organization; and by a collective act of will, expressed in a signed covenant with God, the congregation typically rejected the idea of nominal Christianity as one's birthright and elevated an in-tense personal holiness above catholicity and unity as the proper mark of the true Church. In Robert Browne's *A Booke which sheweth the Life and Manners of all True Christians* (1582), the concept of the "gathered Church" is clearly defined:

> The Church planted or gathered is a company or number of Christians or believers, which, by a willing covenant made with their God, are under the government of God and Christ, and keep his laws in one holy communion: because Christ hath redeemed them unto holiness and happiness for ever, from which they were fallen by the sin of Adam.[11]

Wesley kept and expanded upon this part of his Puritan heritage, for though he revered Anglican services of worship he was also attracted to the tradition of the "gathered Church," and when he established a regular service for the sake of "joining in a cov-enant to serve God with all our heart and with all our soul" (Wesley, 2 : 339; cf. Matthew 22 : 37) he made perhaps his most original contribution to the forms of English worship.

Congregational covenants and special services were the natural concomitants of personal covenants made from time to time by Puritan and Evangelical alike; leaders of the Great Awakening were reared in the tradition of renewing moral commitment with God's help. The diary of a Baptist minister, John Collett Ryland, shows the fierce determination with which these vows were often made:

> June 25. Ev.10—1744. Aet. 20 years 8 months 2 days. If there's ever a God in Heaven or Earth, I vow, Protest and Swear in God's Strength—or that Gods permitting me, I'll find him out and I'll know whether he loves or hates me or I'll dye and perish Soul and Body in the Pursuit & Search.[12]

Ryland's yearning for God illustrates the Evangelicals' deep concern for the state of their souls, but private covenant-making among both Nonconformist and Anglican (or Methodist) Evangelicals more frequently stressed the less self-preoccupied goal of spiritual betterment. Matthew Henry's incorporation of covenant vows into the sacrament of baptism was later reflected in *The History of Baptism* (1790) by Robert Robinson, the Baptist minister popular at Cambridge during Wordsworth's matriculation (see pp. 18–19); and Robinson, like Henry, sought the Spirit's guidance in the quest for perfection.[13]

Methodist spiritual autobiography, with its self-examination for the sake of recording and assuring moral progress, was another form of individual covenant-making; and Wesley, besides instituting a covenant service, instructed his followers in the making of personal vows. In *Directions for Renewing our Covenant with God* (1780) he laid down guidelines for rededication to the service of God and man and thus suggested the means of responding to the Spirit's assistance. Among his specific directions were "the setting aside of time" to pray for the Spirit's help, a careful searching of the heart, a reliance upon the promise of "grace and strength" from the Holy Spirit, and a firm resolution to be faithful; the covenanter was then ready to "set upon the work" of Christian charity.[14] Perhaps more than the Nonconformists, Wesley regarded the covenant as a safeguard against undue introspection.

And finally, the Evangelicals aspired to spiritual perfection and in their terms came close to succeeding because of their peculiar, if not unique, theological emphasis on the uneasy but fruitful combination of difficult acts of will and spontaneous influxes of grace. John Fletcher by all accounts came nearest to attaining moral excellence, and he includes a concept of the Spirit's witness, as well as an important covenant concept, in his definition of perfection as "that maturity of *grace* and *holiness,* which established adult believers attain to under the Christian dispensation" (Fletcher, 4 : 201; my italics).

In equal measure, then, Christians needed graces of the Spirit and independent vows to be holy in order to achieve or at least to seek perfection, defined by Wesley not as error-free thinking or sinless behavior but as the simple or not so simple mingling of the Spirit's assistance and the Christian's covenant effort to love God and his neighbor with all his heart, mind, and soul (Sugden, 2 : 148; Newton Flew has suggested, in *The Idea of Perfection in Christian Theology,* that this doctrine might be viewed as the principle of concentration on each moment while trusting in divine aids: "faith is no mere single response but a continuous succession of responses to the divine Giver").[15]

This same combination of spiritual grace and personal effort, however full of an uneasy tension, inheres in biblical sources for this doctrine and therefore rested on good authority until the Evangelicals took it up in full earnest and thereby unconsciously began the modern (or rather "Romantic") process of softening distinctions between the acts of God and the efforts of men. On the one hand, the Book of James testifies that "by *works* was faith made perfect" (2 : 22), but the New Testament also associates certain *graces* with the quest for perfection: the author of Hebrews asks "the God of *peace*" to "make you perfect in every good work to do his will" (13 : 20–21); the writer of James exhorts his readers to "let *patience* have her perfect work, that ye may be perfect and entire, wanting nothing" (1 : 4); and Christ Himself associates one of the graces with sanctification: "And for their sakes I sanctify myself, that they also might be sanctified through the *truth*" (John 17 : 19; my italics).

And both the Evangelicals and the Bible emphasize that this virtual partnership of man and God in the goal of perfection is of lifelong duration; indeed, the Christian's moral excellence will be fully or nearly realized only at the end of a lifetime of growing in grace and acting out of charity. Fletcher wrote that "Christian Perfection" is, in part, "the cluster and maturity of the graces, which compose the Christian character" (Fletcher, 4 : 201); and his stress seems to be on maturity. Watts wrote that Christians achieve the full "glory" of joy in good action as they mature; at last they abundantly receive the "fruits of sanctification" in their "hearts and lives" (Watts, 2 : 597; 3 : 179). And the Bible also stresses the end of life, when the greatest possible perfection receives its due reward: the "Spirit of God" helps create "a love made perfect, that we may have boldness in the day of judgment" (1 John 5 : 17); and Christ's sanctification of men anticipates the end of time when "they may be made perfect in one" (John 17 : 22–23).

In 1814, when Wordsworth taught his son that God is a Spirit, he had already written most of his best poetry, including a total of some twenty thousand lines in *The Prelude* and *The Excursion* alone. His fatherly teaching relates directly to that poetry and does not indicate an unfortunate conversion from a praiseworthy epistemological skepticism to a pious and complacent orthodoxy. He was indeed orthodox in old age, of course; and as a young man he was sometimes full of doubt and always epistemologically precocious and sophisticated; but throughout his career he wrote poetry founded not only upon the rather obvious and simple idea that God is a Spirit but on all the precise and definable corollaries to that general doctrine.

For like a composite Watts and Wesley, or like an embodiment of both the Puritan and the Evangelical strains in a spiritually awakened England, or like a prophet of the intimate God and the apotheosized Man, he embraced in his life and incorporated in his works the beliefs or forms of belief associated with the Third Person of the Trinity during his day and during his yesterday: he adopted and adapted the concepts of conversion and covenant, the language of God's witness through particular graces, and the ideal of steady growth into perfection or sanctification; and all of these quasi-doctrinal and clearly religious ideas form the underlying assumptions and constitute the primary on-

tology of *The Prelude, The Excursion,* several familiar works of
the so-called Great Decade (1798–1808), and much of the un-
familiar poetry both early and late.

Wordsworth no less than Wesley saw perfection as the happy
condition of habitual responsiveness to spiritual overtures (and
not as some ideal state of complete sinlessness); and he not only
delineated this goal throughout his work but, in *The Prelude,*
recounted his personal efforts to achieve it, testified to the help
he received, and generally expressed his faith in human effort
strengthened by grace:

> A gracious Spirit o'er this earth presides,
> And o'er the heart of man: invisibly
> It comes, directing those to works of love
> Who care not, know not, think not what they ao . . . .
> [V.516–19]

These lines and much of Wordsworth's poetry grew out of what
he knew were strong spiritual aspirations and what he felt was
an experience of grace. The evidence suggests, indeed, that he
sometimes thought himself inspired by the Spirit; and if in fact
he ever thought so, such inspiration need imply no reduction in
the stature of his Muse, whom he addressed in language con-
ventionally applied to the Holy Ghost, that holy force whose
condescensions were hailed by another "Puritan" poet trained,
as William Wordsworth was, in the precepts and revelations of
spiritual theology. For, somewhat like Milton, he gives thanks in
religious terms to "the heavenly Muse": "surpassing grace / To
me hath been vouchsafed" (see Book I of *The Recluse* ["Home
at Grasmere"]; *PW,* 5 : 317). In the "Prospectus" to *The Excur-
sion,* moreover, Wordsworth invokes the "prophetic Spirit" Who
fills a "temple in the hearts / Of mighty poets" and prays that
this Spirit—"if such / Descend to earth or dwell in highest
heaven!"—will bestow on him a gift of insight enabling his po-
etry, in its effects, to resemble the characteristic operations of the
Extraordinary witness:

> That my Song
> With star-like virtue in its place may shine,

> *Shedding* benignant influence . . . .
>                         [ll. 26–27, 83–90; *PW*, 5 : 5–6; my italics]

It is true that in this same poetic statement of purpose he passes
Jehovah unalarmed, but he shows no such disdain for the New
Testament dispensation, for he seeks "a greater Muse" than
Milton's partially Hellenized Urania, and to find that more
Hebraic Spirit he ascends to "breathe in worlds / To which the
heaven of heavens is but a veil" (ll. 25–26, 29–30, 33–35). And his
"fear and awe" of "the Mind of Man" rest not upon the mind's
self-sufficiency but upon its desire at once to wed "this goodly
universe / In love and holy passion" and to reach not only for
higher things but for a higher being to whom the poet's mind,
at least, is willing to pray:

> If such theme
> May sort with highest objects, then—dread Power!
> Whose gracious favour is the primal source
> Of all illumination,—may my Life
> Express the image of a better time,
> More wise desires, and simpler manners;—nurse
> My Heart in genuine freedom:—all pure thoughts
> Be with me;—so shall thy unfailing love
> Guide, and support, and cheer me to the end!
>                         [ll. 38–40, 53–54, 99–107]

## The Prelude

In 1851, soon after *The Prelude* appeared, F. D. Maurice
shared an insight with Charles Kingsley:

I am sure that you are right, Wordsworth's Prelude seems
to me the dying utterance of the half century we have just
passed through, the expression—the English expression at
least—of all that self-building process in which, according to
their different schemes and principles, Byron, Goethe, Words-
worth, the Evangelicals (Protestant and Romanist), were all
engaged, which their novels, poems, experiences, prayers,
were setting forth, in which God, under whatever name, or

in whatever aspect, He presented Himself to them, was still
the agent only in fitting them to be world-wise, men of ge-
nius, artists, saints.[16]

*The Prelude* suggests that God does fit Wordsworth to be an
artist, as Maurice's parallelism indicates; but the poet-artist makes
clear that the role of divine influence is more extensive than that;
for *The Prelude* also implies that God puts within his reach the
goal of a spiritual perfection analogous to and consistent with the
doctrine of Christian perfection as taught by the Evangelicals.
His persona seeks a kind of sanctity understandable in terms of
their quest for perfection, their process of self-building; and as
an autobiography the poem suggests that he became something of
an Evangelical "saint" as well as an "artist."

Maurice could not have realized that *The Prelude,* written
from 1798 to 1805, was so far from being the "dying utterance" of
the process of self-building, that it was in fact the quintessential
literary expression of that partially Evangelical phenomenon—
written at the height of the revival itself. But we shall see that
Evangelical theology of the Spirit illuminates the important
events of Wordsworth's autobiography of adulthood—a pro-
tracted experience of conversion in late adolescence, a spiritual
crisis during the Revolution, and a final recovery through the
ministrations of his sister. In an important sense the poem is an
account of his covenant with God: characteristically he seeks the
things of the Spirit; but he testifies that, when his will fails him,
grace reconfirms the original regeneration.

It may be helpful to establish the general presence of spiritual
vocabulary before turning to the pivotal events of Wordsworth's
maturity; the idiom of spiritual doctrine pervades *The Prelude.*
From the beginning, in fact, the graces emerge as one of the main
subjects. The poet, seeking a "British theme," at last finds "in-
spiration"

> for a song that winds
> Through ever changing scenes of votive quest
> Wrongs to redress, harmonious tribute paid
> To patient courage and unblemished truth,

> To firm devotion, zeal unquenchable,
> And Christian meekness hallowing faithful loves.
>
> [ll. 168, 180–85; 1850]

And this first cluster of graces—gentleness, patience, truth, meekness, faith, and love—could imply or be intended to imply the spiritual source of his inspiration and certainly heralds, in any case, the thematic importance of man's colloquy with God's Spirit from whom alone such grace derives (through "His great correction and controul," for example, the poet's mother receives "a grace / Of modest meekness" [V.274, 290–91; 1850]).

His spiritual idiom, in fact, reveals that like the Evangelicals he distinguishes between an Extraordinary and an Ordinary witness. The short and sudden nature of the former sometimes appears to characterize his own experience, as when, during a time of rapture, he stops "short" on Esthwaite's Lake and receives a lesson in humility (I.457, 484; see pp. 55–56); or when, catching his first sight of the Vale of Grasmere in Book I of *The Recluse* (of which *The Prelude* was to have formed a part), he is overpowered with a "sudden influx" that leads him to proffer "thanks to God / For what hath been bestowed" (ll. 7, 83–84; *PW*, 5 : 313, 316). And in Book VIII he acknowledges and celebrates man's experience of receiving an Extraordinary witness, of being

> rapt away
> By the divine effect of power and love,
> As more than anything we know instinct
> With Godhead . . . .
>
> [ll. 636–39]

Rarely, however, is the Extraordinary witness implied or described in its unalloyed form of joyous rapture or the sudden influx of love shed abroad in the heart; at times, indeed, Wordsworth seems to regard it as a phenomenon of youth unnecessary in manhood. As a boy for whom nature is all-sufficient, he experiences "a rapture often, and immediate joy, / Ever at hand" (VIII.487–88); but as he matures, these Extraordinary emotions are soon replaced by a growing regard for his fellow man, by a

"gentleness of love" unknown before (l. 492); and the "grace"
(l. 488) of maturer spiritual experience seems Ordinary in the
precise and honorific meaning of the term. Indeed, there is noth-
ing precisely Extraordinary about many of his early memories,
which, after all, perform their renovating function during the
round of "ordinary" existence (XI.264). The "ordinary" sight of
the Girl with the Pitcher, for example, precedes his visionary
acquirement of humility and a sense of duty (XI.309, 311; see pp.
59–61); and even the glorious vision on Mount Snowdon, de-
scribed toward the end of the poem, takes its humble and inaus-
picious beginning in the "ordinary" talk of the travelers at the
foot of the mountain (XIII.17).

But such a vision, with its accompanying "sense of God," is
always possible for minds that are

> ever on the watch,
> Willing to work and to be wrought upon,
> They need not *extraordinary* calls
> To rouze them, in a world of life they live,
> By sensible impressions not enthrall'd,
> But quicken'd, rouz'd, and made thereby more fit
> To hold communion with the invisible world.
>                                    [ll. 72, 99–105; my italics]

Such minds, sustained by "religion" and "faith," are "truly from
the Deity" (ll. 106, 111). The thoroughgoing Evangelicalism of
this passage specifically resists any reliance upon the mind-en-
trapped knowledge of the senses and implies not only the cove-
nant willingness to exercise initiative and resolute effort but also
a receptivity to the Ordinary divine assistance; such interaction
characterizes man's relationship to God as understood by the
Evangelicals and as intimated by Wordsworth's praise of men
who live in this world but whose ordinary responsiveness to an-
other, quite apart from any extraordinary instincts for divinity
or Godhead, keeps them from being defined, delimited, and
overwhelmed by emanations from the implicitly secondary, and
perhaps not even knowable, realm of gross, alien, and alienated
matter.

*The Prelude* suggests, indeed, that the Ordinary witness benefits ordinary men, who can therefore rest more assured in their experience of the primary realm of the spirit than in their dubious and problematical knowledge of the world of sense and common sense. And their experience gives them strange skills of expression; even those "among the walks of homely life," "whose very souls perhaps would sink / Beneath them" were they asked to express "their thoughts in lively words," speak an unverbal but strong and eloquent speech of the spirit, a mental picture-language filled with the quiet and unspectacular signs of an Ordinary witness:

> Theirs is the language of the heavens, the power,
> The thought, the image, and the silent joy;
> Words are but under-agents in their souls;
> When they are grasping with their greatest strength
> They do not breathe among them: this I speak
> In gratitude to God, who feeds our hearts
> For his own service, knoweth, loveth us
> When we are unregarded by the world.
>
> [XII.263–79]

These "meek men" (l. 268) have a quiet joy that is far from the rapturous one attending Extraordinary spiritual experience, but they acquire sustenance and strength from such fruits of the Spirit as meekness, joy, and power; and though "unpractis'd in the strife of phrase" (l. 267) they have strange powers of communication—they practice a kind of tongueless glossolalia—because they have received the power of communion, the power of representing their thoughts to a God who nourishes them in turn. Thus they resemble the Apostle Paul, who claimed no "excellency of speech" nor "enticing words of man's wisdom" but spoke, nevertheless, "in demonstration of the Spirit and of *power:* That our faith should . . . stand . . . in the *power* of God" (1 Corinthians 2 : 1–6; my italics). And Wordsworth's gratitude to God— itself a spiritual gift according to Watts—seems owing to his recognition of the demonstrated "power" so widespread among the lower classes of his day, due in no small measure to the ministry of John Wesley.

The Extraordinary witness (or its Wordsworthian analogue)

does not fade entirely from his spiritual life; the ideal is a mixture of the two kinds of grace. The first may initiate an encounter but soon yields to the milder graces of longer duration, so that the varying intensities of a given experience are conceived as a single phenomenon (as among the Evangelicals). He recalls the times, for example, when Coleridge displayed a variety of graces and somehow even managed to share his seemingly Extraordinary/ Ordinary spiritual experience. When they first met, he seemed affected by the more sudden and dramatic witness: he was "placed on this earth," the poet believed, "to *love* and understand, / And from thy presence *shed* the light of *love*" (XIII.249–50; my italics). As their friendship progressed, the poet began to profit from his companion's apparent access to the more subdued and Ordinary witness: "Thy *gentle* Spirit to my heart of hearts / Did also find its way" (ll. 252–53; my italics); and the word *also* implies a distinction between the two kinds of grace exemplified in Coleridge's life. Wordsworth particularly cherishes his friend's Ordinary spiritual grace, from which he learns to admit "closelier gathering thoughts / Of man and his concerns" into his own spiritual life (ll. 257–58); and he therefore seems to know that the mild or "gentle Spirit" is one of the graces believed (by Watts and Taylor) to support the charitable duties of ordinary existence.

Because of Coleridge's influence during these inspired early days (a time when he preached, albeit as a Unitarian, the new spiritual dispensation),[17] the poet feels that the "deep enthusiastic joy" he knew in youth, as well as his former "rapture of the Hallelujah sent / From all that breathes and is," are now "chasten'd, stemm'd, / And balanc'd" by a sense of duty and the grace of truth (ll. 261–65). Like Watts and Wesley, who regarded the unspeakable joy and rapture of the Extraordinary witness as marks of the only proper enthusiasm, he sees a certain validity in the joy and rapture of his earlier experience; also like those leaders, however, he associates milder fruits of the Spirit, such as truth, with the ordinary duty so central in Christian morality, and seems to place even greater emphasis on the common spiritual influences and their salutary effect. In Book XII he expresses

a desire to do for others what his Christian friend has done for
him. Through his poetry he hopes to

> teach,
> Inspire, through unadulterated ears
> Pour rapture, tenderness, and hope, my theme
> No other than the very heart of man
> As found among the best of those who live
> Not unexalted by religious hope . . . .
>
> [ll. 237–42]

Extraordinary "rapture" remains a theme, but Ordinary "hope"
receives the double emphasis.

*The Prelude* suggests, moreover, that the performance of duty
depends as much on covenant vows and resolutions as on the
Spirit's witness; for Wordsworth is as willing "to work" as "to be
wrought upon," as willing to give promises as to receive grace. In
writing he relies on spiritual aid—

> a higher power
> Than Fancy gave assurance of some work
> Of glory
>
> [I.77–79]

—and even demonstrates one of the Pentecostal gifts of the Spirit
when he tells a "prophesy" to the "open fields"; but such grace
accompanies arduous labor (his "spirit" is "singled out" for "holy
services" [I.60–63]). This religious sense of duty, reflecting the
Puritan covenant ideal of intense personal holiness, dates from
his days at Cambridge, where he believed himself to be a "chosen
Son" with "holy powers," elected or set apart not only to "feel"
but "to work" (III.82–84). During his London visits of the early
1790s (see pp. 26–29), the latter-day Pentecostal "tongues" of the
Evangelicals might have strengthened his predisposition to moral
effort; for London pulpits, as he now declares, gave him "power
to search the Soul" (VII.547–48, 1850); and thus one of the spiri-
tual graces seems to have initiated a kind of self-examination that
was also to be found among Wesley's most basic "directions for
renewing our covenant with God."

The entire poem, in one sense, is a covenant reciprocation of such grace; for in the first book Wordsworth makes his solemn vow of spiritual introspection: "I through myself make rigorous inquisition" (ll. 158–59). But the poem also seems to observe the last of Wesley's directions for covenant-making whenever the poet moves beyond introspective soul-searching to make faithful "resolutions." He regrets the times at Cambridge when he failed to achieve a "calm *resolve* of mind, firmly address'd / To puissant efforts"; but when he begins *The Prelude* "as a Pilgrim *resolute*," and when he completes it as a pilgrim nearer, if not to the goal of spiritual perfection, then to the final destination of life and hence to the moment of spiritual truth and promise, he demonstrates fidelity to the most difficult resolution of his life: "to grapple with some noble theme" (III.353–54; I.91, 1850; I.139; my italics).

*The Prelude* also suggests that the combination of spiritual aid and covenant effort does lead to perfection or sanctification, and Wordsworth's evident employment of this important doctrine seems consistent with the views of Watts and Fletcher, who saw Christian perfection with all its moral "glory" as the effect of man's interaction with the Spirit of God. In childhood when he steals the boat, the "Spirit of the universe" begins *"sanctifying"* the passions of Wordsworth's "human Soul" (I.428, 434, 439; my italics; see pp. 50–53); in 1790, after he takes the lower Alpine road, his soul is "strong in itself," "blest in thoughts / That are their own *perfection* and reward" (VI.545–47; 609, 1850; my italics; see pp. 62–65). In his youth the "Spirit" makes him "recognize / A grandeur in the beatings of the heart" (I.440–41) and thus holds out the possibility of man's spiritual excellence; and in the Alps he comes to recognize the glory of his own soul, which now reflects the moral strength of a new "perfection."

Such glory does not denote inherent or congenital worth but signifies moral and charitable endeavor; as a poet Wordsworth vows to write of an active and enduring "love," "for the glory that redounds / Therefrom to human kind" (XII.247–48). *The Prelude* is itself a "glorious" work (I.157), perhaps because it heralds the moral perfection to which man can attain with the Spirit's guidance. In Book X he implies that truth from the spirit of heaven gives men the grace, despite their earthly afflictions, to keep faith and achieve sanctity (ll. 409–10, 423–28); he seems, therefore, to conceive of his poetic career as an imitation of Christ, who sanctified himself that men "may be sanctified through the truth."

Wordsworth's versified analogues to spiritual doctrine, then, pervade the poem. And they can be said collectively to represent its predominant and most readily discoverable world-view; these analogues are not simply helpful in the way they convey a reliable impression of the work as a whole: they are crucial as aids to analyzing and interpreting it as spiritual autobiography. For just as the early memories of Evangelicals compare with his account of a developing humility during the formative years, so their doctrine pertaining to adulthood contributes an organizing principle to his further account of progress during the ripening and ripe years of maturity and grace, a principle that gives this later chronology and this remaining narrative its beginning, middle, and end. The poem suggests, first, that the Spirit guides him throughout undergraduate days (cf. pp. 16–24), a period containing his "conversion" experience, his dramatic spiritual about-face during the Long Vacation of 1788. Then, after graduation in 1791, he goes to France (where he finds little unmediated guidance and sometimes neglects to seek it), undergoes severe testing of the spirit, suffers a dark night of the soul, and generally fails to meet the secular challenge to his faith. But when he settles at Racedown, Dorset, in 1795, he recovers and thereby sets in motion the joyful ending of his account, a comedic and substantially Christian denouement by which the agencies of Coleridge (who, as suggested above, plays the role of Faithful to his Christian), and more notably his sister Dorothy (whose ministrations he describes in language evoking the Spirit's operations) reconfirm his faith, heighten his spiritual receptivity, and strengthen his moral determination and resolve.

*The Prelude,* in short, is written by one whose faith is strong because it has survived a crisis. From a position of strength and with all the advantage of hindsight and reverent retrospective, the author pauses to review his progress not just from the youthful passions of pride to the chastened humility of adolescence, but from an apparent conversion in young manhood, through the tribulations and trials in that and any other period, to the sanctified vision of maturity. And we shall see that Wordsworth sees, as he looks backward and girds himself for further forward progress, a striving toward perfection through a series of covenant vows, a spiritual yearning sustained at many points, from the dawn of his childhood to his realization of poetic identity, by the fruits of the Spirit of God.

The adult pattern of spiritual life, as shown in Books III, IV, and VI, begins at Cambridge where the persona seems guided by the Spirit or by some higher Power, and where he takes an alternately passive and active role in spiritual communion; the poet does not call the Spirit by name but employs words evoking the dramatic Evangelical pattern: an interaction between condescending grace and aspiring will. Book III examines both characteristics of the persona's role. On the one hand he awaits visitations; he often leaves his comrades and goes into the fields to receive "strength and consolation," two common benefits of the Spirit's witness, and be "awaken'd, summon'd, rous'd, constrain'd," common effects of the Spirit's initiative (ll. 108–09). But he also responds to these compelling overtures (Book III stresses his active role); he begins searching both outside himself and within:

> . . . I look'd for universal things; perused
> The common countenance of earth and heaven;
> And, turning the mind in upon itself,
> Pored, watch'd, expected, listen'd . . . .
>
> [ll. 110–13]

His mannner of reciprocation, born of heightened awareness and at once extroverted and introspective, is characterized not so much by an experimentally based rejection of external reality, or an introverted retreat into the selfhood of epistemological timidity, as an almost systematic yearning to know, or at least to explore, the spiritual basis of both being and existence. And his reciprocation is followed by a more intimate spiritual communion through which, first, he enjoys "Incumbences more awful" (l. 115), and then responds again, aspiring to "community with highest truth" (l. 120). With related terminology, Watts describes a similar kind of spiritual colloquy: the Holy Ghost stirs up the soul "to a most diligent search . . . making it unwearied in this toil and labour of self-examination" so that it may at last be wrought upon by "the Spirit of truth" (Watts, 1 : 707); and in Wordsworth's experience also, the Spirit appears to inspire both self-examination and a yearning for truth.

Book III now suggests that the persona's subsequent behavior shows the genuineness of his encounters. The poet seems concerned to distinguish them from mere enthusiasm or fanaticism; like Wesley he emphasizes that the genuine witness is known by its fruits. He confirms the Christian context of the phrase "highest truth" when he testifies to receiving three other gifts of the Spirit, and he offers this cluster of graces as the public evidence of a private realm that "only liv'd to me, / And to the God who look'd into my mind":

> Some call'd it madness: such, indeed, it was,
> If child-like *fruit*fulness in passing *joy,*
> If steady mood of thoughtfulness, matur'd
> To *inspiration,* sort with such a name;
> If *prophesy* be madness . . . .
> [ll. 143–44, 147–51; my italics]

Like the Evangelicals, then, he reacts to the charge of enthusiastic madness by invoking the traditional marks of genuine spiritual encounter (the fruit of joy, the gift of inspiration, prophecy itself—all denote in Watts's theology the true witness and not mere enthusiastic frenzy); he can therefore conclude, "It was no madness" (l. 156).

Indeed, the main emphasis of these lines, and of their context, is on the common graces, the milder spiritual fruits that are far removed from enthusiasm and its excesses. A few lines further down, for example, the poet shows little interest in one of the richest spiritual gifts and receives instead such modest presents as he can hold within: the Pentecostal gift of "signs" forms no part of his unspectacular experience, because such "outward things / Done visibly" are superfluous to one who speaks, as he does, "of my own heart" and of "what pass'd within" (ll. 174–76). And his gift of prophecy is similarly unspectacular if it connotes, consistent with a context stressing muted spiritual experience, Watts's idea of "freedom of speech" (and hence facility and force of personal testimony) more than, say, a dramatically Pentecostal foretelling of the future.

Wordsworth's own life, in any case, constitutes such a prophecy; for he projects a "Power" (l. 171) reminiscent of the grace that once gave eloquence to Paul and later imbued the heavenly language of Wordsworth's silent men with the quieter eloquence of moral force and forceful example. And his spectacular and extraordinary experience is common enough to be considered genuine and perhaps therefore sufficiently ordinary to be unfanatical. For his "breathings for incommunicable powers," his aspirations to seemingly inhuman or superhuman abilities, are in fact no more unusual than the "godlike hours" felt and known by all (ll. 188, 192); and his enthusiastic and indeed isolated and solipsistic kind of strength can sometimes be more prideful than properly exalted and so should be less desired, and cherished less, than his communicable and less self-enhancing power. But his inhalations for rare might, and his experience of godlike moments, and his consequent ascension to a superhuman if not supernatural plane, though hardly so dependable or practical as the common, natural, yet still spiritual power that goes out to men in the world below, need never effect his fall into fanaticism (and hence near-solipsism), since his apotheosized and apotheosizing faculties of mind and spirit positively suggest his reflection or bold embodiment of Watts's conviction that even wise and judicious men, through the Spirit's witness, may believe themselves divine and God to be ensphered and circumjacent; for of such "Divinity" does Wordsworth speak (l. 171), a divinity manifestly imparted and willingly received, freely given and properly claimed.

The Cambridge years, then, produce a spiritual balance and a spiritual possibility; but they do not consistently reveal such gifts of strength and purpose and such godlike reciprocation; for they include a period when Wordsworth's aspiring will (in concert with his gift of moral engagement and spiritual interaction) weakens, flags, and yields temporarily to worldliness of mind and a vain independence. The Long Vacation of 1788, the period described throughout Book IV, threatens to produce a misdirected "progress" from the spiritual elevation described in Book III to the dubious destinations of lofty pride and low unspirituality; but the summer finally yields a forward, forthcoming, and properly upward progress toward the distant but attainable heights of covenant resolve and communing will.

The book presents, therefore, an intense and concentrated period of spiritual development, a time when prideful highs fall short of spiritual elevation and worldly depths prove shallow in comparison with the fundamental profundity of an ever resurfacing life of the spirit. The book, indeed, is a maze of autobiographic patterns: the poet chastens, stems, and balances his bold but sometimes justifiable assertions of divine potentiality with painful and hence equally bold inquisitions into sin and error; and he suggests that nothing short of epiphanal interventions, persistent overtures, and a particular instance of decisive influx, can restore his communion with God and with his better self. And in his confession of need and celebration of grace he reconfirms his recovery: he examines his motives, admits his recalcitrance, recounts his transformation, acknowledges his debt, stresses his consequent charity and covenant resolve, and generally records his progress.

In contrast to Wordsworth's later recidivism, he shows in early summer signs of grace and spiritual-mindedness; for he greets his Dame in gratitude and joy, perhaps then sharing what he now extends—a blessing sent from heaven; and he receives from Hawkshead's Church "a gracious look" (ll. 13–15, 19–22, 29). Thus he shows a mind both graced and gracing. But he also shows, this early in the season, another and a less spiritual state of mind, a pride and passion chastened once and now recurring: he takes "a little pride" in his appearance, in his habiliments and gay attire (ll. 65–66); and he knows once more those low desires, the weariness and restlessness of natural pride; for he sees an emblem of his languor and rebelliousness in the "froward brook" now "box'd / Within our Garden," the "unruly Child of mountain birth" thus "left to dimple down / Without an effort and without a will" (ll. 39–44).

Thus stubborn, vain, and full of lassitude, he retrogresses

further still, indulging the worldliness of a morally neutral aesthetic; he wishes to retrace those "dilatory" and spiritually digressive walks on which as a boy he fed additional guilty passions, "the fermentation and the vernal heat" of a sensuous, self-intoxicated, and unspiritual verse: he wishes to dwell once more upon "some fair enchanting image in my mind / . . . full-form'd like Venus from the sea" and thus to value some vague shape of an ideal Beauty (as distinct, perhaps, from the palpable form of a real and loving woman lineal from old Adam's seed); and he wishes once more to gaze within, "affecting private shades / Like a sick lover," and like a lover in love with self and therefore not with God or man (ll. 94–96, 99, 104–05).

In these first lines of *Prelude* IV, then, the poet implicitly distinguishes between his spiritual and his worldly states of mind; and though he generally glories in the vestiges and traces of grace and strength (he feels more shame than pride in his habiliments, remembers his walks with much more joy than sadness [ll. 66, 122, 125]), he also suggests, in however subliminal and preliminary a fashion, that the debilitating passions of self begin to sap his strength and qualify his bliss; and we may therefore feel that the apples of discord could spoil the fruits of the Spirit.

Both here and throughout the book, however, help attends such weakness. In early summer, for example, languor and unruliness sometimes come to terms with spiritual mediation from his motherly Dame ("She guided me; / I willing, nay—nay—wishing to be led" [ll. 56–57]); and flirtations with the exclusive but alluring poetry of sense and self sometimes submit, on those early summer walks, to seeming strictures from his faithful dog, an equally reliable if more unlikely mediator, whose stern "admonishment" and "timely notice" of approaching strangers interrupt the young man's introverted reverie and warn him "to give and take a greeting" that might head off the "piteous rumours such as wait / On men suspected to be craz'd in brain" (ll. 115–20).

The "rough Terrier," then, is not only "preordain'd / To hunt the badger and unearth the fox / Among the impervious crags" (ll. 87–89), but is now assigned to pursue his master, or at least to attend him and watch over him in an apparent effort to pene-

trate the defensive perimeters of a passionate and cunning pre-
server of self. The dog is not, therefore, so unlikely a mediator of
spiritual truth, but indeed prefigures an unmediated message that
comes, if not from those hounds of heaven that sought the Evan-
gelicals ("I am hunted by spiritual hounds" exclaimed Cowper
to Hayley [29 July 1792—OED]), then from some more gracious
but equally persistent influence, some Spirit who touches the
stubborn and elusive young poet on one of those dilatory walks
toward the middle of the summer and then delivers, through a
witness Extraordinary in certain manifestations, a direct but
Ordinary message of an unmistakably moral import. For sud-
denly the youth is rapt, has swellings of the spirit, and sees the
apotheosized and apotheosizing vision:

> How Life pervades the undecaying mind,
> How the immortal Soul with God-like power
> Informs, creates, and thaws the deepest sleep
> That time can lay upon her . . . .
>
> [ll. 155–58]

And then he reflects the Ordinary spiritual fruits, "the milder
thoughts of love," the comfort, peace, and hope enabling men
to perform the acts of duty and acquire the unsolipsistic self-
lessness of a covenant morality and engagement:

> . . . how on earth,
> Man, if he do but live within the light
> Of high endeavours, daily spreads abroad
> His being with a strength that cannot fail.
>
> [ll. 143, 152, 157–62]

Conceiving "amplest projects," envisioning "a peaceful end / At
last, or glorious, by endurance won," he comes close to embracing
that same kind of moral effort believed by the Evangelicals to
effect or prefigure the serene glory of spiritual perfection (ll.
165–66).

He comes close without quite doing so; for on this occasion,
though he clearly responds to condescensions and overtures, and
though he therefore renews to some extent his spirituality, he

still displays some willful resistance and reveals some spiritual blindness. He receives, for example, the gift of strength; but he does not see that he was weak ("Strength came where weakness was not known to be" [l. 145]); and he therefore does not seem to derive full benefit from this particular condescension (he catches only a "glimmering" view of the unfailing strength that spreads abroad its being [l. 154]).

He also receives new comfort (as prelude to consolations from the other mild graces); but he seems either unaware of his new gift or indifferent to it; for though he has indulged a spiritually desolate and hence necessarily disconsolate worldliness, he does not admit his need for such a grace: "a comfort seem'd to touch / A heart that had not been disconsolate" (ll. 143–44). And despite his fleeting access to Godlike power—his enraptured and extraordinary assurance of an immortalizing faculty; despite an insistent and overpowering restoration, knocking like an intruder at the door of his weariness and discontent; and despite his awareness of an attendant respiration "short and quick" as the Extraordinary witness in its short and sudden manifestation (l. 176), his weakness remains stubbornly "unacknowledg'd" (and therefore mortalizing and dispiriting [l. 148]); and his uncleansed perceptions "again and yet again" mistake the *spirit* or *ruah* of God, the breathlike sound "now here, now there," persistent and recurring, for the finite pantings of his mortal terrier, his faithful but "off-and-on" companion (ll. 175–79).

His blindness and recalcitrance, moreover, contribute to the complacency and half-hearted self-examination in his covenant response: he weighs himself in the balance but is pleased with what he finds and undisturbed to find but little (ll. 148–50). And little more than idle fancy fills the following summer days, when "a swarm of heady thoughts"—

> gawds,
> And feast, and dance, and public revelry,
> And sports and games

—crowd out the things of the Spirit and seduce him from the zeal and yearning that were his as an "unworldly-minded Youth" (ll. 273–81). Wordsworth knows, as well as the Evangelicals did, to shun such worldly frivolity; for he was chastened in childhood and stirred to diligent self-examination at Cambridge. But now "these vanities" cause "an inner falling-off" from the heights of his "new-born feeling"; they prey upon his strength and press upon the "religious dignity" of his mind (ll. 270, 288–93, 296–97); and self-satisfied complacency thus interrupts "the course / And quiet stream of self-forgetfulness" (ll. 293–94).

His summer worldliness is most apparent when he passes the night in a throng of maids and youths, a "promiscuous rout" and "festal company" (ll. 316–18). This assemblage, this "medley of all tempers," contains a mixture of humors and passions: "Old Men" look upon maids, perhaps, instead of the "Matrons staid" (ll. 317–20); and this mixture is decidedly unspiritual and sensuous. "Unaim'd prattle" assaults the ear; "glancing forms" attract the eye and then move on (ll. 322–23). And tapers glitter: "young love-liking," warm and glowing as candlelight, intemperate as the rising flame and straight wick of passion and sexuality, mounts up "like joy into the head" and tingles "through the veins" (ll. 322, 325–27).

It is, of course, too much to say that Pilgrim's Progress reverts to Rake's when Wordsworth joins this more Hogarthian than Bunyanesque company and its "dancing, gaiety, and mirth" (l. 320); his touch is light, his memory tinged with sympathy and nostalgia. But we may conjecture that his undertones, his hints at the undirected passions and flirtatious conduct of disorderly and vulgar rioters (as distinct, say, from simple celebrators of an emerging and "natural" pubescence), cast at least a whispering voice to his previous underbreathings of the finitude and ephemerality in unspiritual sensuous experience. Intimations of mortality bring "a gentle shock" to the boy of Winander (see pp. 56–58), and the revelers' "slight shocks of young love-liking," denoting rising passion, intimate the shocks that flesh is heir to, the shock of declining sensuality (tapers glitter but soon die). The "Old Men," though hardly preredemption postlapsarians, nevertheless are nearer to being dirty-minded greybeards than good chaperones; and if they recall the "old man" of lusts and decay, their charges do so too; for the youths show no sign of putting on the New Man of holiness but instead indulge their desultory talk and sensual pleasure.

Like them, Wordsworth revels all the night. But on the morrow he shows signs of assuming a New Manhood; for at that time he feels a rich, strange, and potent sea-change of the spirit. The Evangelicals recorded precise times of their strange warmings of the heart, and he commemorates the "one particular hour" (l. 315) of his heartfelt transformation: the transfigured sea lies laughing in the distance as he envisions, considerably after the cock crows, soon after the rout disperses, just after dawn breaks, and when the sky is bright with day, the magnificent and glorious morning; he beholds, suddenly transformed if not transfigured, the solid mountains bright as clouds; he sees laborers going forth into the fields and hears the accompanying melody of birds; and he is deeply moved by his watershed, his baptismal and sacramentarian, experience: "to the brim / My heart was full" (ll. 328–41).

When least expected, and at the depths of his inner falling-off, his Extraordinary/Ordinary encounter with a Nature suffused with spiritual light (l. 335; see chapter 4) delivers Wordsworth from vanities and cleanses the doors of his perception. Prattling, dinning, shuffling, all the noises of dissociated sense, fade to sounds of purifying laughter and spiritual melody (ll. 333, 338; cf. Ephesians 5:19); fragmentary impressions and confused close-ups of feet, tapers, forms, instruments, the appurtenances, appearances, and objectified appendages of lustful, dissembling, and raucous revelers, are all now dim in comparison with the pictorial clarity, the translucent wholeness, and the solid substantiality of a mountain-height, foreground meadow, and background sea all blended in and by and for his new-created, now-creating mind and spirit.

And his new sensuous and aesthetic faculty of distancing and focusing—techniques attributable, perhaps, to his awareness of sublime aesthetics (see pp. 139–44) in combination with his proto-impressionism and pointilism of the verbal medium—has its religious counterpart in his new "sense" of spiritual truth and perspective (for his spirit's encounters with the Spirit do not utterly deny the senses or even question their capacity to give reliable experience and at least some knowledge of what is real and permanently valuable). Exaltation supplants the unspiritual "joy" of sensual pursuit (l. 326); "intense desire" and physical "passion" yield at last to "thought and quietness" (ll. 310, 313); and the account, insofar as the testifier seems converted from his worldly-mindedness, recapitulates, reconfirms, and bodes spiritual progress. Its significance, moreover, is increased by his subtle modification and adaptation of biblical meaning for the purpose of contributing at least a hint of divine forgiveness to the already complex implications of divine grace and the already resonant general concept of dramatic and pivotal change.

The Gospel of Mark foretells an apocalypse: at the cock-crowing or in the morning Christ will come in the clouds to judge mankind in great power and glory (13 : 26, 35). Wordsworth's passage, of course, presages no such fearful terror; but his account assuredly absorbs some of the atmosphere, reflects much of the language, and intimates the obverse doctrine (Christ may bring judgment but wants to redeem). The crowing of his cock, the melody-making of his new bird of spiritual potency, announces a cloudy but glorious and magnificent New Day of forgiveness and renewal. For the persona is no longer suspended, as in some earlier spots of time, between grace and damnation, but is here and throughout the rest of Book IV restored and, like the New Man, filled with "melody" and "Spirit" (ll. 338, 344; cf. Ephesians 5 : 18–19). And the crowing, therefore, in concert with the harmonizing and communicable powers of a fruitful and joyous Nature, tell a prophecy that is glorious to hear but far more millenial than apocalyptic in its immediate and far-reaching effects. The cock, together with the clouds, the sea, the meadows, mountains, and the men, make up a world that is solid and real; a world to be seen and therefore believed; a world luminescent and sacramental, with significations to be read, interpreted, heeded, and applied; the Spirit's means of mediated grace and His efficacious setting for the unexpected, sudden, timely, and unmediated gift of redemption.

And finally, Wordsworth's New Day is one of rededication and covenant resolve. For like Wesley, who described the covenant as a solemn act of rededication, "an affair of the heart attended with eminent blessing" (Wesley, 4 : 39); like William Black, the Cumbrian Methodist preacher who went into the woods and fields to make his covenant prayer (in which he reaffirmed "the sacred vows and engagements that I am under to thee" and promised to sin no more—*Lives,* 3 : 160); and like John Fawcett, the Whitefieldian Baptist minister who wrote perhaps the most famous of all covenant hymns ("Blest be the tie that binds / Our hearts in Christian love"), the poet promises as he walks through "humble copse / And open field" to keep his "vows" and covenant "bond" "else sinning greatly"; and he rejoices in the blessedness and full heart attending and supporting his now-dedicated Spirit (ll. 341–45; 321–22, 1850).

Toward the end of the summer, when Wordsworth extends the hand of practical charity to the godly veteran (see pp. 32–33), he fully honors these terms of his covenant; for he establishes a human bond that demonstrates his moral dedication and shows the sincerity of his spiritual vows. Earnestly he commends the "poor friendless man" to the "charitable care" of a laborer, undoubtedly one of those who tilled the fields on the morning of his covenant resolve:

> ". . . and, take it on my word
> He will not murmur should we break his rest;
> And with a ready heart will give you food
> And lodging for the night."
>
> [ll. 456–59]

The persona himself performs a charitable act and thereby joins, on a symbolic level, the ones who labor to bring in the New Day of the kingdom of God within and among the hearts of men. And *Prelude* IV, as a chapter in Wordsworth's spiritual autobiography and as an account of how covenant resolutions succeed weakness of will toward the end of an experience of forgiveness and grace, suggests to us who see how he shaped Evangelical thought that he was soon to join the laborers of his new day and age who felt called upon to gather the harvest of a spiritual vineyard and bring in sheaves of men; and who fulfilled, in historic measure, their personal and collective covenants to do so.

The imagery, of course, is reminiscent of that letter in which the poet speaks of himself as "a Fellow-labourer" in the same vineyard with Wilberforce (*EY,* p. 685); and the context of the imagery, including Book IV, all of *The Prelude,* and Wordsworth's very life, compares with the parable in which Christ likens the kingdom of God to a vineyard filled with laborers (Matthew 20 : 1–16). The association of the parable and its primary metaphor with an important exemplar of Evangelicalism was obviously a major concept for the maturing poet and perhaps even the structuring principle and chief source of symbol for Book IV, and for his experience in general as distinct from his written account of it.

For in 1788, the eleventh hour of the Great Awakening, the height of the harvest season, and the year of Wordsworth's "call," many Evangelical laborers in the English vineyard of God's kingdom had gone forth already—the Wesleys, Whitefield, Berridge, Hill, Simeon, Robinson, Newton, Cowper, Hopper, Black, and Fletcher. A few, such as Mathews, Wrangham, Clarkson, Wilberforce, and Dorothy Wordsworth, were seemingly chosen, if not to usher the kingdom in, at least to assume at its height a kind of leadership both spiritual and intellectual; and the poet's career during the 1790s (except, perhaps, for the period of his French experience), and most of his literary and spiritual labors thereafter, following upon and flowing from his covenant/conversion of 1788 (an experience told just when Wordsworth labored most productively), suggest that in a late season of Christian history and after a period of frivolous activities, heady thoughts, and idleness of spirit, he was summoned from the marketplace of worldliness and signally included in their number in order to undertake, not just the spiritual activity of practical charity, but the allied intellectual enterprise of writing poems, as he put it, that would serve "the good of the immortal soul" (*LY, 2 :* 1007). *192656*

And so it is essential to remember, in terms of the contrast between Books III and IV, and in terms of the commonplace that his vocation was somehow prophetic and inspired, that Wordsworth's religious and professional identity, despite, or in part because of, all his technical discipline, spiritual aspiration, and moral effort, derived evidently from a decisive moment of influx when he received a gift both free and clear, and when he perceived a phenomenon wholly external in origin, wholly independent from his own mind and spirit, and wholly influential.

For if indeed he consciously identified with the laborers for whom he had so clear an affinity, and if indeed he did so in 1788 or as he wrote Book IV, he claims in this particular passage no special credit for joining their labor—he takes no strong initiative in covenant resolve. In fact, he is almost totally passive: he is subjected to One Who molds, shapes, commands, and sends; he is persuaded that this Other can keep that which he has committed; and he is then led to feel that he can take a new responsibility in and for his own commitment:

> I made no vows, but vows
> Were then made for me; bond unknown to me
> Was given, that I should be, else sinning greatly,
> A dedicated Spirit. On I walk'd
> In blessedness, which even yet remains.
>
> [ll. 341–45]

"Covenants," said Wesley, are a "scriptural means of grace," the fruit of which shall remain forever (Wesley, 2 : 339; 4 : 478); and a similar conviction may account for the joyful tone of much of Book VI, where Wordsworth suggests that heartfelt rededication obtains much favor over a long span of time—clusters of spiritual gifts characterize his experience during the later Cambridge period. The book records

> the birth and growth
> Of *gentleness,* simplicity, and *truth,*
> And *joy*ous *love*s that hallow innocent days
> Of *peace* and self-command,
>
> [ll. 271–74; my italics]

and thus describes a plateau in the terrain of his journey; his covenant/conversion ushered in, not a spiritual kingdom immediately established for and recognized by large numbers of workers and idlers outside his innermost circle, but certainly a time of especial blessedness within that circle and in his renewed study of mathematics and Newtonian physics. "Almost / Through grace of Heaven," geometric science gives "transcendent *peace"* and "frequent *comfort"* (ll. 137, 157–59, 188–89; my italics); and meditation upon "the frame / And laws of Nature" gives "a still sense" of

> the one
> Surpassing Life, which out of space and time,
> Nor touch'd by welterings of passion, is
> And hath the name of God.
>
> [ll. 145–46, 151, 154–57]

Spiritual aid, therefore, attends Wordsworth's rededication to the earnest pursuit of knowledge (as distinct from his searching and hoping for spiritual experience); the language and method of science give him an other-worldly "sense" of spiritual perspective and thereby constitute, like Nature in the conversion episode, an efficacious medium of grace. And this private discovery of grace prepares him and motivates him to spread his experience out from self (and perhaps even share his knowledge with others); for Book VI implies that the gifts of God's Spirit, though received, perhaps, in intimate colloquies or solitary experiences of grace wherever it may be found, can be shared among those who love each other.

The poet spent the summer of 1789 at Penrith with his sister and Mary Hutchinson, and in *The Prelude* he recalls not only revering Mary, a spirit meek of heart, but also receiving from Dorothy, who "seem'd / A gift then first bestow'd," an extraordinary "joy / Above all joys" (ll. 211–12, 217–18, 237–38). That community of spirits makes him think, as he writes the book in April 1804, of his friend on the island of Malta; and to the absent Coleridge, a man of temperance and peace, he now sends the additional graces of joy and strength in the hope that "fresh spirits" and "loving thoughts," themselves a "gift" borne on "gales Etesian," would soon come in return (ll. 257–60, 290). These deeds of love, then, are supported by grace. And toward the end of Book VI, in his memory of France during the summer of 1790, the poet suggests that his receptivity and covenant resolve continued to be strong at the end of his spiritually significant Cambridge period; for he remembers how "Locarno's Lake" (Maggiore), "spreading out in width like Heaven," radiated *"power"* that was

> *gracious,* almost might I dare to say,
> As virtue is, or *goodness,* sweet as *love,*
> Or the remembrance of a *noble deed,*

> Or *gentlest* visitations of pure thought
> When God, the giver of all *joy*, is *thank'd*
> Religiously . . . .
>
> [ll. 589, 610–15; my italics]

The scene is picturesque, but Wordsworth does not so much display the conventional emotions of an impressionable youth abroad (responding as one should to natural beauty) as he demonstrates, in a supernaturally natural setting for the observance and mastery of spiritual phenomena, the spiritual graces and covenant capacity of a maturing young man, and hence the familiar and "Evangelical" interaction and interdependence among the graces, the pilgrim, and his fellow travelers.

The summer covenant of 1788, though genuine and long-lasting, was not to bear fruit perennially. In the following books the persona descends from the plateau of his Cambridge years and, soon after his "Evangelical" New Birth, once more (and for the last time) loses a major struggle with worldly vanity. He has found relief from the burden of sin; and he has enjoyed the favor of grace; but he must now (like Christian) struggle with the powerful and temporarily overpowering temptations of Vanity Fair. Wordsworth travels to Saint Bartholomew's Fair soon after receiving his degree in the spring of 1791. His strong faith, his "early converse with the works of God," shields him against the "blank confusion" and the worldly allurement of "trivial objects" and "low pursuits" (VII.695, 700–02, 718); but his London experience, testifying to strength of conviction and firmness of resolve, also foreshadows the spiritual pitfalls of his sojourn in France from November 1791 to December 1792, a year when the worldliness of the secular Revolution (and hence the temptations of a more alluring and more confusing fair) challenged his faith and temporarily interrupted his growth in grace: he was "favoured" with "*power*," "*love*," "*joy*," "*truth*"— "*Prophetic* sympathies of genial *faith*"—

> Until that natural graciousness of mind
> Gave way to over-pressure of the times
> And their disastrous issues.
>
> [XI.44–48; XII. 48–49, 1850; my italics]

Book IX, it is true, holds out the tantalizing possibility that the Revolution would foster discrete acts of charity and provide the context for perfection of faith (more than, say, the realization of a Godwinian perfectibilitarianism); [18] but Book X dispels this hope, relates the particulars of his loss of faith and lapse from covenant vows, and thereby shows that Wordsworth, like many others, falls prey to the false lure of an earthly New Jerusalem to be built only by the hands of men in power.

For a time, then, he forsakes the goal of that kind of perfection or moral excellence that may be reached through charity or the love of one's neighbor; for when he succumbs to the temptations of secular glory and assumes that God's kingdom is temporal in nature, he no longer practices acts of kindness or seeks spiritual companionship: rather, he wanders in blank confusion until the return to England where Dorothy, at the height of her "Evangelical" powers (see pp. 24–25), helps to restore the transcendent peace of his Cambridge days.

The opening paragraphs of Book IX suggest the chaos of events that began to trouble Wordsworth when he arrived in Orleans. The "revolutionary Power," he recalls, tossed "like a Ship at anchor, rock'd by storms":

> I star'd and listen'd with a stranger's ears
> To Hawkers and Haranguers, hubbub wild!
> And hissing Factionists with ardent eyes,
> In knots, or pairs, or single, ant-like swarms
> Of Builders and Subverters . . . .
>
> [ll. 49, 55–59]

He strives to retain his now-threatened faith: somewhat self-consciously, he adopts "the guise / Of an Enthusiast" and once more feels "some strong incumbences" (ll. 66–68). But the secular world proves no fair testing-ground for the spiritual strength of a young man who now can find no moral anchor and must therefore feign revolutionary fervor: "I look'd for something that I could not find, / Affecting more emotion than I felt" (ll. 70–71). "To me," he remembers, "all things" appeared "loose and disjointed"; his affections were "left / Without a vital interest" (ll. 105–07); and his faith, which survived an excursion through

Saint Bartholomew's Fair, seemed to waver in the face of greater
worldliness and graver temptations.

In the early months of 1792 Wordsworth moved from Orleans
to the garrison city of Blois where he met Michel Beaupuy, an
officer sympathetic to the revolutionary cause; and Book IX im-
plies that Beaupuy interpreted the Revolution from a religious
point of view ("in perfect faith" he understood "the events / Of
that great change" [ll. 304–05]) and was therefore able, like the
rough Terrier, the motherly Dame, the Alpine Peasant, the Girl
with the Pitcher, and sundry manifestations of nature, to mediate
spiritual guidance for the shaken youth. For whatever the actual
character and theology of this Catholic nobleman, and whatever
his allegiance to French rationalist philosophy, Wordsworth per-
ceives him primarily as a man of faith; and he describes him in
terms consistent with Evangelical theology of the Spirit (and
thus seems to stress the way a religious but now frightened young
man from England would have conceived the piety and selfless-
ness of one whose ideals were nourished in another land).

An ideal resembling Christian perfection, for example, emerges
from their conversation—their deep discourse in which the na-
ture of faith is as much considered as "the end / Of civil govern-
ment and its wisest forms" (ll. 328–31); one of their "dearest
themes"—

> Man and his noble nature, as it is
> The gift of God and lies in his own power,
> His blind desires and steady faculties
> Capable of clear truth
>
> [ll. 361–65]

—is reminiscent of the Evangelicals' covenant interaction be-
tween man and God, a relationship characterized by human
effort sustained through grace, a fellowship culminating in
sanctification. "Perfect faith," to the noble Beaupuy, arises from
the interworking of moral will and the gift of grace; for an
extraordinary "radiant joy" and an ordinary "meekness" urge
him to "works of love" on behalf of "the mean and the obscure"
(ll. 297–99, 313, 321–25). And to the admiring youth, therefore,
he seems to be one of those "single spirits that catch the flame

from Heaven," embodying this "deep sense / In action," sharing his gift and affording it "outwardly a shape / And that of bene-diction to the world" (ll. 375, 407–09). Such service is sanctioned "by an authority divine" (l. 414).

We can now, in the light of his faith as described in Book IX, see the religious implications of a familiar anecdote illustrating Beaupuy's charitable response to the misery of French peasants:

> And when we chanc'd
> One day to meet a hunger-bitten Girl,
> Who crept along, fitting her languid self
> Unto a Heifer's motion, by a cord
> Tied to her arm, and picking thus from the lane
> Its sustenance, while the Girl with her two hands
> Was busy knitting, in a heartless mood
> Of solitude, and at the sight my Friend
> In agitation said, " 'Tis against *that*
> That we are fighting," I with him believed
> Devoutly that a spirit was abroad
> Which could not be withstood, that poverty
> At least like this, would in a little time
> Be found no more . . . .
> 
> [ll. 510–23]

This episode, of course, anticipates the prevailingly secular hu-manitarian sentiment of twentieth-century socialism (such con-cern for the poor can be found not only among Rousseauists and French revolutionaries but also atheistic Russian Communists); but the episode also, and more importantly, epitomizes Beaupuy's religious view of the Revolution as a time when "love, now a universal birth, / From heart to heart is stealing" ("To My Sis-ter"; *PW*, 4 : 59); for Wordsworth implies, through his por-traiture of his new guide as a man with perfect faith as well as social ideals, that the spirit shed abroad in France was both a political phenomenon and an extraordinary religious inspiration for the many individual acts of "love . . . / For the abject multi-tude" (ll. 509–10) that he and Beaupuy fervently hoped would be performed by men motivated as much by the spirit of charity as by the hope of Utopia. He beheld during these early days of the Revolution a dispensation of love, a gracious endowment comparable to the spirit of Evangelical charity (and indeed to the spirit that led him to scorn aimless governmental efforts to aid indigents such as the Old Cumberland Beggar).

In the terms of Book IX, then, the true Revolution is spiritual and establishes its sway in each man's heart when each man's isolated charitable deeds at once show change in his life and shed grace throughout his sphere of action. Beaupuy fights not to put himself or some faction into power—not, indeed, with any regard for the usual terms of temporal conquest—but to alleviate the suffering of his nearest neighbor. And his perfect faith, insofar as it bears the fruit of charity, parallels the Evangelical goal of Christian perfection. Book IX suggests that the poet finds a perfect exemplum in his life and teachings and then regains a sense of spiritual direction from one who does not need to adopt a guise of faith. Beaupuy, "gracious" and "enthusiastic to the height / Of highest expectation" (ll. 299–301), is a genuinely fervent revolutionary of the human spirit; and Wordsworth, in moments of similar enthusiasm, might have gone so far as to call him a vanguard fighter for the kingdom of God within and among the hearts of men.

Another kind of kingdom, however, was soon to prevail; Beaupuy "perish'd fighting" (l. 430) and never enjoyed the chance to temper the increasing temporality and dangerous secularity of his countrymen's revolutionary fervor. On 29 October 1792, after the September massacres in which the forces of Marat, Danton, and Robespierre slaughtered three thousand suspected Royalists, Wordsworth arrived in Paris amid the rising extremism of the Jacobin Club and detected a widespread falling-off from all the principles for which Beaupuy had stood: "Heaven's best aid is wasted upon men / Who to themselves are false" (X.119–20, 1850). At first, Book X suggests, Wordsworth remains true to a faith recently fortified by Beaupuy's ideal of renewal through good works inspired by grace; he continues, for example, to read political events with spiritual eyes. At a time when men are strong only through their impiety, he seems to recognize that nothing short of a Pentecostal manifestation of the Spirit's witness can save France from herself and teach her that civil liberty

cannot be rightly understood apart from seeking and receiving
the spiritual truth that makes men free indeed:

> —my inmost soul
> Was agitated; yea, I could almost
> Have prayed that throughout earth upon all men,
> By *patient* exercise of reason made
> Worthy of liberty, all spirits filled
> With zeal expanding in *Truth*'s holy light,
> The *gift* of *tongues* might fall, and *power* arrive
> From the four quarters of the winds to do
> For France, what without *help* she could not do,
> A work of honour . . . .
> [ll. 116; 133–42, 1850; my italics] [19]

In the apparent hope of mediating such guidance (and thereby
taking up Beaupuy's great revolutionary work), he considers be-
coming a leader of the moderate Girondins; though "little *graced*
with *power*,"

> Yet would I willingly have taken up
> A service at this time for cause so great,
> However dangerous,

for he knows that "tyrannic Power is weak," unspiritual, "hath
neither *gratitude,* nor *faith,* nor *love*" (ll. 132, 135–37, 168–69;
my italics).

France's need for such moral and spiritual leadership increased
in geometric proportions: the "goaded Land wax'd mad" during
the period following Robespierre's death by guillotine (28 July
1794), a period when "even thinking minds / Forgot . . . whence
they had their being" (ll. 313, 347–48); the "best in individual
Man," in fact, was no longer "proof against the injuries of the
day" (ll. 667, 677). Those who were "strong in love" knew "hope
and joy," "lively natures" were "rapt away"; but these seemingly
Extraordinary emotions arose from extreme worldliness of moti-
vation: the germ of earthly power yielded such false fruit, for
these men moved among "the objects of the sense" and dealt
with "whatsoever they found there / As if they had some lurking
right" to do so (ll. 690–91, 708–09, 714–16). And Frenchmen of

milder character, those of gentle mood and peaceful temper,
perverted their inborn receptivity to such ordinary grace, finding
unspiritual and materialistic "stuff at hand" "to exercise their
skill," their pride in their autonomy,

> in the very world which is the world
> Of all of us, the place in which, in the end,
> We find our happiness, or not at all.
>                                    [ll. 718–28]

The context of this much-quoted passage, a verse-paragraph in
which Wordsworth diagnoses the spiritual malaise of France,
suggests that he intends these lines to be taken ironically; for
this mundane sentiment, though it represents the dangerous and
erroneous viewpoint of the French, far from represents his own
mature viewpoint, and indeed epitomizes the blithest and bleak-
est secularism of the Revolution: in the most general terms of
*The Prelude,* a worldly frame of mind, or an attitude that finds
no spiritual meaning in the world, can lead to no happy "end."

The lines do represent Wordsworth's immature viewpoint. As
a young man in France, bereft of Beaupuy and thus weakened in
spirit, he never finds the will to pray for grace nor does he ever
succeed to Beaupuy's command of the now-paralyzed forces of
spiritual renewal. Book X shows, indeed, that like many rational-
ists of the day he begins to place his trust in man's unaided effort
and thus forgets that noble nature is the gift of God. As he writes,
Wordsworth confesses to committing "juvenile errors" of faith
after returning to England in December 1792 and before joining
Dorothy at Racedown in 1795 (l. 638): having already missed the
opportunity of hastening the spiritual kingdom abroad, he con-
tinued naïvely to believe that the world following the death of
the tyrant Robespierre would "march firmly toward righteousness
and peace" (l. 583); but this hope for two of the spiritual graces
turned out to be as false as the promise of love, gentleness, and
peace among the French. The whole earth wore the beauty
of great promise, but toward the end of the Revolution and
throughout the reign of Napoleon an uncontrolled greed for
conquest proved his early vision of a French latter Eden to be
cruel illusion, a fanciful product of "false imagination," "beyond

the limits of experience and of truth" (ll. 702–03, 848–49). In retrospect he understands that the "light of circumstances," worldly wisdom, was an insufficient "guide," even when "flash'd / Upon an independent intellect" such as his own, through the moral complexities of that age (ll. 829–30).

The light of spiritual guidance, however, is restored to him through the book of nature (see chapter 4) and the agencies of Coleridge (see above) and his sister; Book X and other closing books testify especially to Dorothy's important role in preserving Wordsworth for the kingdom's work. Her admonition, sudden as the Spirit's Extraordinary witness, gives him "saving intercourse" with his "true self" and helps him recover from the false enthusiasm, the near- and unreligious fanaticism, of his French experience: new strength and peace, graces known in "earlier life," are now enlarged through her witness and ministrations, and are indeed "never more to be disturbed" (ll. 911–16, 925–27).

Wordsworth's task of tracing spiritual maturity, his account of a grace quite as amazing and perhaps even as Christian as the experience recorded in the spiritual autobiography of his day, is therefore essentially completed; and the poetic record of his remaining life gives little evidence of temptations or errors as unsettling as the ones he faced and made in France (in the great Ode, for example, he can profess "the faith that looks through death" in part because he entertains no further illusions about the inglorious or unspiritualized aspects of this world [*PW*, 4 : 279, 284]). Toward the end of his account he includes Dorothy among those who have done for him "all that love can do"—

> All that a darling countenance can look
> Or dear voice utter to complete the man,
> Perfect him, made imperfect in himself . . . .
> [XIII.200–03]

She has helped to bring him within sight of sanctity and within reach, therefore, of the main goal in spiritual life. In the future, she warns him, he must not be "reckless of mild grace" (XIII. 228): he must seek the graces that crown maturity in fruitful clusters.

And yet not Dorothy but the Spirit in her, as it seems, per-

manently restores the discipline of his earliest years (the disci-
pline through which God "trains / To meekness, and exalts by
humble faith" [V.227–28]); for near the end of his recorded pil-
grimage, on a "public road" resembling "a guide into eternity,"
Wordsworth receives a mysteriously unmediated and abundantly
supervenient grace akin to but elder and more efficacious than
what Dorothy, Coleridge, or Nature can give:

> . . . there I found
> *Hope* to my hope, and to my pleasure *peace,*
> And steadiness; and *healing* and repose
> To every angry passion.
>
> [XII.151, 178–81; my italics]

## The Excursion

In the Preface to *The Excursion* (1814), Wordsworth compares
his writings to a gothic church, with *The Prelude* as antechapel
and *The Excursion* as a part of the main body (*PW*, 5 : 2), and
this metaphor indicates that he held the latter work in highest
esteem and that he regarded it as even more important, in the
religious sense, at least, than *The Prelude* itself. These implica-
tions, however, have largely been avoided or ignored, for critics
prefer *The Prelude:* They discover no systematic theology in
*The Excursion,* and in general they hold the poem in low esteem
(indeed they see it as the record of Wordsworth's flight from his
own vision).[20]
But we shall see that the implications of the poet's metaphor
are provocative and well worth exploring. For we shall find that
*The Excursion*—an objective, comprehensive, and instructive if
not an intimate, particular, and delightful poem—shows the
catholicity of Wordsworth's religious experience and thus re-
lates to *The Prelude* as *Pilgrim's Progress* relates to *Grace
Abounding* (and indeed as the inclusive and mature if not al-
ways engaging or successful works in the mid and late careers
of modern and hence post-Puritan/Evangelical authors relate to
their "autobiographical" and more attractive, if less formalisti-
cally correct, experimentations).

We shall always prefer *The Prelude,* of course; for like the Romantics and the Evangelicals we live in an epistemological and experiential age, not a metaphysical and dogmatic one; but we can nevertheless exert the effort to dwell upon the implications—for understanding, if not appreciating, *The Excursion*—of Wordsworth's attempt to construct a religious and Evangelicalized edifice sheltering all his literary substructures. For then we may see that, even as Wesley's journal contributed both matter and illustration to his sermons and discourses, even as his ministers' autobiographies prepared them to say what proved so comprehensible to many, and even as Wilberforce's charitable enterprises undoubtedly gave conviction to the objective theology in *A Practical View,* so Wordsworth's almost daily poetical record of grace and consequent charity helped him to write, though not the great philosophical poem hoped for by Coleridge, at least the good religious one received as such by some.

Meditation in the antechapel of Wordsworth's works, therefore, prepares us to enter the main sanctuary where several aisles in particular—the biography of the Wanderer in Book I, his creed in Book IV, the Pastor's tales (Books VI and VII), and the reaffirming aspirations throughout Book IX—echo the spiritual themes first sounded in the antechapel where he framed his personal profession of faith; and the continuity of world-view from *The Prelude* through *The Excursion* suggests that what we have of *The Recluse* follows his spiritual autobiography as night the day. We can undertake, then, an extensive and systematic though by no means exhaustive reading; we can expect to find terms that make sense of *The Excursion* as it relates to and in no way contradicts *The Prelude* and the shorter poems; and we can conclude, leaving aside the question of critical evaluation, that the poem departs in no radical way from Wordsworth's earlier and indeed his lifelong point of view, but reflects instead an undivided and essentially constant mind as harmoniously and as consistently, though with as differing an emphasis, as *Grace Abounding* and *Pilgrim's Progress* reflect the mind of Bunyan in its progression from a subjective toward an objectified presentation of belief.

And though we should suspend our final judgment, though

we may be impatient even now and wish to blame *The Excursion* for being "second-rate" in its muted humanism and "massively depressing" in its unremitting (but perhaps more prudent than morbid) emphasis on suffering and death,[21] we can observe as we concentrate on its theological point of view that it has many stylistic strengths and virtues, and that these are the ones we have found in Wordsworth all along: an assured and steady progression and development from phrase to phrase and from paragraph to paragraph, an unpremeditated force of conviction and hence of expression, a pure simplicity of narration and relation of anecdote, and a gift for spiritualized abstraction. And finally, therefore, we can hold in reserve the possibility of concluding that this most massive and ambitious work, in the huge mansion of which it forms all we have of what was to have been by far the largest room, not only merits more consideration and analysis but commands—and demands—more admiration and respect.

The Wanderer's biography, appearing in the first half of Book I (for a discussion of the second, see pp. 160–61), parallels the poet's autobiography in the two-part division: a strict early training followed by a rich spiritual life. Within the compressed space of only four hundred fast-moving and energetic lines, Wordsworth brings his protagonist from childhood to maturity and thereby demonstrates that he can here accomplish in brief what it took him fourteen books to do in the expression of his chastened self and in the baring of his maturing soul. The Wanderer's parents were "pure livers," "austere and grave, / And fearing God"; the children were therefore taught "stern self-respect, a reverence for God's word, / And an habitual piety" (ll. 113–16). And this parental guidance, worthy of Susanna Wesley's Puritan disciplinary practices, antedates his "precious gift" of communion with "the presence and the power / Of greatness" (ll. 133–40), a recurring adolescent and young adult communion described through the language of Evangelical spiritual experience. As a youth, for example, he has an encounter comparable to the poet's covenant / conversion of 1788—an epiphany during which the sight of a glorious sunrise gives the joy and rapture of an extraordinary witness:

> In such access of mind, in such high hour
> Of visitation from the living God,
> Thought was not; in enjoyment it expired.
> No thanks he breathed, he proffered no request;
> Rapt into still communion that transcends
> The imperfect offices of prayer and praise,
> His mind was a thanksgiving to the power
> That made him; it was blessedness and love!
>
> [ll. 197, 211–18]

In such "ecstasies" the Wanderer seems *"possessed"* but soon acquires the ordinary grace of "patience" and becomes "meek in gratitude" (ll. 221, 236–39); and these extraordinary and ordinary fruits of the Spirit confirm the Evangelical meaning of Wordsworth's introduction of him as a man full of "graces," a man whose mind, like the collective mind of Quakers (who participated in the Great Awakening), was "filled with inward light" (ll. 94–95).

He reciprocates such favor, moreover, by exercising moral will: in childhood he read the lives of Scottish martyrs whose "will inflexible" and solemn "Covenant" with God provided examples of inspired human initiative (ll. 170–75); and as a young man led by the "stern yet kindly Spirit" (a spirit not only attached somewhat pantheistically and somewhat like God on Sinai "to regions mountainous" but also separated from nature as one who "constrains / The Savoyard to *quit* his native rocks"), he chooses to become a "vagrant merchant" traveling with the practically evangelical purpose of going into the world to perform "kind works" and to "suffer / With those whom he saw suffer" (ll. 316, 370–71, 405; my italics). And in this combination of external aid and his own effort lie the means to a personal purity and hence to an evident state of perfection: he "shaped his belief" "to the model of his own pure heart," but "as grace divine inspired" (ll. 411–12). The Wanderer, in short, applies his early training and proves the child-rearing and adult-maturing theories of the poet's "Evangelicalism" in its Nonconformist and northernmost manifestation:

The Scottish Church, both on himself and those
With whom from childhood he grew up, had held
The strong hand of her purity; and still
Had watched him with an unrelenting eye.
This he remembered in his riper age
With gratitude, and reverential thoughts.

[ll. 397–402]

Building upon his firm foundation of spiritual experience, the
Wanderer delivers in Book IV an eloquent profession of faith;
in one sense, therefore, the first half of Book I relates to Book
IV as *The Prelude* relates to *The Excursion:* like Wordsworth's
persona, the Wanderer feels his faith before he formulates it.
And he specifically formulates it in order to save the Solitary,
a skeptic deeply shaken as the poet was by the French Revolu-
tion and therefore fully representative of that modern and often
secular, but potentially religious because experiential, cast of
mind for which Evangelicalism proved such a stay (see *Excur-
sion* II and III). The book, indeed, contains some of Words-
worth's most memorable expressions of Evangelicalism and shows
with what certainty of vision and fluency of conviction he turned
from *The Prelude* to *The Excursion.* The opening lines advo-
cate an intense religion that seems to assign equal importance to
the complementary virtues of trust in God and exertion of will:
men must live "by faith," exclaims the Wanderer—"Faith abso-
lute in God" (ll. 21–22); and he suggests, moreover, that man's
"boundless love" of God's "perfections" strengthens the will to
corresponding human perfections, a

dread
Of aught unworthily conceived, endured
Impatiently, ill-done, or left undone . . . .

[ll. 21–26]

He concludes that the enabling power of grace preserves man's
divine potentialities (ll. 50–51).

Throughout the book, indeed, he suggests that grace is now
and has always been manifested by the fruits of the "all-pervading
Spirit, upon whom / Our dark foundations rest" (ll. 969–70).

From the dawn of creation "joy and love" were the dividends of "communications spiritually maintained" between man and "the articulate voice / Of God" "borne on the wind" (ll. 634–45): Jehovah continued to fill the earth with "hope, and love, and gratitude" throughout early recorded history (l. 660); and even the "brave Progenitors" of the British nation, though without the knowledge of Christianity, escaped idolatry because they knew a "spiritual presence"

> that filled their hearts
> With joy, and gratitude, and fear, and love
> And from their fervent lips drew hymns of praise,
> That through the desert rang.
>
> [ll. 920, 927, 929–32]

Like Watts, Wesley, and Fletcher, moreover, the Wanderer feels that this spiritual force continues to establish communion with men in modern times, restoring them daily with a "touch as gentle as the morning light" (ll. 86–90); and the Spirit's gentle touch suggests his particular reliance upon the Ordinary witness. He remembers the "fervent raptures" and "joy exalted to beatitude" characterizing moments seemingly Extraordinary, when his soul is filled with "holiest love" and all things seem full of glory (ll. 119–23); but like Watts he realizes that men cannot long bear such joy unspeakable and full of glory, for he admits that it is difficult for most men "to *keep* / Heights which the soul is competent to gain" (ll. 138–39), especially when the eyes become

> too dim
> For any passion of the soul that leads
> To ecstasy.
>
> [ll. 181–83]

At full spiritual maturity he is seldom "rapt" in a kind of Extraordinary transport, but he frequently enjoys the more dependable if ordinary gifts of the Spirit—"settled peace," hope, and the comforting sense of support that quells all doubt and banishes trouble (ll. 187–91, 234–36). An ordinary witness suffices for daily living.

The Wanderer in fact does not rely exclusively on grace but puts considerable emphasis on the individual's responsibilities to God and man. The faithful should renew their vows on the "first motion of a holy thought" until their strengthened conscience finally becomes God's most perfect image in the world (ll. 216–27); and this internal controlling principle, analogous to Wordsworth's mature Imagination as described in *Prelude* VI (see pp. 62–65), is the result of disciplined spiritual communion and rigorous moral effort: it is never easy, says the Wanderer, "to converse with heaven,"

> Yet cease I not to struggle, and aspire
> Heavenward; and chide the part of me that flags,
> Through sinful choice. . . .
>
> [ll. 126–32]

Thus he advocates the development of a covenant bond like that accepted by the poet in the summer of 1788, a bond entailing earnest vows to perform the acts of charity that lead at last to glorious perfection; after a lifetime of such covenant-making a man is "glorified," worthy to "dwell with God in endless love" (ll. 189–90).

In these terms of spiritual theology the Wanderer diagnoses the Solitary's spiritual sickness: shame, Watts pointed out, is opposite to the glory sought by men who aspire to perfection; and the Wanderer, himself such an aspirant, suggests that the Solitary is harvesting the "false fruit" of shame by placing too much confidence in "social man" (the skeptic's temporal "hope" in the French Revolution, like that of many well-intentioned Frenchmen and Englishmen during the early 1790s, proves an illusory grace [ll. 261, 290–93]). By the end of the book, however, the Solitary begins to respond to the Wanderer's testimony by inquiring about both grace and covenant resolve as the possible means of regeneration: he entertains a new and more spiritual hope that "showers of grace, / When in the sky no promise may be seen," will fall "to refresh a parched and withered land"; and he now recognizes that God's gifts are "in some degree rewards / For acts of service" (ll. 1093–98).

He is not fully recovered, of course; but when the Wanderer sees his eye kindle as though it were "lit by fire from heaven," he expresses confidence in the skeptic's future restoration to peace and "union with our God" (ll. 1116–22). And in subsequent books he continues his gradual progress: Book V, for example, shows his new regard for the baptismal ceremony, a growing admiration recalling Henry's *Baptismal Covenant*, Robinson's *History of Baptism*, and Wesley's *Directions for Renewing our Covenant with God*. He respects the sincerity of the "aspiring vows" made during this "solemn ceremony," in which a "dedication made" by man and "a promise given" by God combine to insure an "unremitting progress" in "holiness and truth" (ll. 289–92). He now grasps, therefore, the essential characteristics of covenant interaction with the Spirit; and his sympathetic response to baptism is undoubtedly intended to foreshadow his own regeneration, planned for the final portions of *The Recluse*.

The Pastor's tales in Books VI and VII ("The Churchyard Among the Mountains") constitute an important part of Wordsworth's strategy for the Solitary's regeneration, and these simple parables reflecting Evangelical ideals of spiritual theology contain some of the most memorable poetry in *The Excursion* and are, indeed, objectified exempla reminiscent of the spots of time, the poet's more personal and more famous though not always better understood system of morality and testimony of grace (a system and testimony resting no less firmly than the churchyard tales upon the assumption that experience and death are reliable teachers of men). The Pastor's themes can be understood in the light of his faith as described throughout Books V, VI, and VII. In Book V he stresses, in a way reminiscent of the Evangelicals' commingling of spiritual, natural, and biblical theology (see chapter 4), the Spirit of God as much as the Bible: man is empowered

> to perceive
> The voice of Deity, on height and plain,
> Whispering those truths in stillness, which the WORD,
> To the four quarters of the winds, proclaims.
>
> [V.990–93]

The whispered truths, moreover, are the gifts of the Spirit as specified in the Word of God; for at the beginning of Book VI Wordsworth describes the Pastor as a man who spreads the "gen-

uine fruits" of religion (l. 80); and at the end of Book VII the
Wanderer thanks the "gracious" teacher for telling stories of
spiritual grace,

> words of heartfelt *truth,*
> Tending to *patience* when affliction strikes;
> To *hope* and *love;* to confident repose
> In God; and reverence for the dust of Man.
>                                              [ll. 1054–57; my italics]

And in addition to grace the Pastor, like the Wanderer, stresses
the exertion of moral effort; before relating his tales he defines
life as "energy of love / Divine or human" (V.1012–13), thereby
implying the covenant interaction between God and man. Be-
cause of pain, strife, and tribulation, such love will be difficult
for men to achieve and must therefore be consciously exercised;
but the Pastor, whose life reflects the "sanctity of elder times,"
teaches above all else that a kind of perfection can crown con-
stant moral effort sustained by grace: "sanctified" men will "pass, /
Through shades and silent rest, to endless joy" (V.1012–16; VI.76).

In Book VII the Wanderer briefly describes a Lake Country
vicar of his acquaintance, a man of moral "resolution" and "in-
dustry severe," but also a man of "temperance" in whom "all
generous feelings flourish and rejoice" (ll. 323–24, 328, 330); thus
he reflects the proper—indeed the perfect—balance between vir-
tuous effort and reliance upon grace:

> . . . he appears
> A labourer, with moral virtue girt,
> With spiritual graces, like a glory, crowned.
>                                              [ll. 337–39]

The vicar epitomizes the Wanderer's vision of lifelong labor in
the spiritual vineyard (the vision first shaped in *Prelude* IV);
and he also epitomizes the Evangelical ideals underlying not just
the Pastor's faith but all his tales, in which the characters em-
brace or violate one or more tenets of spiritual theology.

Some stories are negative exempla; a widow, in one case,
pridefully relies on the efficacy of resolution apart from grace:
despite poverty she vows to support her only son and faithfully

honors this covenant (she "resolved" to be thrifty and "adhered to her resolve" [VI.720]); but her exclusive "trust / In ceaseless pains," with no acknowledgment of dependence on God, leads her to grow "slack in alms-giving" and to lose her charity (ll. 721–22). Her covenant resolve, therefore, unlike the vicar's resolute industry, remains narrowly one-sided, unsupported by grace. At last she becomes intolerant of lasting "peace": "gentleness" eludes her (ll. 732, 738), and the fruits of the Spirit do not return until she lies on her deathbed, where "divine mercy" or unmerited grace descends and bestows the gift of "meekness" (l. 771).

*Wil*fred Armathwaite sets another bad example: he breaks his marriage vow not so much because he cannot keep perfect faith —a common enough human failing—as because he *will*fully resists redemption by grace. He feels "remorse," to be sure; but he never finds "forgiveness in himself," and therefore loses access to such ordinary graces as peace and comfort and remains impervious to the invitations of the "gracious" Anglican Church, offering "peace and hope / And love" (VI.1096–1111). Armathwaite dies of grief because he cannot "endure the weight of his own shame" and will not accept the available relief (he never knows the glory that should crown a lifetime sustained by grace [l. 1114]). Along with the widow, therefore, he can be judged by the criteria of faith and morality, criteria implicit in the life of the vicar and variously stated throughout *The Excursion;* and both the Solitary and the reader are clearly meant to see the contrast between the spiritual lives of the Wanderer and the Pastor, and those of Armathwaite and the widow.

The Pastor also presents characters worthy of emulation; three men and one remarkable woman excel in one or more of the requirements and rewards of spiritual life. The tale of a miner who perseveres in search of a "precious ore" implicitly analogous to the priceless gifts of the Spirit draws this prayerful response from the Wanderer: "Grant to the wise *his* firmness of resolve!" (VI.261); the tale of a widower with "six fair Daughters" is a fit exemplum of reliance on grace—

> Deprest, and desolate of soul, as once
> That Father was, and filled with anxious fear,

> Now, by *experience* taught, he stands *assured,*
> That God, who takes away, yet takes not half
> Of what he seems to take . . . .
>
> > [VI.1131–35; my italics]

—and is also precisely Evangelical in diction (an assurance of
God's love comprises the distinguishing dividend of Wesley's
theology of experience [Wesley, 11 : 369–70; see Davies, *Worship
and Theology in England,* pp. 205–06]). And the tale of the deaf
Dalesman, like the Wanderer's brief description of the vicar, is
a microcosm of spiritual values. Like the lily of the field (Mat-
thew 6 : 28), he does not work for himself but trusts God more
than his own effort (VII.425) and thereby turns his deaf ears to
the alluring appeals of ownership. Unlike the passive lily, how-
ever, the Dalesman practices the good works indicative of cove-
nant resolve: "duteously" he pursues "the round / Of rural la-
bours" (ll. 418–19), selflessly offering service and hence a kind of
spiritual labor, if not in spiritual vineyards then in the literal
fields of harvest belonging to his farmer-brother and yielding
food to neighboring communities. And as he grows older in this
service (and therefore increasingly sanctified), he often reads the
"word of holy Writ" and thereby sharpens his spiritual senses
to hear the Voice

> Announcing immortality and joy
> To the assembled spirits of just men
> Made perfect, and from injury secure.
>
> > [ll. 451–54]

The echo of Hebrews 12 : 23 (Wordsworth's most explicit biblical
allusion to the doctrine of perfection) suggests that the Dalesman
himself, no longer set apart on earth by his faithful covenant
effort but gathered—or soon to be gathered—into the heavenly
assembly, joins the perfect company of the elect; and the ending
of the narrative bears out the implication: a pine tree near his
grave serves as an emblem of the "sanctity" to which he attained
(l. 479), even as his life, commemorated by the Pastor and there-
fore remembered by those still struggling on the earthly pilgrim-
age, stands as an example of perfection.

The remarkable story of Ellen, the longest, most complex, and most affecting of the tales, rests upon many of the assumptions and displays many of the characteristics of adult spiritual life as understood by the Evangelicals; the narrative's structure, indeed, can be seen in terms of Wesley's distinction between the divine "covenant of grace" and the Christian's "covenant of works" (the former enables the errant soul to "retrieve the life of God"; and the latter, permitting *"continuance* in the favour of God," consists of *"perfect* and uninterrupted obedience to every point" of His law [Wesley, 5 : 70]). For despite or because of an initial error, Ellen receives a covenant of grace; then she makes and honors a covenant of works; and finally, through an exemplary obedience (and hence a constant communion), she finds more favor and receives additional support in time of need. From the Evangelical point of view she is lost in sin at first (she conceives a child out of wedlock), but she responds to overtures of grace and seems by the end to manifest spiritual perfection.

Grace is manifested at the birth of her child—an event described as a gift of joy and thanksgiving (VI.908, 910, 916); and thus the fruit of her "shame" (l. 848) yields to and helps bring forth the glorious and miraculous fruits of God's Spirit. For these graces indicate the mother's own New Birth (an experience as dramatic as the covenant / conversion in *Prelude* IV): she testifies that her mature spiritual life, like that of the Evangelicals at the time of their conversion, begins at a sudden turning-point —the birth of her child:

> There was a stony region in my heart;
> But He, at whose command the parchèd rock
> Was smitten, and poured forth a quenching stream,
> Hath softened that obduracy, and made
> Unlooked-for gladness in the desert place,
> To save the perishing . . . .
>
> [ll. 918–23]

Ellen echoes the Old Testament passage in which God takes pity on the thirsty and spiritually arid Israelites by empowering Moses to extract water from the rock in Horeb (Exodus 11 : 6); and in addition to this exploitation of Jehovah's willingness to condescend, her heart/stone metaphor evokes a complex of biblical covenant imagery: the people's "stony heart" is removed and replaced with "an heart of flesh" "that they may walk in my statutes, and keep mine ordinances, and do them" (Ezekiel 9 : 19–20).

God's law, in effect, is now written on Ellen's heart. She finishes the labor of childbirth and undertakes a spiritual labor; for she makes a covenant of works when she makes evident, soon after her redemptive experience, a new moral commitment: first she regrets that her mother's prayers were seemingly "in vain," and then she moves beyond such idle self-reproach to make a firm resolution: "Yet not in vain; it shall not be in vain" (l. 927). And the good faith of this new covenant is demonstrated by her subsequent conduct: she begins, for example, to feel scruples about relying on the "slender means" of her mother, and "with dutiful content," therefore, she finds employment as a nurse (ll. 940–41).

Many afflictions test her faith: her employers allow no visits to her child; the child becomes ill, then dies within three days. But her strength never fails—with no bitterness she simply mourns "her own transgressions; penitent sincere / As ever raised to heaven a streaming eye!" (ll. 990–91). And she remains strong partly because of access to the graces that now reinforce her covenant of works; at her lowest point, physically languishing because she cannot see her child, she receives them from the Pastor (who suggests he was an agent of the Spirit):

> To me,
> As to a spiritual comforter and friend,
> Her heart she opened; and no pains were spared
> To mitigate, as *gently* as I could,
> The sting of self-reproach with *healing* words.
>
>                    [ll. 1029–33; my italics]

Other graces are manifested as her life nears its end; and they bear witness to her imminent perfection: *"Meek* Saint! through *patience glorified* on earth!" (l. 1034; my italics). Like the Dalesman, then, Ellen leaves the legacy of perfect example: the "sanctity" that broods over her grave will remain "till the stars sicken at the day of doom" (ll. 804–05). And of all the Pastor's exemplary tales, her story bears the fullest resemblance to Wordsworth's autobiography, with its reflection of the fruits of the Spirit sought through resolution and acquired through a grace both extraordinary and ordinary in its manifestations and effects.

The theology underlying these tales carries over into the visionary and doctrinal Book IX, where one last time the Wanderer and the Pastor reaffirm spiritual truths. In a brief verseparagraph (ll. 206–54) the Wanderer summarizes the conviction elaborated in Books I and IV that through spiritual aid man is capable of making a covenant of good works: because of conscience and "freedom in the will" men can know that the "primal duties" are "charities that soothe, and heal, and bless"; and to enhance these moral faculties and strengthen their grace-sharing powers, the Almighty grants the fruits of power, truth, hope, and gratitude to each man, whether "proudly graced" or "meek of heart." With such ordinary and extraordinary aids, men can achieve "holiness on earth," the Puritan goal of covenant-making, and thus be "assured" of heaven even as Wesley experienced the sense of Christian promise.

And to the Wanderer's doctrine the Pastor adds vision in the final lines of the poem: he leads his wife, his son and daughter, the Wanderer, the Solitary, and the poet now completely freed from self, to the top of a hill where they watch a "less than ordinary" sunset (l. 591); and though the scene is commonplace, he is moved to a prayer both ordinary and extraordinary: wondering whether ordinary graces such as hope, righteousness, peace, love, and faith (all still to be found among men) will suffice to help them "triumph over sin and guilt," he fervently asks the "Eternal Spirit! universal God!" for a timely dispensation of the Extraordinary witness and thus makes at last the prayer that Wordsworth could not make in France:

> Almighty Lord, thy further grace impart!
> And with that help the wonder shall be seen
> Fulfilled, the hope accomplished; and thy praise
> Be sung with transport and unceasing joy.
>
> [ll. 614, 663–65, 672–79]

And finally he proclaims his belief that "the elect of earth," his own "little band / Gathered together" like Puritan/Evangelicals entering solemn league and covenant, already receive encouragement while performing the works of charity from the grace and support of that same Spirit of Almighty God:

> Your Pastor is emboldened to prefer
> Vocal thanksgivings to the eternal King;
> Whose love, whose counsel, whose commands, have made
> Your very poorest rich in *peace* of thought
> And *in good works;* and him, who is endowed
> With scantiest knowledge, master of all *truth*
> Which the salvation of his soul requires.
> Conscious of that abundant favour showered
> On you, the children of my humble care,
> And this dear land, our country, while on earth
> We sojourn, have I lifted up my soul,
> *Joy* giving voice to fervent *gratitude.*
>
> [ll. 731–42; my italics]

### The Shorter Poems

When in 1814 Wordsworth compared *The Prelude* and *The Excursion* to the antechapel and main body of a gothic church, he extended the metaphor and called his other poems the "little cells, oratories, and sepulchral recesses ordinarily included in those edifices" (*PW*, 5 : 2). This extension does not so much indicate that he regarded them as less important than the main body and the antechapel as it suggests that he considered them to be religious poems and private colloquies concerned in part, as *The Excursion* and *The Prelude* are, with the theme of mortality. Another and a more suggestive implication of the metaphor is that he regarded all his works as one great poem, and that each of them therefore partakes of a fairly constant and stable mode of thought and expression.

Already, of course, we have dwelt upon this implication; for we have seen that spiritual theology underlies the two longer works and helps to account for the continuity in style and point of view; and we have found that the coherence of his vision is due in large measure to the consistency of its religious content. And we can now proceed on the assumption that these same spiritual themes and this same spiritual idiom can be found throughout the many kinds of verses spanning his career. We can expect to find that, like *The Prelude*, some small poems reflect the poet's own experience and that, like *The Excursion*, others are objective; and we can expect to see that even as experiential theology excelled systematic among the Evangelicals, so Wordsworth's autobiographical oratories, if only because we find them more congenial to our taste, are more successful than his universalizing experimentations.

And finally, if Wordsworth's works are one great poem, we can prepare to apply what we have learned in the sanctuary and antechapel to a representative sampling of the cells, oratories, and recesses, in the belief that our generalizations will hold for all or most of his shorter poems. I will not here undertake detailed explorations of more than a few of even the more familiar recesses in the rest of the cathedral. And I do not wish to force Evangelical patterns on those familiar or unfamiliar recesses constructed, for reasons of variety, experimentation, or simple doubt, with more philosophical or secular than Evangelical building blocks. (The Immortality Ode, for example, though it arrives at "the faith that looks through death," is built upon the Platonic and only vaguely religious idea of "a prior state of existence"; and though Wordsworth came to regard that idea as "far too shadowy a notion to be recommended to faith" [*PW*, 4 : 464], the poem exists under that shadow and does not respond except with reluctance to the most hopeful applications and employments of Evangelical glosses.) But I will here describe the basically spiritual character of many of his poems, and we can then hold in mind, as we have occasion to walk through all the small rooms in his mansion, the possibility and indeed the likelihood that spiritual theology, of the Evangelicals and thence of Christians from the beginning, provides the most immediate and therefore the most helpful background for appreciating the vast but remarkably uniform, if hardly symmetrical, architecture of Wordsworth's mind and vision.

The sustained labor of producing *The Prelude* gave birth to several satellite poems of spiritual autobiography, three of which show the subject's progression from experiences of grace to habitual reciprocation through covenants of works: "Lines, composed a few miles above Tintern Abbey" (1798) was written on the threshold of this period of self-examination, "Resolution and Independence" (1802) appeared at its height, and "Ode to Duty" (1805) represents the maturest viewpoint of these years.

In "Tintern Abbey" the emphasis lies not so much on the doubt, diffidence, and desperation of the speaker, and surely not so much on his recoil from vision or his waning faith,[22] as on his mature experience of grace. Somewhat like Coleridge's Ancient Mariner, and more like the persona's testimony in the closing books of *The Prelude,* the speaker affirms a redemptive event; for the poem is addressed to Dorothy not simply out of instinctive fraternal love but in gratitude for her help during the poet's crisis of faith five years earlier (*PW,* 2 : 259). Thanks in part to her, he testifies now to having encountered a presence or spirit that even yet gives him the fruit of joy in "elevated thoughts" (ll. 94–95, 100) and holds, moreover, that "the affections"—a term signifying not just the emotions but in Evangelical circles the fruits of the Spirit[23]—"gently lead us on." He describes these spiritual "gifts" as an "abundant recompense" for the "aching joys" and "dizzy raptures" of youth—emotions that seem excessively enthusiastic and even unspiritual (ll. 42, 84–87). An ordinary witness of grace, then, suffices for the performance of what Watts refers to as "Christian duty" and what Wordsworth in this poem calls "little, nameless, unremembered, acts / Of kindness and of love" (ll. 34–35).

Even the regenerated poet, of course, sometimes feels the "weary weight" and "fever" of the world and thus backslides (like the reborn Christian at Hill Difficulty) into his restless discontent of *Prelude* XI, where "feverish and tired" he selfishly rushed the Christmas season (ll. 39, 53; see pp. 43–50); but, dependably, his experiential faith, his claim that he yet feels the spiritual "presence," leads him outside himself once more and yet once more to perform the nameless deeds of charity. He thus takes part in his own correction; the "still, sad music of humanity" has "ample power / To chasten and subdue" any lingering pride or discontent (ll. 91–93). And the very words of the poem seem intended as a gesture of kindness and love toward Dorothy; for in future years if solitude, fear, pain, or grief should be her portion, she can remember his affirmation of faith, his moral exhortations, and in so doing receive the graces of *"healing* thoughts" and "tender *joy"* (ll. 143–46; my italics).

In "Resolution and Independence" Wordsworth recounts an instance resembling the influx of Extraordinary grace, an instance, in any case, enabling him to escape the weary burden of self: "I consider the manner in which I was rescued from my dejection and despair almost as an interposition of Providence" (*EY,* p. 366); and his experience, whatever it resembled or was, reestablished his progress toward a kind of spiritual perfection. (The goal of Christian perfection as described by Wesley and defined by Newton Flew is helpful in understanding the tone and structure of his autobiographical poem.) In the first seven stanzas he recalls his deviation from a joyful state of mind, and he devotes the remainder of the poem to his providential encounter with the leech-gatherer, a virtual embodiment, as we shall see, of the kind of spiritual perfection characterized and celebrated by the immediate theological context. With such an example before him, he takes heart again and, as the first step toward regaining spiritual health, makes a prayerful vow to be morally firm, a vow reminiscent of Evangelical covenant resolve. Critics, of course, have seen that the persona escapes an unhealthy self-absorption; and they have also seen that here nature is less instrumental than revelation in effecting his recovery; [24] but we can now elaborate upon these views in terms of the specific spiritual context; and we can see that the poem relates to Wordsworth's characteristic mode of spiritual autobiography.

Flew defines Christian perfection as "a freedom from anxiety and fettering self-consciousness," a freedom symbolized by the birds and flowers in Christ's Sermon on the Mount: the fowls of the air sow not, yet God feeds them; lilies toil not, yet God clothes such "grass of the field" in glorious array and will clothe his children much more so (Matthew 6 : 26, 28–30; see *The Idea of Perfection in Christian Theology,* p. 406). Christ taught, in

short, that necessary material things are added unto those who
seek God's kingdom first (6 : 33). And such perfect trust, symbol-
ized in part by singing birds and grass "bright with raindrops"
(ll. 4–6, 10, 29), characterizes the persona's initially unselfcon-
scious state of mind: "all needful things" "come unsought" to
his "genial faith, still rich in genial good" (ll. 38–39; PW, 2 : 235).
With this implicit trust in God, Wordsworth feels no burden
of "old remembrances," seems "calm" like the rising sun, has no
worldly "care" (ll. 3, 20, 33), and thus resembles Wesley's true
Christian (as described in "A Plain Account of Christian Perfec-
tion"): a man having "no thought of anything past" and being
"at all times . . . calm" and "anxiously careful for nothing"
(Wesley, 11 : 371, 379–80). Such a man, says Wesley, rejoices with
joy unspeakable and full of glory (11 : 380), a properly Extraor-
dinary enthusiasm consistent with perfection and with Words-
worth's memory of Robert Burns as a man "who walked in glory
and in joy" (l. 45) and therefore as a man apparently guided in
his early years by an ideal of spiritual beatitude. Wesley's analysis
of spiritual imperfection, furthermore, compares with the poet's
description of the fears and sadness that interrupted his perfect
peace of mind (ll. 27–28): those full of self-will, wrote Wesley,
fall short of perfection (they suffer from fear of things to come,
anxiously desiring "supplies in want" and "ease in pain" [11 :
379]); and similarly, when the poet is tempted to take heed for
himself, to do his own building and sowing, he begins to have
"fears" about "another day" that "may come" bringing "pain of
heart" and poverty (ll. 27, 34–35, 41–42). His anxiety for self, his
"fear that kills" (l. 113), destroys his perfect trust.

Wesley might have regarded such a lapse as only a temporary
threat to spiritual progress; for he believed that no one can be
entirely free of "such infirmities." But he also believed that since
the "image of God" is periodically "stamped on our hearts" by
the Holy Spirit, perfection or the absence of self-will remains the
proper and realistic goal of every Christian: God calms men's
anxious fear by "sending . . . the Holy Ghost to comfort them,"
teach them, make them "gentle" once again (11 : 374, 378, 381).
Flew formulates the corollary to this doctrine: a man need only
show "responsiveness" or "willingness to receive faith"; perfect

faith is "no mere single response but a continuous succession of responses to the divine Giver" so that "the ideal life is a moment-by-moment holiness." The doctrine and its corollary provide a revealing context for the poem; for though Wordsworth does not say that the Holy Spirit ministered to his weakness, he does imply that his encounter with the leech-gatherer was the result of "peculiar grace, / A leading from above, a something given" (ll. 50–51); and he thus employs a diction decidedly Evangelical (members of the Evangelical party in Oxford earned the sobriquet "Peculiars," perhaps deriving from their synonym for Extraordinary grace in time of doubt [OED]).

And reflecting other Wesleyan ideas and terminology, Wordsworth suggests that the "gentle" leech-gatherer was sent from some far region to teach him by apt admonishment (ll. 85, 111–12); and he shows that the old man possesses a serene cast of mind in contrast to his own sudden, self-centered fear of pain and poverty: the leech-gatherer, for his part, is not at all intent on finding relief from his "hazardous and wearisome" occupation, though his body is bent double as by "some dire constraint of pain"; and he is "poor" but labors not so much to escape poverty as simply to gain "an honest maintenance" (ll. 66–68, 100–01, 105). He seems never to worry, indeed, about what Wesley called "supplies in want." Each day he seeks shelter "with God's good help," and despite the scarcity of leeches he "find[s] them where [he] may" as though he trusts God to provide (ll. 104, 126). He lives one moment at a time, seeking sustenance day by day; and Wordsworth suggests that he gradually came to profit from these exemplary qualities of the old man's character and, indeed, that he responded to the old man's embodiment and mediation of grace.

The response can be seen in light of Wesley's third and fourth rules of covenant-making (rely on God's promise of grace and strength, and resolve to be faithful); for the poet in his banal and conversational greeting speaks better than he knows seeing "promise" in that glorious day: soon, through peculiar grace, he acquires "strength" from the old man's steadfastness (ll. 50, 84, 112). The fundamental trust and responsiveness (submerged in his greeting) find full articulation in his faithful resolution appearing at the end: " 'God,' said I, 'be my help and stay secure, / I'll think of the leech-gatherer on the lonely moor!' " (ll. 139–40).

Wordsworth's exclamation derives from an occurrence toward the end of their encounter: by this time he is "longing to be comforted" and therefore ready to receive faith; but he relapses into weakness when his "former thoughts" and "fears" of pain, misery, and fleshly ills return to him once more (ll. 113, 115–17). Once more, therefore, the leech-gatherer ministers to his need; he responds to the persona's perplexity with a smile of serenity and, confident of finding sufficient leeches, exemplifies a perfect trust again (ll. 120, 126). Now the poet recovers completely: he laughs himself to scorn and finds the grace to exercise his will (his final vow, "firm" as the leech-gatherer's mind, epitomizes the covenant interaction so frequently present in his verse [ll. 137–38]); and in sum he regains his peace of mind through a receptivity to mediated grace, a receptivity leading to resolute effort.

Evil thoughts of self-will, said Wesley, find no room "in a soul which is full of God"; and without evil thoughts men are able to "pour out their hearts" in an "immediate manner before God" having "no thought of anything . . . but of God alone" (11 : 379). Through the leech-gatherer's gift of grace and example of conduct the poet gains access to freedom from such evil thoughts; he then consciously rejects them; and at the end, in a natural and unpremeditated outpouring before the man and God who now fill his mind and restore his soul, he makes public his promise always to do so.

The autobiographical importance of the poem is especially evident in Wordsworth's awareness of the spiritual pitfalls surrounding poets in particular; Burns, after an early joy of spirit, grew despondent, forsook his glorious quest, and finally went mad—perhaps because of the same kind of concern for self that made Chatterton perish "in his pride" (self-will is necessarily the great danger for those who must, by trade, look into their hearts and write [l. 44]). "Resolution and Independence" suggests that Wordsworth, when he took heed for himself, suffered the anxiety of separation or excessive "independence" from God and became

too much like the contemporary poets who deified or apotheo-
sized their spirits (l. 47) apart from the apotheosizing ministra-
tions of the Spirit, and therefore perished in their pride.

Communion with the self instead of God, Wesley taught, may
lead to "improprieties of language, ungracefulness of pronuncia-
tion; to which one might add a thousand nameless defects, either
in conversation or behaviour" (11 : 374); thus he implies that
finding the means of interacting and communicating is difficult
for the self-indulgent. The self-concerned poet's initial behavior,
his inane belaboring of the obvious (" 'What occupation do you
there pursue?' "—" 'How is it that you live, and what is it you
do?' " [ll. 88, 119]), seems unthinking or absent-minded, and to
that extent defective (certainly the awkward rhythms of his in-
appropriate conversation are anything but graceful); and, in
short, the effectiveness of his language and hence the very means
of his livelihood appear to be impaired and threatened by an
introverted self-will.

The misery common among poets, then, seems to be the result
of behavioral and consequent linguistic failings, lapses regarded
by Wesley and by the self-examining Wordsworth as the con-
comitants of pride. The grateful Wordsworth remembers his
delivery from that professionalized solipsism through the agency
of an unselfconscious and therefore "perfect" man who commits
no infelicities of speech. The leech-gatherer, indeed, is blessed
with the gift of "utterance"—"Choice word and measured phrase,
above the reach / Of *ordinary* men" (and he receives his gift
from his strong faith: his language resembles the "stately speech"
of the "religious men" of Scotland, "who give to God and man
their dues" [ll. 94–98; my italics]).

Isaac Watts, subscribing, of course, to the Puritan faith com-
mon in Scotland, taught that lofty "utterance" is a specific gift
of the Spirit's Extraordinary witness. Wordsworth, therefore,
employs a diction suggesting that spiritual perfection, especially
important for the craftsman of words, depends upon communing
with the Spirit in His Extraordinary manifestation and incar-
nation: the old man, his stock in trade in diminishing supply,
manages his stock of words more skillfully at one point than the
worthy wordsmith at his side; soon, however, after the poet

laughs himself to scorn and grasps the extraordinary significance of an encounter filled with sudden and peculiar benefits, he rediscovers the wellsprings of his religious creativity and utters a strain of prayerful resolution. When freed from self-will, said Wesley, men shall know "what they shall speak, nor therefore have they any need to reason concerning it" (11 : 379); and Wordsworth's renewed sense of self-perspective accounts for his final exclamation: unselfconscious once more, he knows what to say and finds and receives the means of expressing it.

And he now knows what to write: the "Ode to Duty," sometimes considered the main document of his putative Stoicism,[25] is in fact another of his labors of love. Paralleling all three departments of spiritual theology, the poem implies his receptivity to grace, honors the ideal of perfect trust, and emphasizes personal vows of morality. The entire ode, in one sense, is a petition for divine support and expresses the hope of receiving from the Godhead the "benignant grace" worn by Duty (l. 42; *PW*, 4 : 83). The poet, moreover, though he never uses the word *perfection* and does not specifically aspire to it, acknowledges the reality of moral excellence among those who possess such unselfconscious peace of mind that they "ask not if [God's] eye / Be on them" (cf. Psalms 33 : 18) and do God's work though they "know it not" (ll. 9–10, 14). And he seems in sympathy with those who hope for a widespread spiritual beatitude in that serene and happy day when "love is an unerring light, / And joy its own security":

> And they a blissful course may hold
> Even now, who, not unwisely bold,
> Live in the spirit of this creed . . . .
> [ll. 19–23]

His emphasis, however, is on the freedom, and indeed the duty, to choose moral progress without the need for frequent visitations or the expressed incentive of perfection as a distant goal (the poem, then, represents the end-point of a natural autobiographic progression from his apparent experience of grace as recorded in "Tintern Abbey" and "Resolution and Independence").

By 1805, it seems, Wordsworth was less dependent upon dramatic instances of aid, more confident in his covenant resolve. Throughout the poem he makes resolute vows to God and pledges his voluntary obedience:

> . . . thee I now would serve more strictly, if I may.
> · · · · · · · · · · · · · · · · · · · · · · · · · · · · · ·
> . . . [I] feel past doubt
> That my submissiveness was choice.
>
> · · · · · · · · · · · · · · · · · · · · · · · · · · · · ·
> Denial and restraint I prize
> No further than they breed a second Will more wise.
>
> · · · · · · · · · · · · · · · · · · · · · · · · · · · · ·
> I myself commend
> Unto thy guidance from this hour . . . .
>                    [ll. 32, 50–51; stanza 6 (1807 ed.)]

Wordsworth now elaborates the brief covenant resolution concluding his lines on the leech-gatherer. He now moves on, in fact, to profess a "spirit of self-sacrifice" (l. 54); like Milton's postlapsarian Adam (*Paradise Lost* 8 : 172–74), he is "lowly wise" (l. 53), ready to cultivate his own garden (perhaps by planting the seeds of common charity to assure the harvest of a spiritual labor). And so, having learned what to write and what to do, Wordsworth seems prepared to translate faith into action.

Long after he completed the Ode, "Resolution and Independence," "Tintern Abbey," and the first version of *The Prelude,* with their collective and particularized methods of acknowledging grace, searching the soul, and making covenant vows, Wordsworth continued from time to time to practice the mode of spiritual autobiography; in a late sonnet, for example, written in November of 1836 after Dorothy became an invalid, he still finds in her "a loveliness to living youth denied" and hopes she will again restore him if his faith should ever weaken:

> Oh! if within me hope should e'er decline,
> The lamp of faith, lost Friend! too faintly burn;
> Then may that heaven-revealing smile of thine,
> The bright assurance, visibly return:

> And let my spirit in that power divine
> Rejoice, as, through that power, it ceased to mourn.
>
> [ll. 8–14; *PW*, 3 : 17]

Despite her age and illness she remains an effective mediatrix of grace. And she remains so in part because she has served that important function for so long and with such selfless love: the final line recalls the 1790s when she first gave him an experience of faith and the additional grace of joy; after more than forty years he acknowledges her role in strengthening his faith (a faith reminiscent of the Evangelical hope of assurance) and expresses the conviction that she does so yet. Thus the poet ends his journey where he began, except that now he is much closer to his idea of perfection, as we can see in the prayerful conclusion of the second "Evening Voluntary" (written on his sixty-third birthday as another late exercise in spiritual autobiography):

> Teach me with quick-eared spirit to rejoice
> In admonitions of thy softest voice!
> Whate'er the path those mortal feet may trace,
> Breathe through my soul the blessing of thy grace,
> Glad, through a perfect love, a faith sincere
> Drawn from the wisdom that begins with fear,
> Glad to expand; and, for a season, free
> From finite cares, to rest absorbed in thee!
>
> [ll. 19–26; *PW*, 4 : 3]

Near his final rest at the end of life, and with perfected faith like that of Ellen, the deaf but spiritually sensitive Dalesman, all the principals of *Excursion* IX, and the persona toward the end of *The Prelude* and in the satellite poems of autobiography, the poet envisions a new beginning through his acute spiritual sense, a sense trained and shaped by grace and sharpened by a lifetime of receptivity, aspiration, and disciplined will.

But Wordsworth wrote in modes other than spiritual autobiography: the poems suggesting the catholicity of his experience and hence the objectivity of his faith and its ultimate independence from his spiritual perceptions were numerous in the early years, and in the later even more numerous than the poems of testimony; for these objective works represent his cherished attempt to express what is true as distinct from what seems true to him; and if they do not always carry the force of conviction that energizes the personal poems, they always carry the weight of a stabilizing, sustaining, and communicable conviction. Wordsworth finds subjective truth and truth to be the same: in disinterested if not dispassionate works of greater or lesser scope and achievement throughout the corpus, in good and bad exempla like those of the Pastor, at strategic points of structure in such ambitious undertakings as *The River Duddon* and *Ecclesiastical Sonnets,* he reaffirms and remythologizes the theology of the Spirit—strict Evangelical upbringing, conversion as a spiritual turning-point, sustenance from the graces, the human capacity for moral response through covenant vows, and the possibility of an earthly spiritual perfection—as it is aptly compressed in the second part of *Ecclesiastical Sonnets* (no. 30): wise men nurtured in the stern religion of Old Testament patriarchs should contend above all else for the perfect faith with which the Spirit of God at Pentecost filled the temples of men's hearts and made them "resolute to do his will" (ll. 9–13; *PW,* 3 : 376).

In 1835, for example, Wordsworth honored all these ideals in his tribute to Charles Lamb (the friend who recognized "natural methodism" in *The Excursion*): for him the "lamp of love" burned with increasing strength "from infancy, through manhood, to the last / Of threescore years, and to [his] latest hour" because he acknowledged "God's grace" in his heart and performed the works of charity (by the end of his life a "sanctified" soul lodged "at the center of his being" ["Written after the Death of Charles Lamb," ll. 30–35, 118–19; *PW,* 4 : 273, 276]); and at various points throughout his career the poet concentrated (with little or no reference to himself) on one or another of these and all other stages of spiritual development from infancy to death.

In *Michael* (1800) he suggests that spiritual nourishment in the early years can be characterized by the kind of loving chastisement to be found in the Christmas episode: the old shepherd, a man of "stern unbending mind," sometimes punishes his son

Luke "with looks / Of fond correction and reproof"—with "staff, or voice, / . . . or threatening gestures"; and the boy grows up "a healthy Lad" thriving on his father's love and "Heaven's good grace." (Michael thus seems to apply the remedial principles of Puritan discipline, the principles applied by Wesley's mother, the Wanderer's parents, and the *Prelude* persona's Father and God: loving chastisement is consistent with grace.)

Wordsworth stresses conversion as a crucial event in mature spiritual life. In *Ecclesiastical Sonnets* (1822) he urges attendance of the Anglican Commination Service (in which God's warnings to sinners are read) because he hopes the resulting congregational repentance will "yield timely fruit of peace and love and joy" ("The Commination Service," l. 14; *PW*, 3 : 398). In the same work he describes the conversion experience as "the pledge of sanctity" or the foretaste of perfection (and his choice of theme does not so much reflect his fascination with the remote experience of a convert who lived before the time of Bede as it shows his awareness of the characteristic turning-point in the spiritual lives of nineteenth-century men ["Conversion," l. 13; *PW*, 3 : 350]). In *Peter Bell* (1798) the wicked potter hears "a fervent Methodist" and then, because of the preacher's words in combination with the admonitions of a moral Nature, renounces his folly and becomes "a good and honest man" (following his "repentance," itself a fruit of the Spirit, he finds access to other graces such as power, gentleness, hope, and joy—all pledges of the sanctity toward which he begins to strive [ll. 949, 951, 959, 961, 965, 1133–35; *PW*, 2 : 376–77, 382]). And in *Michael,* the shepherd, if not converted from an excessive reliance on his own effort and thriftiness (a reliance reminiscent of the widow's "trust in ceaseless pains"—*Excursion* VI), is thrust into a new spiritual life when his heart (like Ellen's) is "born again" following the birth of his child (and his Wesleyanesque "conversion" is attended and extended by an abundance of spiritual graces: Luke brings love, hope, joy, and comfort to his father, who accepts these gifts and offers ordinary graces in return, doing female service for the boy with "patient" mind and "gentle" hand [ll. 148, 151–52, 156, 158, 203, 206]).

Wordsworth suggests, indeed, that the gifts of the Spirit as they are found among these poems of broader scope, come from impulses that bear a close analogy with what the Wesleyans described as communion with the Holy Ghost: he describes the Pastor in *Ecclesiastical Sonnets* as being meek, patient, and full of gentleness and peace ("Pastoral Character," ll. 5–7; *PW*, 3 : 393); stresses the patience and "peace so perfect" of the spiritual and incorruptible Old Man in "Animal Tranquillity and Decay" (ll. 11, 13–14; *PW*, 4 : 247); suggests, in an early sonnet echoing 2 Timothy (1 : 7), that "the children of the God of heaven" receive the gift of "sound, healthy" "minds" ("October, 1803," ll. 6–7, 10; *PW*, 3 : 119); and sometimes, as in "The Last of the Flock" (*PW*, 2 : 45), points to an absence of the graces in figures who fall short of spiritual excellence (the materialism of the shepherd, whose "precious flock" is so dear that he loves his children less each time he has to sell a sheep, makes him lose access to the fruits of the Spirit: " 'No peace, no comfort could I find' " [ll. 75, 81–82, 88]).

The poet, moreover, in nonsubjective poems both early and late, celebrates man's capacity for covenant response to the Spirit's overtures. Filled with graces, Michael finds the strength to begin a sheepfold (the symbol of his "covenant" with Luke) and to vow while building that no matter what Luke does he will love him to the last and bear his memory with him to the grave. (He remains true to his vow, finding "comfort in the strength of love" and hence continued nourishment from the spiritual fruits when Luke fails in his part of the covenant and gives himself to evil courses in the city [ll. 414–17, 445, 448].) *Ecclesiastical Sonnets,* harking back to Puritan concepts of covenant-making, reveres American Puritans who found moral resolution an avenue to perfection ("Blest Pilgrims," "who could not bend," boasted a "will by sovereign Conscience sanctified" ["The Pilgrim Fathers," ll. 9–11; *PW*, 3 : 391]). And "Inscription on a Rock at Rydal Mount" (1838) calls upon readers to embrace the Puritan idea of being gathered together in holiness and set apart from the world in solemn league and covenant to choose the narrow way that leads to salvation:

Wouldst thou be gathered to Christ's chosen flock,
Shun the broad way too easily explored,
And let thy path be hewn out of the Rock,
The living Rock of God's eternal Word.

[ll. 1–4; *PW,* 4 : 389]

Finally, Wordsworth holds out the hope that spiritual perfection can crown not only his own life but the lives of the faithful, and he expresses this hope most notably in the closing sonnets of his two sequences, and hence during his own crowning years. He trusts (at the end of *The River Duddon,* 1820) that he will one day be "Prepared, in peace of heart, in calm of mind / And soul, to mingle with Eternity!" (and thus he echoes the New Testament passage with which Wesley defined perfection as the commitment of heart, mind, and soul to the love of God and man ["Conclusion," ll. 13–14; *PW,* 3 : 260]). He evokes in the last of the *Ecclesiastical Sonnets* the broader, more sharply defined vision of a large host's reaching "the eternal City— built / For the perfècted Spirits of the just!" ("Conclusion," ll. 13–14; *PW,* 3 : 407); and thus alluding to Hebrews 12 : 23 (the favorite text of the deaf Dalesman), he precisely and certainly sounds for a final time the most inclusive and the most challenging spiritual theme to be heard from both the personal and the public voices of his poetry from the beginning to the end of his career.

## CHAPTER FOUR

*WORDSWORTH AND*

*THE BOOK OF NATURE*

The poetry of Wordsworth, in part because of the influence of Thomas Burnet's *Sacred Theory of the Earth* (1681), incorporates the eighteenth-century commonplace that man can see the sublimity of God in the asymmetries and wild variety of nature;[1] and this religious commonplace, descended from the doctrine that the book of nature declares God's glory (Psalms 19 : 1–6), is rather violently yoked to aesthetics by a well-known theory of the relation between his nature poetry and its eighteenth-century background. In *Mountain Gloom and Mountain Glory,* Marjorie Hope Nicolson gives insufficient weight to the religious character of Burnet's influence in particular and eighteenth-century thought in general when she concludes, with particular reference to the Simplon Pass section of *The Prelude* (VI.562–640, 1850), that Wordsworth reflects "the Aesthetics of the Infinite" as he leads us from the wild and asymmetrical Alps, "through Space, to Eternity and Infinity, with awe and reverence for the power of God, to the serene and tranquil peace that passes all understanding" (p. 393).

Wordsworth sometimes stands in awe of the natural manifestations of God's sublimity; but he does not base his poetry upon totally "aesthetic" ideas of the infinite, ideas acquired from nature's nobler prospects. At the Simplon Pass, the legible "Characters of the great Apocalypse, / The types and symbols of Eter-

nity, / Of first and last, and midst, and without end" (ll. 570–72),
are read not so much on mountain peaks as in the "blossoms
upon one tree" (l. 569), the small objects discernible in the valleys
and among the lowlands. And Wordsworth's eye for detail, as
well as for grandeur, is apparent in his most admiring descrip-
tions of mountain glory, in passages that invite us not only to
marvel at nature's larger vistas and then to fill with pleasurable
fear but also to read each natural leaf, at whatever altitude, for
profit. To the Wanderer (and to Wordsworth's readers) nature
reveals sublimity "on the lonely mountain-tops"; but even there,
the things of this world impart didactic truths as well:

> O then how beautiful, how bright, appeared
> The written promise! Early had he learned
> To reverence the volume that displays
> The mystery, the life which cannot die;
> But in the mountains did he *feel* his faith.
> All things, responsive to the writing, there
> Breathed immortality, revolving life,
> And greatness still revolving; infinite:
> . . . . . . . . . . . . . . . . . . . . . . .
>            . . . Low desires,
> Low thoughts had there no place; yet was his heart
> Lowly; for he was meek in gratitude,
> Oft as he called those ecstasies to mind . . . .
>     [*The Excursion* I.219, 221–29, 234–37; *PW*, 5 : 15–16]

The Wanderer acquires from nature's book a reverent sense of
magnitude and infinity—two of the attributes of God's awesome
presence in the world; but he also receives instruction and sup-
port, moral wisdom and spiritual insight, for the passage sug-
gests that "all things" teach him humility and offer him the hope
of immortality. He learns a moral lesson—to be meek and lowly;
and his spiritual hope, like the things of nature from which it
comes, is "responsive to" and hence consistent with "the written
promise," the biblical hope of everlasting life (the cyclical con-
tinuity of nature's revolving life serves to intimate, even to pro-
claim, the beauty and brightness of an otherworldly immortality).
The passage reflects, at a very great distance and in the poet's

own way, the medieval concept that nature-scripture, no less than the Bible, directly expresses God's mind and conveys moral or allegorical significance.[2] Here, and elsewhere in his poetry, Wordsworth affirms that the Volume of Creation, like the written Book, shows forth divine grandeur in ways both delightful and overwhelming, and also teaches morality and records the promises of faith.

We are prepared to examine the context of Wordsworth's spiritual reading of nature; for we are familiar with the spiritual context of his religious thought in general. We have seen that he was nurtured in the strict precepts of a fundamental faith; and we have seen that he developed his narrative patterns and borrowed his most characteristic themes from what he absorbed of the doctrinal configurations in spiritual theology. Thus far, then, we have attempted to understand the spiritual character of his thought and vision (as distinct, say, from political, scientific, and pantheistic approaches to his view of Man, Nature, and even God in Nature) because his view of God and, indeed his relation to God's Spirit, considered entirely apart from any context and subject matter except the appropriately and exclusively theological ones, have not been sufficiently understood or even sufficiently allowed. But of course we must consider Wordsworth's Evangelicalism as it contributes to his view of nature; for however important the topics thus far, we cannot study the man for whom "poet of nature" is an apt if somewhat vague and general label and much longer postpone such a consideration without seeming to ignore what is both obvious and centrally important.

We are certain to have ideas already, and well-grounded ones, concerning Wordsworth's view of nature, for we have made enormous strides away from the truism that he loved nature for itself and toward a variety of persuasive and well-informed arguments that the word was theoretically and critically resonant and the concept philosophically complex and fruitful.[3] But the word also possessed theological significance. Having come so far in our study of the Evangelical character of his thought, we are now ready to entertain the possibility of what I shall try to show: that in his theory and practice, as they relate to his generally religious cast of mind and his specifically spiritual shape of character,

Wordsworth held views consistent with, and even partially in-
debted to, the well-formulated natural theology of the Evangeli-
cal Movement. For already we have noted Lamb's suggestion (in
his description of *The Excursion* as "natural methodism") that
Wordsworth's enthusiasm for nature is a definably religious en-
thusiasm; already we have found that nature is often the vehicle
for a mediated grace; already we have discovered that the objects
of nature, when sacramental and full of biblical associations, are
rich sources for his religious symbol-making; and before moving
on, we may once more cite (at the risk of some excess) the poet's
letter to Wilberforce and point out how pleased he was that the
Evangelical shared his own desire never to indulge a literal-
minded reading of nature, never to value "material forms . . .
for their own sake" (*EY,* pp. 684–85).

Wesley called Burnet "one of the first-rate writers" and thought
his *Sacred Theory* "one of the noblest tracts which is extant in
our language" (Wesley, 3 : 385–86); but he was not interested in
Burnet's taste in scenery so much as he recognized and admired
the fundamental orthodoxy of his theory of the earth. (Burnet,
after all, fashioned his theory from the uneasily coexisting but
equally venerable Christian views of nature as expounded, for
example, by Martin Luther and John Calvin, concluding that the
Alps, despite, or perhaps because of, their seemingly haphazard
arrangement, were "the best [Work] that could be made of
broken Materials" and also, quite positively, an emphatic mani-
festation of God's magnitude and glory.) [4]

Like Burnet, Wesley formulated a theory of the earth at once
recognizably traditional and admirably independent. In fact,
Wesley's spiritual and indeed his "natural' allies among Evan-
gelical leaders, too, not only held that nature's book reveals the
glory of God but also, on the basis of their observations of the
natural world and therefore of their characteristic reliance on ex-
perience, gave particular currency and a great deal of renewed in-
terest to the corollary and formerly less spectacular doctrine that
nature-scripture informs its readers about God's morality and in-
spires them with His promises. And their impassioned phrasing
of Renaissance and Puritan—indeed, of medieval—traditions of
natural theology, provided Wordsworth a conventional but lively

idiom with which to express his own idea of nature as a volume containing, in addition to phrases reminiscent of the Bible and suggestive of grace, and in conjunction with columns and paragraphs on the greatness of God, lengthy passages and entire chapters given over to the inculcation of moral emblems and the intimation of types of things to come.

We shall see that the evidence, without detracting from the re-creating, idealizing, and unifying functions of his primary and secondary faculties of imagination, and indeed contributing positively to our understanding of a creative process perhaps more comprehensible than Coleridgean and complicated, shows conclusively what we have seen all along—that Wordsworth possessed the religious heritage that thrived in his own day. Furthermore, this evidence challenges the widespread and general view that he secularized inherited theology and particularly refutes the specific view that his myth of nature is entirely his own creation.

We can expect to find, then, that Wordsworth and the Evangelicals made similar efforts to interpret the spiritual content of the world. We can hope to define his theology of nature. We can establish the close parallels, and some direct links, between representative poems from all periods of his career and the Evangelical emphasis on a traditional and positive reading of nature. We can observe that his emphasis, like theirs, was compatible with Burnet's religious fascination with grand and glorious prospects but gave its fullest attention to the more straightforwardly didactic and the more accessibly sustaining passages in God's other book. We can realize that, like the many Evangelicals who were less aesthetically minded than the few followers and diluters of Burnet, he studied nature through the eyes of an experiential faith and saw spiritual truth and promise in the meanest flower that blows. (We are sufficiently aware of his response to beauty and sublimity, his delighted fear of the world's lovely power, and need not because of that awareness entertain the astonishing notion that he could see God's glory in that of the mountains and be *primarily* an "aesthetic" poet.) We can undertake to test, in a limited way prelusive to further experimentations, the usefulness of his natural theology in the enterprise of practical criticism. We can draw out some implications of his natural theology for his view of science and against the view that he was a pantheist. And we can see that the sharp parallels between his most basic theory about and his most characteristic practice regarding the natural world and its symbolic value, and the literature written and widely disseminated by the concurrent exemplars of the religious mainstream, throw new light on the essence of his insularity and offer new evidence for the continuity of his thought.

Wesley taught that "the Book of Nature is written in an universal Character, which every man may read"; the book "consists not of Words, but Things, which picture out the divine Perfections" (Wesley, 1 : 229). In *Meditations and Contemplations* (1748), popular among the Evangelicals, James Hervey identified some of the natural "things" that seemed analogous to the "words" of books: he described nature as "that stately Volume, where every *Leaf,* is a spacious Plain—every *Line,* a flowing Brook—every *Period,* a lofty Mountain"; and he suggests, moreover, when he insists that every page is rich with "sacred Hints," "lively Sermons," and "excellent Lessons," that the things of nature picture out divine perfections.[5]

His metaphors, in any case, more commonplace than ingenious, recall the Evangelicals' figurative interpretation of natural objects (a mode of seeing they all acquired from the spiritual reading of Scripture): the dependence of their interpretation upon their Bible-reading is made explicit, for example, by John Newton, who believed a thorough knowledge of God's Word to be the best preparation for a first-hand understanding of the book of nature:

> The lines of this book, though very beautiful and expressive in themselves, are not immediately legible by fallen man. The works of creation may be compared to a fair character in cypher, of which the Bible is the key; and without this key they cannot be understood. . . . They who know God in his word, may find both pleasure and profit in tracing his wisdom in his works. . . . Perhaps they have no idea of the magnitude or distance of the sun; but it reminds them of Jesus the Sun of righteousness, the source of light and life to

their souls. The Lord has established a wonderful analogy between the natural and the spiritual world. . . . Almost every object they see, when they are in a right frame of mind, either leads their thoughts to Jesus, or tends to illustrate some scriptural truth or promise. This is the best method of studying the book of Nature; and for this purpose it is always open and plain to those who love the Bible, so that he who runs may read.[6]

And yet "dependence" is too strong a word; for the Evangelists' figurative interpretation of nature, as suggested by Newton's obvious and probably unprecedented emphasis on nature's wonderful analogies for their own sake, quite apart from any immediate or precisely allusive groundings in biblical passages, was indeed strong enough and reliable enough to affect their spiritual reading of Scripture. Their strange warmings of the heart, when inspired by nature as the medium of grace, were sometimes so intense as first to shape their perceptions of all surrounding phenomena and then to color their future experience with the equally external, but less venerable and less available, Word of truth. Witness the conversion experience of John Furz, one of the Methodist preachers. How reminiscent this is of Wordsworth's covenant / conversion of 1788 (both include a primary emphasis on the spiritual efficacy of nature and a consequent and secondary emphasis on that of the Bible):

> I was in a new world. If I walked into the open field, every thing showed forth the glory of God. If I looked at the sun, my heart said, "My God made this, not for himself, but us." If I looked on the grass, the corn, the trees, I could not but stand and adore the goodness of God. My Bible also became a new book: it was sweeter to my soul than honey to my tongue. [*Lives*, 2 : 333]

Often for the Evangelicals the Volume of Creation possessed as much authority as the Bible itself. This was only natural, for the book of nature was necessarily more often open and therefore quite an influence—on their reading and interpretation of the transcribed Logos as well as on their lives and actions. So there is no contradiction in Wesley's reading his Bible in natural forms as he rode on horseback to his Sunday sermon. For God's works only glossed God's words.

It is in this tradition that Coleridge, toward the end of a life-time of scanning the Volume of Creation, observes about "the great book of [God's] servant Nature": "That in its obvious sense and literal interpretation it declares the being and attributes of the Almighty Father, none but the fool in heart has ever dared gainsay: But . . . it is the poetry of human nature, to read it likewise in a figurative sense, and to find therein correspondences and symbols of the spiritual world." [7]

His observation is worth remembering, since Wordsworth's emphasis—like Coleridge's and Newton's—lies upon discerning individual truths of the Spirit as distinct from and in addition to simply accumulating evidences of God's existence or hints of His character; the poet, indeed, believed that his figurative, moral, and spiritual reading of nature's book served his purposes as author, as shaper of symbols and steward of values. Words-worth's nature poetry, of course, does lead the reader's thoughts to God and Christ: the centuries-old conviction that natural objects can "remind" the Christian of the Godhead is germane to his practice (W. P. Jones, for example, has shown that his fre-quent references to divine attributes such as power, wisdom, and goodness derive in part from the characteristic vocabulary of astronomy and natural history as taught by the physicotheologians —John Ray, Richard Bentley, Samuel Clarke, William Derham, William Wollaston, and others).[8]

The doctrine that nature declares God's magnitude, a doctrine underlying Furz's testimony that all things show forth the glory of God, is implicit in his several accounts of the sublimity in meadows, mountains, and the sea; and Newton's analogy between the natural and the spiritual worlds is specifically reflected in his poem commemorating the building of Rydal Chapel (no. 13 of the "Miscellaneous Poems" [1823]), a poem in which the image of the "wished-for Sun" makes the poet "mindful of Him Who in the Orient born / There lived, and on the cross His life resigned" (*PW*, 4 : 168). But his nature poetry concentrates, to a greater ex-tent than we have ever recognized, on Newton's second important point: that an object may "illustrate" specific truths and promises; for we shall see that such illustrations, figuratively presented in the book of nature, were the most important parts of William Wordsworth's works: "the spirituality with which I have endeavored to invest the material Universe, and the moral relation under which I have wished to exhibit the most ordinary appearances." [9]

The Evangelicals exhibited the "moral relation" of "ordinary appearances" through their inherited system of emblems and types (the two categories of symbols drawn from nature); and, like Wordsworth, they exercised their vested spiritual power to discern a practical, moral significance among the subjectified objects and the mind-independent phenomena underlying a Nature inscribed by God and read by men. Their natural emblems comprised a kind of didactic symbology dating back, for example, to the 1630s, when Francis Quarles expressed the following concept of the emblematic universe: "Before the knowledge of letters, God was known by Hieroglyphics. And indeed what are the heavens, the earth, nay, every creature, but Hieroglyphics and Emblems of his glory?" [10]

In his 1823 edition of Quarles's *Emblems, Divine and Moral* (1634) the Evangelical Augustus Toplady, author of the emblematic hymn "Rock of Ages," praised the "elegancy" of Quarles's "ocular language" and described his poems as being "very consistent with the evangelic doctrines." Another Evangelical, John Ryland, also praised "the depth of evangelic fervour" underlying Quarles's poems (pp. vii–viii). And the movement's enthusiastic rediscovery of this early emblem-book is not surprising in light of the widespread practice, among their Puritan forebears, of what J. Paul Hunter has called "the emblematic method." Illustrations of this can be found among the works of John Bunyan: in *Pilgrim's Progress*, for example, a spider's venom is an emblem of man's sin, and a hollow tree with leaves is an emblem of the hypocrisy of those "whose outside is fair and whose inside is rotten." [11] The Evangelicals' sponsorship of a new edition indicates their interest in continuing and enriching the tradition of regarding objects as emblems of divine attributes (as Quarles suggested) and also of moral truth (as the Puritans taught).

In his spiritual autobiography Thomas Olivers, one of the

Methodist preachers, testified that he had "often received in-
struction" "even from a drop of water, a blade of grass, or a
grain of sand" (*Lives*, 1 : 208–09). He did not specify the content
of this instruction, but Newton, in one of his *Olney Hymns* ("Hay-
time," no. 35), shows how specific a particular lesson could be:

> The grass and flow'rs, which clothe the field,
>     And look so green and gay,
> Touch'd by the scythe, defenceless yield,
>     And fall, and fade away.
>
> Fit emblem of our mortal state!
>     Thus in the scripture glass,
> The young, the strong, the wise, the great
>     May see themselves but grass!
>
> [Newton, 6 : 177]

His allusion to the Book of Isaiah (who warns that "flesh is grass"
[40 : 6]) exemplifies the Evangelical employment of biblical meta-
phor as the means of deciphering the hieroglyphics and emblems
of nature's book.

In Book V of *The Excursion,* the Solitary expresses his dis-
satisfaction with traditional "emblems" "from the visible world"
(ll. 333–34; *PW*, 5 : 164): he acknowledges that three of the most
commonplace emblems ("the torch, the star, the anchor"), re-
spectively denoting, according to Quarles, God's "regen'rate fire"
kindling "lifeless will," the wayfaring pilgrim's divine guidance,
and the Christian's spiritual hope,[12] provided "safest guidance"
and "firmest trust" during England's past, before the modern
turmoil of the French Revolution (ll. 333–36); but in the present
day the Solitary sees little evidence that "individual Souls," few
of whom are free "from passion's crooked ways," derive signifi-
cant benefit from such object lessons as these (ll. 353–54).

The Poet, Wordsworth's persona in *The Excursion,* agrees with
"the general tenor" of the Solitary's complaint (l. 369); and
though Book V offers no substitute, the poet's work as a whole
does suggest a new kind of emblemology, in which the observer is
no longer asked to accept the morals somewhat arbitrarily attached
to certain objects. Instead he is now empowered, like the Puritan-

Evangelical reading his Bible, to interpret for himself the various spiritual meanings of any natural image and its correspondent object: the Evangelicals' doctrine of verbal inspiration (teaching that each biblical word comes from God),[13] in concert with their reliance upon natural objects to illustrate His emblematic truths, is analogous to the poet's faith in the book of nature where the humblest object carries deep moral and religious meaning. And just as their careful tracing of God's wisdom in the emblematic works of nature rivals their characteristic explication of every jot and tittle in passages throughout the Bible, so Wordsworth's famous faculty of focusing his eye on the object, his deliberate and unapologetic numbering of the streaks of the tulip, is due in part to his Protestant training. In a sense, Wordsworth and the Evangelicals together could be said to have contributed to the modern transfer of veneration from the Word to the laws of nature; and they also could be said to have unconsciously hastened the day of a literary naturalism and a modernistical quasi scientism almost religious in its single-minded passion.

The clearest prose statements detailing Wordsworth's theological and implicitly emblematic views of nature appear in a letter of December 1814 to Catherine Clarkson, the wife of his Evangelical Anglican friend Thomas.[14] The letter takes exception to Miss Patty Smith's criticisms of *The Excursion,* and the poet begins by refuting her contention that the poem fails to distinguish "between Nature as the work of God, and God himself" (*MY,* 2 : 618). He goes on to clarify his beliefs about God's precise relationship to nature, first by rejecting (as did the Evangelicals) [15] the deistic notion of "the Supreme Being as bearing the same relation to the Universe, as a watch-maker bears to a watch" and then by implying, through as strong an association between nature and the Bible as can be found among the Evangelicals, that God relates to nature as an author relates to his book; he speaks of "the innumerable analogies and types of infinity . . . which I have transfused into that poem from the Bible of the Universe, as it speaks to the ear of the intelligent, and as it lies open to the eyes of the humble-minded" (*MY,* 2 : 617–18).

His nature, then, apparent to the spiritual senses of the chastened, humanized, and purified man, is the open and always available book of God; his nature, at once "the breath of God" and "His pure Word by miracle revealed" (*Prelude* V.221–22, 1850), is a volume filled, as the Bible is, with moral and spiritual truths. And the letter to Mrs. Clarkson implies that the moral lessons in nature's book can be perceived only through the spiritualized senses: Miss Smith construed the works of nature as she read his poems—"in cold-heartedness, and substituting the letter for the spirit" (*MY*, 2 : 618); and her approach was an especially wrong-headed one to poems described in *The Prelude* as having achieved a

> Conformity as just as that of old
> To the end and written spirit of God's works,
> Whether held forth in Nature or in Man.
>
> [IV.357–59]

Wordsworth thought himself able to write poems of a spiritual nature partly because of his skill in scanning the Volume of Creation, his grasp of what Coleridge called its "correspondences."

Though Miss Smith did not comprehend Wordsworth's theological interpretation of nature, Mrs. Clarkson's husband, in his *Portraiture of Quakerism* (1806), did. Like John Wilson (who stresses "the reverential awe . . . with which [Wordsworth] looks upon the whole system of existing things, and the silent *moral connections* which he supposes to exist among them," in short the "feeling of religious obligation" with which he "turns his mind to nature"),[16] Clarkson describes his perception of moral truths in the book of nature. He argues that many of Wordsworth's "instructive poems" present "teaching by external objects" as a "consequence of impressions from a higher power." And he then quotes "Expostulation and Reply," with its advocacy of a "wise passiveness" amidst "this mighty sum / Of things for ever speaking" (*PW*, 4 : 56), as a notable example of the instructive and hence emblematic poems.[17] He also discusses at some length the natural theology he finds in Wordsworth's poetry.

Though Clarkson, like Wesley and Newton, acknowledges that

"the beauty of creation" is "spiritually connected" with the "character of God," so that "the attributes of the divine being" are to be found in natural phenomena, he stresses even more the degree to which a Christian might learn "some lesson for his spiritual advantage," even "without any motion of his will," if he would stir abroad to contemplate the sun, clouds, blossoms, leaves, and crops (2 : 43, 127–28). "Natural objects," says Clarkson, may excite only "natural ideas"; but the "spiritual man," reading with "spiritual eyes," would acquire from the emblematic things of nature particular lessons. So if a man see "the frolics and gambols of a lamb," he would begin to understand "the beauty and happiness of innocence"; a "stately oak laid prostrate by the wind," he would "be spiritually taught to discern the emptiness of human power"; "the little hawthorn that has survived the storm," he would learn "the advantage of humility"; and "the change and the fall of the autumnal leaf," he would be duly reminded of his inevitable death (2 : 127–28).

Wordsworth read these remarks with great interest and approval.[18] And no wonder. After the misreadings of the many Patty Smiths, it must have been delightful to have a Clarkson. To see the connection between his friend's observations and his own practice over the years, we may note the Wanderer's summary declaration that the "all-pervading Spirit, upon whom / Our dark foundations rest," could never have intended that "the earth we tread" should exist "only to be examined, pondered, searched, / Probed, vexed, and criticized" (*Excursion* IV.972–78); to echo Clarkson, such literal-minded and unspiritualized perception of natural objects would excite only natural and finite ideas.

The poet's spiritual ideas about nature can be seen in his evocation of some of the emblems mentioned by Clarkson. So, in the Intimations Ode, the young lambs bounding to the tabor's sound are associated with the happiness and innocence of youth (*PW*, 4 : 279); the blasted hawthorn (*Prelude* XII.301, 1850) in the Christmas episode, where the persona progresses from restless discontent, through a chastisement associated with a stormy day (XI.357, 370), to reverent submission before God, is an emblem of the disadvantage of pride and hence, in Clarkson's phrase, the advantage of humility—the boy falls under the stroke of a moral

Nature (see pp. 43–50); and one of religion's "emblems" "from
the visible world" in Book V of *The Excursion* is the "falling
leaves" of autumn, "foretelling agèd Winter's desolate sway"
(ll. 332–34, 409–10).

Such didactic interpretation of natural objects, when noticed
at all in his poetry, has been attributed to Wordsworth's assumed
familiarity with the poetry of Henry Vaughan or the *Castara* of
William Habington,[19] but students of Wordsworth need not
search so far afield since examples of the emblematic method
were everywhere in Evangelical thought. As a means of treat-
ing the theme of pride, in any case, he experimented with a
method closely akin to that of Bunyan, Newton, and Olivers. In
"Lines left upon a seat in a Yew-tree" (*PW*, 1 : 92–94), an early
poem written over a ten-year period (1787–97), he tells of a man
who at first sustained his soul only "with the food of pride" but
who finally acquired spiritual nourishment by "tracing . . . / An
emblem of his own unfruitful life" in the "barren rocks" and
"gloomy boughs" near the lake of Esthwaite (ll. 23–24, 28, 31–32);
and the moral is baldly stated:

> Stranger! henceforth be warned; and know that pride,
> Howe'er disguised in its own majesty,
> Is littleness . . . .
>
> [ll. 50–52]

Later he varied his method somewhat, perceiving in natural
emblems sometimes an admonition against restlessness and some-
times an illustration of some virtue of spiritual life such as love
or peace of mind, but always basing his figurative reading on the
observable characteristics of the object. In an undated poem en-
titled "On the Banks of a Rocky Stream" (*PW*, 4 : 208), Words-
worth responds to the "eddying balls of foam" within a whirl-
pool by seeing there "an emblem of our human mind / Crowded
with thoughts that need a settled home" (the moral in the em-
blem is decidedly religious: "Stranger, if such disquietude be
thine, / Fall on thy knees and sue for help divine" [ll. 1–4, 7–8]).
In an untitled lyric composed in 1829, the play of shadows on a
lawn yields "an apt emblem" "of Worldlings revelling in the
fields / Of strenuous idleness." (In the same poem, however, the

grass beneath these shadows serves as a more positive emblem, a sign of "the genuine life / That serves the steadfast hours" [ll. 4–6, 14–15; *PW*, 4 : 102].)

A similar kind of contrast, one made between two emblems, appears in the sixth Evening Voluntary ("Soft as a cloud"), where yellow daisies are associated with the "petty pleasures of the garish day," and the "tender green" of the surrounding grass with the "staid simplicity" of a "disencumbered spirit." (The lesson implied by this contrast is explicitly stated in terms consistent with a familiar phenomenon of the twilight hour, when grass becomes more visible than the daisy: "An emblem this of what the sober Hour / Can do for minds disposed to feel its power" [ll. 9–10, 12–13, 15, 18–19; *PW*, 4 : 7–8].) And as late as 1840, in a sonnet addressed to Isabella Fenwick, the dim-sighted poet continued spiritually to perceive the emblems of nature (he accurately observed the Evening Star and then went on to see a moral meaning in it: the characteristic twilight manifestation of Venus suggests the qualities of loyalty and steadfastness requisite for a relationship founded on love; because it "comes at close of day to shine / More heavenly bright than when it leads the morn," the planet is "Friendship's emblem" [ll. 1–3; *PW*, 3 : 412]).

These poems, of course, make up just a few leaves of a lifetime album thickly foliated with natural emblems similar in moral import and didactic intention. On the emblemological branch of Wordsworth's natural theology, moreover, they simply make up some of the leaves specifically inscribed with the word itself: unnamed and more subtle but equally moral examples of his emblematic method can most notably be found throughout the subjective chapters in his life's work. *The Prelude*, for example, is filled with the lessons Wordsworth learned while reading the Volume of Creation. Like Clarkson and apparently unlike Patty Smith, he sees among the "works" of nature "apt illustrations of the moral world, / Caught at a glance, or traced with curious pains" (XIV.315, 319–20, 1850); he painstakingly observes the phenomena of nature; he schools himself to discern, sometimes in an instant and sometimes over the course of several years' gestation, the spiritual underpinnings of specific objects. And, in short, he fully furnishes his mind with nature's "illustrations";

for he assimilates a system of pictorialized morality, a system he believes to be as objective and as authoritatively sententious as Quarles's familiar emblems encaptioned with God's truth. And he learns, in the Evangelical manner, a set of natural exempla tested and proved in the laboratory of spiritual experience and therefore made not only his own but a very part of his soul and spirit. The huge cliff in the boating episode (I.409), the unearthly sky and undistinguishable sounds in the woodcocks passage (I.330–31, 349), the letters fresh and visible near the moldered gibbet-mast (XI.291, 299), the girl struggling against the wind (XI.306, 308), the froward brook unwillingly boxed within the garden (IV.40–41), the twilight hour on Esthwaite's Lake (I.452–53), and the summer season of renewal and reformation (IV.1–504)—all take on significance in a mind habituated to emblematic associations, alert for natural teachings about impending judgment and steadfastness in adversity, about willingness to bear the restrictions and limitations of earthly existence, about mortality and its chastening effects, about the spiritual advantage of staid Puritan simplicity and a genuine life of humility, about moral disadvantage in the disquietude and discontent attending crowds and revelers as yet encumbered by ephemeral distractions, about the worldly depths of idleness and the spiritual heights of a naturally mediated grace.

Wordsworth thus draws upon his wide experience in the figurative interpretation of nature's book: he finds moral meaning in its metaphors and makes that spiritual sense his own in a mental emblemology deeply felt but fully valid in the world and fully consistent with a body of religious truths discoverable by each and hence sharable by many. Through "Nature's secondary grace," which empowers him to interpret literal objects with spiritual eyes, he gains a varied and constant experience, not only in listening to her mighty sum of things forever speaking, but also in reading her circumjacent pages lying always open, as Nature and the Bible were to Wesley when he sought daily guidance through a kind of characteristically experiential bibliomancy, to whatever "natural" chapter and verse best served the needs of a given hour or most providentially attracted the running reader's shining eye:

But I believe
That Nature, oftentimes, when she would frame
A favor'd Being, from his earliest dawn
Of infancy doth open out the clouds,
As at the touch of lightning, seeking him
With gentlest visitation; not the less,
Though haply aiming at the self-same end,
Does it delight her sometimes to employ
Severer interventions, ministry
More palpable, and so she dealt with me.

[I.362–71]

It seems proper, indeed, to draw a not so odious comparison between those godly men of his own time (and earlier) who wrote of what they read in nature, and Wordsworth who wrote from an experience demonstrably spiritual and perhaps unique among all men either godly or unreligious, modern or ancient, who ever gave much thought to natural teachings of whatever kind, religious or philosophic and scientific. And if it is not proper, it is nevertheless irresistibly tempting to go further and say what his emblems (in particular the specifically named and seemingly less subjective ones) suggest: that he characteristically presses his cleansed and spiritualized senses into the practically evangelical service of expressing, through a conventional, communicative, and sufficiently eloquent idiom, what can be as true for others as for him. And we may imagine what could well have happened: common men—affected by the Evangelical Movement, imbued with natural theology, and represented by the well-known Evangelical readers of Wordsworth's poetry (see pp. 34–36)—could well have read his nature-poetry as a commentary on the book of nature. They could have tested his interpretation against their own. And with a Protestant respect for a text external to themselves and discernible by their own and fellow commentators' trained and practiced spiritual eyes, and in the faith that a best reading exists apart from but accessible to the perceptions of regenerated men, they could have synthesized their readings and his; and they could thereby have reached a deeper, more objective understanding of God's works.

These possibilities are consistent with Wordsworth's high regard for the intelligence of those many countrymen whose literacy with regard to both of God's books could most easily have come from the zealous but educated popularizers of theology; for Wordsworth undoubtedly saw that even those common people who were illiterate and who, like his barber in Grasmere, knew their poetry only from hearing it read, were sometimes staunchly Protestant "priests" skilled in nature's ways, steeped in nature's teachings. What seems certain, in any case, is that Wordsworth and the Evangelicals, through their empirical and scholarly reverence for the smallest words and phrases in God's other Volume, joined forces in order to delineate a harmony of nature's gospels and thus to establish a deeply considered and fully workable *formsgeschichte* Englished and applied in particular to the Lake Country texts in Britain's chapter of that cosmic Book for men who run and are not weary.

The second kind of religious symbol to be found in Wordsworth's nature poetry—and one as central to his symbology as his emblems—is specified in the letter to Catherine Clarkson: "from the Bible of the Universe" he draws "innumerable . . . *types* of infinity" and transfuses them throughout *The Excursion* (*MY*, 2 : 617–18; my italics). These types, flowing both from the Bible and from the authoritative Book of Nature into his own book of verse, are founded not simply on the Evangelical (and medieval) tradition of types of persons, objects, or events of Old Testament history, prefiguring persons or things revealed in the new dispensation, but also on Renaissance and Puritan (and not always allusively biblical) typologies of the end of life and time. In short, they are based on his idea of types as the biblically or theologically resonant words of a natural "Old Testament" prefiguring the death and immortality of himself and other men, and also the composite Word of a natural "New Testament" containing Revelations of its own end and prefiguring, not some third, more spiritualized Book of God, but indeed the new heaven and new earth itself. Wordsworth's typology also prefigures a new and final dispensation of a divine boundlessness and immensity no longer mediated by the mountains—no longer imaged in the things of earth—but now directly manifest as the Lord of Heaven.

George Landow has shown that the Evangelicals, with their elaborate interpretation of biblical detail, gave special currency to the long tradition that "the rock in Horeb," from which Moses drew water (Exodus 11 : 6), typifies Christ from whom flow streams of mercy.[20] And the Pastor, in the story of Ellen, draws on that tradition in order to foreshadow a grace explicitly spiritual and implicitly christological: the quenching stream of the parchèd rock typifies the flowing mercies that nourish the mother and give her New Birth (*Excursion* VI.919-20—see pp. 121-23). The poet, in his "Answer to the Letter of Mathetes" (published in *The Friend* [1809] and addressed to his admirer John Wilson), draws on Renaissance typology in reminding his young reader of man's mortality. Quarles does so for his young readers by warning that God will someday puff out our taper, and Wordsworth advises every schoolboy to dwell on the implications of a "dying taper," seeing the figure first as an "image of departing human life," then as "the life of a venerated parent, of a beloved brother or sister . . . gone to the grave," but finally as "a visible *type* of his own perishing spirit" (thus interpreted, the flickering candlelight should encourage "steady remonstrance, and a high resolve").[21] His heartfelt commentary upon this commonplace means of foreshadowing the end of life serves to reinforce the possibility that the glittering tapers at the midsummer dance (*Prelude* IV.316-45) at once typify the revelers' transitory sensual pleasure and prefigure their inevitable death. (Remonstrance and resolve, in any case, clearly characterize the next day's "call" experience, when the magnificent sunrise contrasts with the young man's worldly night, chastens his spirit, and inspires his determination to pursue, else sinning greatly, some vocation high and moral [see pp. 95-100].)

The verses prefatory to *Pilgrim's Progress* defend Bunyan's allegory of the end of time by citing God's own use of "Types, Shadows, and Metaphors" (Wharey, p. 4); and verses in the middle and at the end of *The Excursion* typologically illustrate not only a sense of an ending but an assurance of a new beginning; for the Pastor views the world as the "local transitory type / Of

thy paternal splendours" (IX.619–20), and the Wanderer, for
whom the sinking sun typifies the setting of this world and pre-
figures the rise of another, feels no despair at the prospect of a
cataclysm causing "the universe" to "pass away" but rather is
"filled with bliss / And holiest love" in the steady faith that
God's Volume of Creation, though not indestructible like the
Logos, remains a glorious "work" "because the *shadow* of thy
might, / A step, or link, for intercourse with thee" (IV.100–02,
116, 120–21; my italics).

"The religious man," said Wordsworth, "values what he sees
chiefly as an imperfect shadowing forth of what he is incapable
of seeing" (*PW*, 2 : 412). Such a man, then, sees in part; and
what he reads, in the precious book still before him, is by no
means easy to construe; but what he reads nevertheless yields a
fully sufficient typology unto and against the day not only of
God's paternal splendors but also of His *son*ly ones. The poet, in
the poem on building Rydal Chapel, interprets the *sun* as a
figure for Christ, "Who from out the regions of the *morn*, / Is-
suing in *pomp*, shall come to judge mankind" (ll. 15–16; *PW*,
4 : 168; my italics). And his persona in the "conversion" passage
beholds the *sun*rise, the memorable *pomp* of the magnificent
*morn*ing (*Prelude* IV.330–31; my italics), falls under the stroke
not of Christ, but of a moral and spiritual Nature in her most
solemn state, and receives forgiveness implicitly from Christ and
manifestly from the efficacious dispensation of his and his Fa-
ther's redeeming grace.

And finally, both for himself and for others, the poet sees "the
types and symbols of Eternity" (*Prelude* VI.571), and hence the
foreshadowings of everlasting life, in "the blossoms upon one
tree" (l. 569), or the natural objects capable of new life and
growing upon the one natural Object that once seemed to take
all life away, but in fact soon symbolized the hope and expec-
tation of a new life without end. Walking with John Constable
in the spring of 1812 Wordsworth interpreted this naturalized
typology of the New Life and valued the visible world expressly
because it spoke to him and sharply shadowed forth a Christian
immortality that filled him with joy and caused him to exclaim
that "Everything seems full of blossom of some kind, and at
every step I take, and on whatever subject I turn my eyes, that

sublime expression of the Scripture, 'I am the resurrection and the life' seems as if uttered near me" (cf. John 11 : 25).²² And though he was reticent about speaking glibly on what he was not yet capable of seeing (see pp. 9–10), he continued to scan the open pages of the book of nature for the signs and prefigurements of immortality, and at certain moments to see "types beneficent" of God's "redeeming love" and promises fulfilled:

> Sin-blighted though we are, we too,
>   The reasoning Sons of Men,
> From one oblivious winter called
>   Shall rise, and breathe again;
> And in eternal summer lose
>   Our threescore years and ten.

["The Primrose of the Rock" (1831), ll. 36, 42–48; *PW*, 2 : 304]

For Wordsworth, then, the book of nature is an invaluable guide for "the religious man." Such a man reads with a spiritual eye to unseen levels, and he learns, therefore, what morality is, what hopes can be. He learns, however, with considerable effort; for though he properly values what he sees with his bodily eyes, he finds in the visible world only an "imperfect" shadowing forth. And since he knows that natural objects, though full of spiritual significations, are still the temporary means of expressing and conveying what is permanent and hence more valuable, he must take care to read aright: he need only scan the page before him since each part of so organic and metonymical a Work contains the whole and hence suffices—he concerns himself with the lucid pericopes in nature's text and not with the lengthier passages and overall structure of a Book so thick. And we can say that Wordsworth, like his hypothetical reader, scanned with care: he noted the foreshadowings of a final chapter but dwelt contentedly on the middle words and sections as signs and significations of what he should know and what he could feel. He never valued material forms for their own sake; for he strove to sharpen the spiritual senses wherewith he often saw indeed.

Moreover, he never underestimated the task of reading aright: he respected Clarkson and Wilberforce for doing so, was disappointed in Miss Smith, and tended to depict his fictional characters, not just in terms of whether they embrace or violate the

tenets of spiritual theology (see chapter 3), but also according
to whether and how well they read the omnipresent book of
natural theology (and they do not always measure up to the ideal
of the religious man who values what he sees because the visible
world derives from and points to the unseen spiritual realm).
He rarely judges harshly when they read cold-heartedly, sub-
stituting the letter for the spirit; but he characteristically dis-
criminates among the various phases of their spiritual develop-
ment in terms of changes in their ways of reading nature's book.

We have seen already how Wordsworth's own persona under-
goes such changes—suddenly when he sees the morning light,
and more subtly each time the light of nature enlightens his
mind and elevates his spirit—and now we can see that two nota-
ble characterizations in his nonsubjective poems, the Wanderer
in Book I and Leonard in "The Brothers" (1800), correspond to
his own development in figurative interpretation: we can discern
subtle changes even in the honorific figure, and in the one of
more ambiguous character we can observe the more sudden and
dramatic perceptual fluctuations that constitute decisive influ-
ences on his emerging soul, and hence the distinguishing device
of the portrait as a whole. And we can also observe, in these
brief overviews, that Wordsworth's idea of nature (or, more pre-
cisely, his natural theology) enhances the practical criticism of
his works, not just in contributing to our understanding of their
seemingly pure descriptions but actually resonant allegorizings
of birds, blossoms, meadows, mountains, and the sea, but also,
and more importantly, in demonstrating one last time their thor-
oughgoing preoccupation with the state of the human spirit.

At Margaret's cottage the Wanderer is at first unable to find
consolation for the overwhelming fact of human existence: that
"we die, my Friend, / Nor we alone, but that which each man
loved" (ll. 470–71). Aware of her suffering (her poverty, her loss
of husband and child), he does not see the abounding summer
flowers; instead he sees the "shrouded" cottage-yard and broods
over "the useless fragment of a wooden bowl" (ll. 462, 493). Sud-
denly remembering her strength of spiritual perception, he
checks his indulgence in melancholy—"how foolish are such
thoughts! / Forgive them" (ll. 496–97)—and rehearses the long
story of her faithful endurance in the midst of adversity. At the

end of his narrative he recalls that, despite her own doubts, she was able at last to regain her spiritual sight of the "one tree" of blossom—the Christian type of resurrection:

> . . . [she] learned, with soul
> Fixed on the Cross, that consolation springs,
> From sources deeper far than deepest pain,
> For the meek Sufferer.
>
> [ll. 936–39] [23]

And after stressing her spiritual vision, he asks a rhetorical question clearly relating to his original condition of spirit: "Why then should we *read* / The forms of things with an unworthy eye?" (ll. 939–40; my italics).

Thus he seems to recognize that at first he had misread the book of nature (blossoms, as Wordsworth suggested to Constable, are types of the resurrection). Margaret's example, then, corrects his error and restores his spiritual reading: he now modulates a description of nature into a figurative interpretation of nature's types and symbols of eternity, and he thereby rediscovers the religious hope and consolation inherent not only in Margaret's guiding biblical symbol but in the more immediate emblemology of peace and typology of New Life:

> I well remember that those very plumes,
> Those weeds, and the high spear-grass on that wall,
> By mist and silent rain-drops silvered o'er,
> As once I passed, into my heart conveyed
> So still an image of tranquillity,
> So calm and still, and looked so beautiful
> Amid the uneasy thoughts which filled my mind,
> That what we feel of sorrow and despair
> From ruin and from change, and all the grief
> That passing shows of Being leave behind,
> Appeared an idle dream, that could maintain,
> Nowhere, dominion o'er the enlightened spirit
> Whose meditative sympathies repose
> Upon the breast of Faith. I turned away,
> And walked along my road in happiness.
>
> [ll. 942–56]

"The Brothers" is an ambitious early poem in which the Bible and the book of nature nourish the spiritual lives of Leonard and James: their Anglican priest remembers giving Leonard a Bible ("and I'd wager house and field / That . . . he has it yet" [ll. 283–84; *PW*, 2 : 9]); and the Volume of Creation is equally influential (their custom of meditating beside one of their favorite mountain streams leads the priest to exclaim that "God who made the great book of the world / Would bless such piety" [ll. 266–67]). The poem, then, contains a spiritual context for the naturalized figuralism and emblemology.

The priest uses "natural" illustrations to emblematize earthly love and prefigure its renewal after death: his images—"roebucks . . . bounding o'er the hills," "two springs which bubbled side by side," "two young ravens on the crags"—symbolize the bond between the brothers, who "had much love to spare, / And it all went into each other's hearts" (ll. 141, 247–48, 277–78). His description of the mountain farmer, reaping "an acre of his neighbour's corn" (l. 10), suggests that nature provides a congenial setting for such brotherly love. His description of the robust Leonard walking "through the slippery fords, / Bearing his brother on his back" (ll. 258–59), shows how nature calls forth acts of kindness. And finally, his typological idiom suggests that such strong and selfless love as Leonard's survives after death. James is buried on "the third day" (l. 381); and this "natural" detail, referring to a custom in the Lake District, alludes to the day of resurrection—the Christian hope of everlasting life—and thus foreshadows the eternal day of the brothers' love.

The poem concentrates on Leonard's character. His boyhood was lovingly nurtured by the Bible, the book of nature, and an Anglican Church imbued with the Evangelical emphasis on strict Sunday observances (see pp. 22–24):

> The very brightest Sunday Autumn saw,
> With all its mealy clusters of ripe nuts,
> Could never keep those boys away from church,
> Or tempt them to an hour of sabbath breach.
>
> [ll. 269–72]

Leonard does not always resist temptation, however: when he becomes a sailor he necessarily shuts up the most familiar pages of spiritual strength and comfort and finally abandons figurative interpretation altogether. He goes to sea, of course, with the good intention of escaping the family poverty "chiefly for his brother's sake" (l. 305). But the "tiresome indolence" he endured in the tropics, where he "would often hang / Over the vessel's side, and gaze and gaze" at his reflection in the sea (ll. 54–55), fosters a distortion in his perceptions; he relapses into the emotions of natural pride and indulges a kind of solipsistic fantasy: "by feverish passion overcome," he thinks he sees, in addition to his own beloved image, reflections of the mountains, hills, sheep, shepherds, and rural dwellings of his boyhood (ll. 59, 62–64). Spiritually at sea, he surrenders to a narcissistic introversion that betrays him to illusion and almost drives him mad.

Leonard returns to the sources of spiritual health; but his recovery is not immediate; for he misconstrues the most literal level of the book of nature when he

> *imagined* that he saw
> Strange alteration wrought on every side
> Among the woods and fields, and that the rocks
> And everlasting hills themselves were changed.
> [ll. 96–99]

The hills from which he derived his strength do not change at all, of course; and the priest tries to dispel the illusion when he remarks that a chasm thought by Leonard to be different now is in fact "much the same" as ever (l. 137). But the youth can no longer read the permanence of love in nature's book; instead, he can now only "trace the finger of mortality" (l. 129); and he does not venture to ask "Tidings" (or good news) "of one so long and dearly loved" but goes in a morbid and faithless condition of spirit "to the solitary church-yard" (ll. 78–80). There he remembers only the conventional and "unnatural" symbols: he is disappointed to find no familiar memorial images, no "Cross-bones nor skull," no "type of our earthly state / Nor emblem of our hopes" (ll. 171–72); and thus he reverses terminology (the "earthly state" yields *emblems* as much or more than types; religious "hope" depends upon *figuralism*) and thereby reveals how much he has forgotten of the "nature" of religious symbology.

But the priest now reminds him that nature is a richer and more immediate source of the symbols of love and consolation than any derivative and extrabiblical icons:

> . . . for our immortal part! *we* want
> No symbols, Sir, to tell us that plain tale:
> The thought of death sits easy on the man
> Who has been born and dies among the mountains.
>
> [ll. 180–83]

And Leonard, toward the end and after the priest's review of natural and spiritual wisdom, regains the spiritual sense and exclaims "My Brother!" as though James were somehow present (l. 411). Before returning to sea as a wiser—and an eventually "grey-headed"—"Mariner," he asks forgiveness for his lapse in love and faith (ll. 430–31, 435) and in this resembles Coleridge's Mariner, who also confesses past error and undergoes spiritual change. But Leonard's transformation, like his error, is not dramatic, nor does it need to be. It takes place far from exotic seas, in a rural England filled with all necessary types and emblems of love and hope. There, with the help of the priest, he learns to re-read the consolations and commands in nature's book; and then appears the living image of his brother.

H. W. Piper has shown that Wordsworth was influenced by the antimechanistic and pantheistic theory of certain *philosophes* who reacted against Isaac Newton's separation of matter and motion by emphasizing that matter, far from being inert, is the active effect of a system of forces within the natural world; [24] and he has contributed to our understanding of the poet's quasi-scientific view of nature as an "active universe"; for even as a boy he saw "one life" in all the things around him (*Prelude* II.429–30), and at Cambridge he saw the things of nature "feel, / Or linked them to some feeling":

> . . . the great mass
> Lay bedded in a quickening soul, and all
> That I beheld respired with inward meaning.
>
> [III.126–29]

We do well, then, to consider two of Piper's suggestions: that Wordsworth wished to counteract the view that dead weight and lifeless mass are the chief characteristics of matter, and that he was indebted for his vision of the world's "quickening soul" to the biological and pantheistic emphases in French theories of the active universe (as expressed, for example, by Diderot: "the world, like a huge animal, has a soul . . . and the world may be God").[25] We can accept the second only in part, for his idiom is more religious than scientific and more orthodox than pantheistic: the "inward meaning" of nature's breath is not confined to the concept of organicism as the sum of reality, but undoubtedly includes the central tenet of his "natural piety": that moral truths are radically immanent in nature and deeply felt by men. Even "the great *mass*" is partly a religious phrase, suggesting that nature has sacramental significance. And the "quickening soul," reminiscent of "the soul of the world" as scientifically and pantheistically understood in France, has an English and therefore a more immediate source or analogue in Bishop Berkeley's more theological than philosophical concept of the *animus mundi,* of the world as the language of God or a divine perception (perhaps he contributed to Wordsworth's development of a religious empiricism).

We can accept the first without reservation; he personifies "the great mass" because he finds it full of life. But we can heighten the suggestion by adding that he also found the great mass full of Spirit, and by observing that he was able to reconcile natural science with natural theology, and pantheism with his view of nature as a book of spiritual truths. Wordsworth did so, for example, by qualifying the pantheistic elements of his boyhood vision in religious terms. Not only does he recognize that his youthful concept of the one life in all things could be error and that some other faith might find "easier access to the pious mind" (II.435–36), he also suggests that his own faith, though grounded in nature and in the love of nature, is as much for those as for any other reasons not finally unorthodox: he communes "With God and Nature" (l. 446), Creator and created. And at Cambridge, where he perceives the quickening soul embedded in the great mass, he also perceives a life and animation

apart from nature—indeed, a God external both to his soul and
to that of his world, which "only liv'd to me, / And to the God
who look'd into my mind" (III.143–44). Also at Cambridge, he
discovered spiritual valences in objects organic and inanimate
(he saw the things of nature feel and felt them teach as well):

> To every natural form, rock, fruit or flower,
> Even the loose stones that cover the high-way,
> I gave a *moral* life . . . .
>
> [III.124–26; my italics]

We have seen examples of the emblematic morals in Words-
worth's natural images, depicturing and sustaining his life of the
spirit; and we can conjecture that, insofar as his poetry strives
to link religious morality to a just representation of living mat-
ter, his interest in scientific pantheism helped him base his ob-
ject lessons upon what he could learn from the objective realm
of observable phenomena. But we can remember above all else
that he carries the pantheism of the new science only so far and,
indeed, that he subordinates that pantheism to the natural the-
ology underlying his impassioned distinction, in the letter to
Catherine Clarkson, between nature as the work of God and God
himself.

And we can go so far as to coin a phrase, *naturalized emblem-
ology,* to epitomize Wordsworth's idea of the relation between
matter and spirit. His emblems are "naturalized" in the sense of
being fully observed and faithfully rendered; they draw some of
their vitality from his respect for the method of life science,
doubting and disproving the inertness of matter. His concern to
perceive the object before learning its lesson, to prove upon his
pulses the vitality of nature and hence her active claim on his
very life and will, assured that he would never merely imitate
the traditional emblemology of nature and never merely dilute
already conventional (though deeply realized) materials. For his
acknowledgment of the active universe, in addition to his re-
ligious conviction, helped him convey the life and energy as
well as the didacticism of his natural emblems and types: "In
the mountains did he *feel* his faith," said Wordsworth of the
Wanderer.

Nevertheless, the more important term is "emblemology"; for though he valued the vitality of matter he also valued its spiritual content. Science, for him, could not disprove, could help discover, truths incarnate in the world; such truths he sought to show. Like the Evangelicals who saw the world as it was and, for that reason, shaped emblems capable of renewing the spirit of modern empiricism, Wordsworth desired above all else to stress spirituality in the objects that he measured to appeal to man's "discerning intellect," to reach the merely "sensual" and arouse them "from their sleep / Of Death" ("Prospectus" to *The Excursion*, ll. 52, 60–61; *PW*, 5 : 4–5), to fashion a spiritual language from earth's fluent material. And like the Evangelicals who provided a model of faith grounded in phenomena, he fruitfully combined a characteristically English empiricism and perceptual sophistication, and a characteristically English reliance on experience as the source of spiritual as well as scientific and philosophic truths.

We have come to recognize Wordsworth's epistemological awareness, his effort to grasp the object and recall himself from the abyss of solipsistic idealism; and we can recognize that his experiential faith sufficed to give him a kind of philosophic and a definably theological assurance that the great I AM, at once the subject and the object, at once the Creator and created, exists outside the subject-self, perceives the object-self, dwells within the perceiving self, and rises above the chastened self.

We can see, moreover, how his defined theology of nature serves to remind us of what is both obvious and sometimes forgotten: that some of the reasons for his international reputation are at once British in origin and religious in character. He is sometimes—and properly—called the most English of the major British writers, and indeed we may adopt a safe principle in seeking to establish his intellectual milieu—we may assume until it is proved otherwise that continental influences are less significant than insular ones. (Donald Greene, commenting on the intellectual backgrounds of English literature, has called our attention to some truisms of Britain's history: that her culture has always been affected by her insularity, especially in matters of faith. It is therefore dangerous "to lump together English liter-

ary and intellectual phenomena with those of a Continental
movement such as 'the Enlightenment' or 'Romanticism' with-
out making due allowance for the stubborn idiosyncrasy of the
English.") [26] The French Enlightenment, with its espousal of a
reason not always checked by humbling experience, differed from
the experiential point of view that lay at the heart of scientific,
philosophic, and religious thought in England; and *philosophes*
such as Diderot, writing about science but not habitually prac-
ticing its method, were not as close to Wordsworth's humbly ob-
servant cast of mind as the Evangelicals, whose impressive fac-
ulty of emblematizing is partially owing to their almost botani-
cal scrutiny of nature.

England's influence on other nations, of course, was often
considerable; an emblematic symbology grounded in tradition
but useful to the modern world was one of her intellectual ex-
ports to the movers of western romanticism. Scholars have noted
the effect of Bunyan and the Methodists on the influential phe-
nomenon of German Pietism, and we can therefore ask whether
Klopstock's composition of *evangelischen Pilgerlieder,* or Noval-
is's analogy between the inner light and the light of nature, or
Goethe's view that God is known through the medium of the
world, at all depended for characteristic expression on England's
theological gifts to Germany. (Certainly the typology practiced
by New England Puritans, whose fathers came from England,
contributed what Charles Feidelson, Jr. has called "a symbolic
mode of perception" to the world-pictures of Emerson, Thoreau,
Melville, Hawthorne, and Whitman.) [27]

We could find, therefore, that the Protestant thought common
to two continents and America's mother country provides an ad-
ditional means of studying Wordsworth from the standpoint of
comparative literature (I have not suggested that the context of
his symbology is confined to his time and place). I do suggest,
however, that he drank from the stream near one of its main
sources; for we have seen that the religious quality of his enthusi-
asm for nature, and perhaps even a personal awareness of the
natural methodism in his poetry, account in part for his celebra-
tion of the "one common truth" underlying his faith and that of
the Evangelical Wilberforce (*EY,* p. 685); and we can conclude

that, because the Evangelicals' spiritual reading of the book of nature directly bears upon his most basic themes and methods, he was an especially important exemplar—indeed a pathfinder— of a way of seeing and writing at once traditional, viable, local, and widespread.

And finally we should note that his belief and theory, the patterns of his religious and professional thought about Nature (as about the Spirit), were remarkably stable over the years. We are accustomed to looking for major changes,[28] and can find considerable evidence for the variations that must occur during any lifetime of eighty years. We can see them, for example, in his emblematic theory and practice. "Lines left upon a seat in a Yew-tree" and the spots of time suggest that the first third of his career is marked by his attempt poetically to incorporate natural objects as emotionally suffused emblems of moral truth. Book VI of *The Prelude* (with its discovery of the "types and symbols of Eternity"), the letter to Mrs. Clarkson and the "Essay, Supplementary to the Preface" of 1815 (with their vision of the earth as a Bible infused with types of infinity and shadowing forth a more perfect world), and *The Excursion* with its prophecy of the new heaven and new earth—all suggest that his Apocalypse in mid-career, like that of Blake as he grew older, became increasingly spiritual and other-worldly. But the sixth Evening Voluntary, where grass emblematizes staid simplicity, and the untitled lyric of 1829, where grass symbolizes the genuine life that serves the steadfast hours, suggest that his dimming bodily eyes toward the end of his career turned once more to this world and looked steadily at the object as his strong and practiced vision continued to invest material form with spirituality.

We need not attach undue importance, however, to such generalizations about chronology; for we have seen emblems in *The Excursion,* and types as early as "The Brothers" and as late as "The Primrose of the Rock." The consistency and long-standing integrity of Wordsworth's practice are the outstanding features of it: throughout his life the progress of his art, the train of his thought about matter and metaphor, form a sequence. And the only change is his shift away from subjectivity toward the objectivity of the poet laureate who, like Wesley, was suffi-

ciently well known and sufficiently well understood to restore
the spirit of his century and teach it how to feel.

The traditional picture, then, of Wordsworth as a poet of na-
ture concerned about the heart and deeds of men is true but
incomplete and sometimes sentimental. When we are aware of
his affinity with a world-view that produced a profound (if not
entirely praiseworthy) modification of English thought, we see
him in the context he believed he belonged in. The view of a
nature that warms the hearts, informs the minds, and provides a
standard of value for the actions of men is a view he held. It is
a view he shared with Wesley and Wilberforce. Only if we insist
on divorcing Wordsworth from the influence of the dominant
moral and spiritual leaders of the very ones among the lower
orders whose language he, like Wesley, recommended and some-
times consciously used, can we justify ourselves in disregarding
his debt to Evangelical thought. We are in a defensible critical
position if we not so much ask whether he was in the community
that regarded nature as the second book of God and felt the in-
fluxes of unmediated grace, as examine him in his debt to—his
contribution to—Evangelical England, and investigate the nature
of his alliance with a prevalent mode of thought and feeling.
This chapter, and this book, have begun that inquiry in earnest.

# NOTES

## Introduction

1 The following studies provide an adequate introduction to the Evangelical Movement: J. H. Overton, *The Evangelical Revival in the Eighteenth Century* (London: Longmans, Green, and Co., 1886); Vernon F. Storr, *The Development of English Theology in the Nineteenth Century, 1800–1860* (London: Longmans, Green, and Co., 1913); L. E. Elliott-Binns, *The Early Evangelicals: A Religious and Social Study* (London: Lutterworth Press, 1953); Ford K. Brown, *Fathers of the Victorians: The Age of Wilberforce* (Cambridge: Cambridge University Press, 1961). For the most comprehensive recent work, see Horton Davies, *Worship and Theology in England from Watts and Wesley to Maurice, 1690–1850* (Princeton: Princeton University Press, 1961); subsequent citations of Davies's argument appear in the text. Throughout this study I capitalize the word *Evangelical*, not to indicate a particular sect or denomination, but to refer to the specific eighteenth- and nineteenth-century spirit of renewal in both Anglicanism and Dissent.

2 Lane Cooper, *Evolution and Repentance* (Ithaca: Cornell University Press, 1935), p. 16.

3 For the view that the modern experience of solipsism and religious doubt became entrenched about the time of the English Romantic Period (1798–1832), see, for example, J. H. Van den Berg, *The Changing Nature of Man: Introduction to a Historical Psychology*, trans. H. F. Croes (1961; rpt. New York: Dell, 1964), pp. 228–36; and Owen Barfield, *Saving the Appearances: A Study in Idolatry* (London: Faber and Faber, 1957). For religious and philosophical skepticism in Wordsworth and other English Romantics, see L. J. Swingle, "On Reading Romantic Poetry," *PMLA* 86 (1971) : 974–81; James D. Boulger, "Christian Skepticism in *The Rime of The*

Ancient Mariner," in *From Sensibility to Romanticism,* ed. Frederick W. Hilles and Harold Bloom (New York: Oxford University Press, 1965), pp. 439–52; C. E. Pulos, *The Deep Truth: A Study of Shelley's Skepticism* (Lincoln: University of Nebraska Press, 1954); E. W. Marjarum, *Byron as Skeptic and Believer* (Princeton: Princeton University Press, 1938); Geoffrey H. Hartman, *The Unmediated Vision: An Interpretation of Wordsworth, Hopkins, Rilke, and Valéry* (New Haven: Yale University Press, 1954), pp. 160–73; and Edward E. Bostetter, *The Romantic Ventriloquists: Wordsworth, Coleridge, Keats, Shelley, and Byron* (Seattle: University of Washington Press, 1963). Bostetter argues that Romantic poetry is timid in spirit and uncertain in vision, and he contends that the skeptical Solitary in Wordsworth's *Excursion* is a projection of the author's religious doubt.

4 Russell Noyes, *Wordsworth and the Art of Landscape* (Bloomington: Indiana University Press, 1968), p. 229.

5 Saul Bellow, *Herzog* (New York: Viking Press, 1964), pp. 204–05.

6 M. H. Abrams reemphasizes the optimistic character of Romanticism but argues that Wordsworth and the other Romantics participated in the "reinterpretation of religious ideas, as constitutive elements in a world view founded on secular premises"; see his major study, *Natural Supernaturalism: Tradition and Revolution in Romantic Literature* (New York: W. W. Norton, 1971), p. 13 and passim. Basil Willey's essay "On Wordsworth and the Locke Tradition," in *The Seventeenth-Century Background: Studies in the Thought of the Age in Relation to Poetry and Religion* (1934; rpt. London: Chatto & Windus, 1949), pp. 296–309, foreshadows the recent concern with Wordsworth's skepticism by arguing that the Locke tradition left him in a demythologized world, in which he had to create both value and meaning. The myth that he created, in Geoffrey Hartman's view, is that nature seeks to make the mind independent; see Hartman's important work of criticism, *Wordsworth's Poetry 1787–1814* (New Haven: Yale University Press, 1964), pp. 33–69.

7 In the title of his volume of sermons—*Thirteen Practical Sermons; founded upon Doddridge's Rise and Progress of Religion in the Soul* (1800)—Wrangham acknowledges his debt to the famous Congregational hymnwriter, who admired and corresponded with Wesley.

8 Cited in Edith C. Batho, *The Later Wordsworth* (Cambridge: Cambridge University Press, 1933), p. 300.

9 G. R. Balleine, *A History of the Evangelical Party in the Church of England,* 3d ed. (London: Longmans, Green, and Co., 1933), pp. 170–75; Davies, *Worship and Theology in England,* pp. 19–24, 184–91.

10 Wesley, 2 : 227, 263, 285, 409, 481; 3 : 51, 274, 316, 394, 458; 4 : 13, 73, 99, 101, 180, 208, 272.
11 For Wesley's religious background see, for example, Luke Tyerman, *The Life and Times of the Rev. John Wesley, M. A.,* 3 vols. (New York: Harper & Brothers, 1872); Grace Elizabeth Harrison, *Son to Susanna: The Private Life of John Wesley* (London: I. Nicholson and Watson, 1937); John C. Bowmer, *The Sacrament of the Lord's Supper in Early Methodism* (Westminster: Dacre Press, 1951); Davies, *Worship and Theology in England,* pp. 19–24, 184–91.
12 In 1738 Wesley "walked and sang" with his brother Charles and Isaac Watts, and Wesley saw to it that a few of Watts's hymns were always published in Methodist hymnbooks. In 1782 Wesley published part of Watts's "Treatise on the Passions" in *The Arminian Magazine.* See T. B. Shepherd, *Methodism and the Literature of the Eighteenth Century* (London: Epworth Press, 1940), p. 124.
13 For the beginnings of Methodist and Anglican Evangelicalism see, for example, J. S. Reynolds, *The Evangelicals at Oxford, 1735–1871* (Oxford: Basil Blackwell, 1953); Davies, *Worship and Theology in England,* pp. 210–17; Elliott-Binns, *The Early Evangelicals,* pp. 161–69.
14 Henry Bett, *Early Methodist Preachers* (London: Epworth Press, 1935), p. 9.
15 Cited in Walter Wilson, *The History and Antiquities of Dissenting Churches and Meeting Houses* (London, 1808–14), 2 : 51.
16 For Wesley's interests in education and in Doddridge's school at Harborough, see J. H. Whiteley, *Wesley's England: A Survey of XVIIIth Century Social and Cultural Conditions* (London: Epworth Press, 1938), pp. 331 ff. In September of 1745 Wesley addressed the students at Doddridge's school (Tyerman, *The Life and Times of the Rev. John Wesley,* 1 : 490).
17 Wesley encouraged the itinerant ministers in and around Cambridge and perhaps had heard of Robinson, who was one of the most colorful preachers in the area; see Charles Smyth, *Simeon and Church Order: A Study of the Origins of the Evangelical Revival in Cambridge in the Eighteenth Century* (Cambridge: Cambridge University Press, 1940), pp. 175–78. For Wesley and the Quakers, see Stephen Hobhouse, *William Law and Eighteenth Century Quakerism* (London: G. Allen & Unwin, 1927) and Francis R. Taylor, *The Life of William Savery of Philadelphia, 1750–1804* (New York: Macmillan, 1925). Writing to Quakers about the common ground of Quakerism and Methodism, Wesley observed as early as 1745, "You, as well as we, condemn 'all ungodliness and unrighteousness of men.' . . . You agree, that we are all taught of God, and to be 'led by His Spirit' " (Wesley, 8 : 184).

18  For the Evangelical influence on English character, see Whiteley, *Wesley's England*, p. 375; for the possible effects of charitable activity on population growth, see Dorothy George, *London Life in the Eighteenth Century* (1925; rpt. London: London School of Economics, 1951), pp. 36–42, and Donald Greene, *The Age of Exuberance: Backgrounds to Eighteenth Century English Literature* (New York: Random House, 1970), pp. 5–8.

19  Macaulay's sense of the revival's importance is discussed in Bett, *Early Methodist Preachers*, p. 3.

20  William Edward Hartpole Lecky, *A History of England in the Eighteenth Century* (London: Longmans, Green, and Co., 1883), 2 : 521; Augustine Birrell, *The Collected Essays & Addresses of the Rt. Hon. Augustine Birrell, 1880–1920* (London: J. M. Dent & Sons, 1922), 1 : 324–25.

21  Lord Bolingbroke's comment to Lady Huntingdon is cited in James Downey, *The Eighteenth Century Pulpit: A Study of the Sermons of Butler, Berkeley, Secker, Sterne, Whitefield and Wesley* (Oxford: Clarendon Press, 1969), p. 187. Besides encouraging the Sunday school movement, George III always spoke of the Methodists with respect; see Lecky, *A History of England in the Eighteenth Century*, 3 : 13. Hill's observation is cited in Shepherd, *Methodism and the Literature of the Eighteenth Century*, p. 235.

22  Robert Southey, *The Life of Wesley; and Rise and Progress of Methodism*, 3d ed. with notes by the late S. T. Coleridge (London: A. Knox, 1846), 1 : 184. For evidence that Wordsworth owned a copy of Southey's popular work, see *Transactions of the Wordsworth Society*, 6 (10 May 1884) : 226.

23  In a letter to Wordsworth (early January 1815 [?]), Lamb regretted that the editor of *The Quarterly*, William Gifford, had left out much of Lamb's argument that *The Excursion* is characterized by "natural methodism." Lamb seemed to think that such a description of the work would have pleased Wordsworth: "I regret only that I did not keep a copy. I am sure you would have been pleased with it, because I have been feeding my fancy for some months with the notion of pleasing you." See E. V. Lucas, ed., *The Letters of Charles Lamb to which are added those of his sister Mary Lamb* (London: J. M. Dent & Sons and Methuen & Co., 1935), 2 : 149. See also Lord Jeffrey's "Wordsworth's *Excursion*," *The Edinburgh Review, or Critical Journal* 24 (November 1814) : 14.

24  When the Wesleyan Methodists became Nonconformist in 1795, and when members of the Countess of Huntingdon's movement, led at first by the loyal Anglican George Whitefield, joined the ranks of Dissent in 1782, they left the mainstream to become weakened tributaries more and more diluted in the coming years by further splits. Evangelical Anglicans like Wilberforce and Wrangham, with whom Wordsworth readily identified, stayed in

the center and conserved enough strength to affect in their turn the important Oxford Movement, for which, we have seen, Wordsworth felt sympathy. John Wesley would have been grateful for the lasting effects of his ministry within his own beloved Church.

25 Louis Cazamian, *A History of English Literature: Modern Times,* trans. W. D. MacInnes (London: J. M. Dent & Sons, 1927), 2 : 218; Oliver Elton, *A Survey of English Literature* (1912; rpt. London: Edward Arnold, 1965), 2 : 49–51; William J. Courthope, *A History of English Poetry* (London and New York: Macmillan and Co., 1905), 5 : 327–59. R. D. Havens observes that Wordsworth was "fundamentally religious," but Havens does not think it possible to describe his faith: "Any study of Wordsworth's religion must inevitably come to the conclusion that no formulation of his beliefs is possible"; see *The Mind of a Poet: A Study of Wordsworth's Thought* (Baltimore: The Johns Hopkins University Press, 1941), 1 : 179, 197. H. J. F. Jones's chapter on "The Baptised Imagination" in *The Egotistical Sublime: A History of Wordsworth's Imagination* (London: Chatto & Windus, 1954) is brief but deals provocatively with the way Wordsworth's Christianity affected the imagery in his later work. James Benziger's *Images of Eternity: Studies in the Poetry of Religious Vision from Wordsworth to T. S. Eliot* (Carbondale: Southern Illinois University Press, 1962) argues that Wordsworth, in the absence of traditional belief, created religious meaning from the forms of nature. In a recent comprehensive study of religion in English poetry, A. S. P. Woodhouse does not discuss his poetry written before *Ecclesiastical Sonnets* (1822) and thus seems to share the widespread assumption that he became religious only in his later years; see *The Poet and His Faith: Religion and Poetry in England from Spenser to Eliot and Auden* (Chicago: University of Chicago Press, 1965), pp. 187–92.

The presence of transcendental ideas in Wordsworth's writings has been attributed to the Cambridge Platonists, Newton, Shaftesbury, Boehme, Rousseau, d'Holbach, Volney, Spinoza, Kant, and Plato—among others—but the exact nature of these influences remains cloudy. See Joseph Warren Beach, *The Concept of Nature in Nineteenth-Century English Poetry* (1936; rpt. New York: Russell & Russell, 1966); Newton P. Stallknecht, *Strange Seas of Thought: Studies in William Wordsworth's Philosophy of Man and Nature* (1945; 2d ed., Bloomington: Indiana University Press, 1958); H. W. Piper, *The Active Universe: Pantheism and the Concept of Imagination in the English Romantic Poets* (London: Athlone Press, 1962); Geoffrey Durrant, *Wordsworth and the Great System: A Study of Wordsworth's Poetic Universe* (Cambridge: Cambridge University Press, 1970).

26 Lord Cecil's view is cited in Frederick C. Gill, *The Romantic*

*Movement and Methodism: A Study of English Romanticism and the Evangelical Revival* (London: Epworth Press, 1937), p. 13.

27 For Wordsworth's indebtedness to the Bible and to John Bunyan, see Abbie Findlay Potts, *Wordsworth's Prelude: A Study of Its Literary Form* (Ithaca: Cornell University Press, 1967), pp. 67–71; for Abrams's provocative speculations, see "English Romanticism: The Spirit of the Age," in *Romanticism Reconsidered: Selected Papers from the English Institute,* ed. Northrop Frye (New York: Columbia University Press, 1963) and *Natural Supernaturalism,* pp. 134–40. Geoffrey Hartman acknowledges Wordsworth's radical Protestantism and latter-day Puritanism but does not think that he was "directly aware of his Puritan heritage"; see *Wordsworth's Poetry 1787–1814,* pp. 5, 273, 346.

28 Archdeacon William H. Hutton observes that "the age of Wesley and Whitefield introduced what may be called a new romanticism in religion, just as the Lake School, half a century later, may be said to have destroyed the classic tradition of the older poetry"; see *The Cambridge History of Literature,* ed. A. W. Ward and A. R. Waller (Cambridge: Cambridge University Press, 1913), 10 : 363. E. H. Sugden, editor of *Wesley's Standard Sermons,* draws a parallel between Wordsworth's perception of "the spiritual in nature" and Wesley's "expression of the indwelling Spirit of God" (Sugden, 2 : 343–44 n.). James Downey suggests that both Whitefield's preaching and Wordsworth's poetry exemplify "the spontaneous overflow of powerful feelings" (*The Eighteenth Century Pulpit,* p. 20). See also F. Brompton Harvey, "Methodism and the Romantic Movement," *The London Quarterly and Holborn Review* 159 (July 1934) : 289–302.

29 A. W. Harrison, "Romanticism in Religious Revivals," *The Hibbert Journal: A Quarterly Review of Religion, Theology, and Philosophy* 31 (July 1933) : 582.

30 Cited in Batho, *The Later Wordsworth,* p. 288 n.

31 For a discussion of these doctrines as expounded by Whitefield and Wesley, see Davies, *Worship and Theology in England,* pp. 151–53.

32 Elliott-Binns discusses the three emphases in *The Early Evangelicals,* pp. 387–90, 420–23.

33 For Wesley's practice of extemporaneous prayer and preaching, see W. L. Doughty, *John Wesley, Preacher* (London: Epworth Press, 1955) and Davies, *Worship and Theology in England,* pp. 184 ff. For Wesley's adherence to "the Calvinistic doctrine of Election" see Wesley, 10 : 205–09. He admired *Directions for Believers Covenanting with God* (1665) by the Presbyterian divine Joseph Alleine, and instituted a Covenant Service in 1755; see Wesley, 2 : 339 and Davies, *Worship and Theology in England,* pp. 198–99.

34  For a discussion of the contents and historic effects of Wesley's *Christian Library*, see Reginald Doidge, *John Wesley's Christian Library* (London: Epworth Press, 1938), pp. 3–16, and Henry Bett, *The Hymns of Methodism in their Literary Relations* (London: C. H. Kelly, 1913), pp. 39–51.

## Chapter 1

1  Emile Legouis, *The Early Life of William Wordsworth, 1770–1798*, trans. J. W. Matthews (1897; rpt. New York: Russell & Russell, 1965), p. 470.

2  George McLean Harper, *William Wordsworth: His Life, Works, and Influence* (1929; rpt. New York: Russell & Russell, 1960), 1 : 3.

3  George Wilbur Meyer, *Wordsworth's Formative Years* (Ann Arbor: The University of Michigan Press, 1943), p. 5.

4  Mary Moorman, *William Wordsworth: A Biography* (Oxford: Clarendon Press, 1957–65), 2 : 106.

5  For Dr. Johnson's love of biography, see, for example, Joseph Wood Krutch, *Samuel Johnson* (New York: H. Holt and Co., 1944), p. 465.

6  Gill, *The Romantic Movement and Methodism*, p. 20.

7  Wesley made five visits to Kendal, nine to Ambleside, twelve to Carlisle, and twenty-five to Whitehaven. See Wesley, 2 : 157, 159, 227, 263, 270, 284, 408, 479; 3 : 50, 51, 84, 184, 207, 231, 254, 275, 316, 394, 458; 4 : 13, 73, 99, 101, 180, 204, 208, 271, 272, 331, 417, 486.

8  For Wesley's admiration of Hill, see Fletcher, 3 : 555. On 12 February 1772, Wesley recorded his reaction to Woolman's *Some Considerations on the Keeping of Negroes* (1762): "I read a . . . book published by an honest Quaker, on that execrable sum of all villainies, commonly called the Slave Trade. I read of nothing like it in the heathen world, whether ancient or modern. And it infinitely exceeds, in every instance of barbarity, whatever Christian slaves suffer in Mahometan countries" (Wesley, 3 : 453). For Woolman's visits to Westmoreland, see John Woolman, *A Journal of the Life, Gospel Labours, and Christian Experiences of . . . John Woolman* (Dublin: R. M. Jackson, 1776), p. 233. For Hill's visits to Kendal and Penrith, see Rowland Hill, *Journal through the North of England and Parts of Scotland* (London: T. Gillet, 1799), p. 7.

9  Maldwyn Edwards, *After Wesley: A Study of the Social and Political Influence of Methodists in the Middle Period (1791–1849)* (London: Epworth Press, 1935), p. 172.

10  Schneider, *Wordsworth's Cambridge Education* (Cambridge: Cambridge University Press, 1957), pp. ix–x, 112–63.

11    For Wordsworth's reminiscences about Middleton, see *LY, 3* : 1228.
      For evidence that he knew Gisborne, see Emma Nixon, *A Brief
      Memoire of the Life of John Gisborne* (London: Derby, 1852), pp.
      42–43, as cited in Schneider, *Wordsworth's Cambridge Education,*
      pp. 66, 272.

12    J. L. Creed, "The Master's Address: St Johns College in Words-
      worth's Time," *Wordsworth at Cambridge: A Record of the Com-
      memoration held at St Johns College, Cambridge in April 1950*
      (Cambridge: Cambridge University Press, 1950), p. 6.

13    Schneider, pp. 9, 13.

14    Philip Doddridge, *The Evidences of Christianity,* ed. Francis
      Wrangham (London, 1820), p. 3.

15    Cited in Schneider, p. 139.

16    See John Wesley, *Thoughts Upon Liberty* (Bristol, 1772), p. 3; and
      David Hume, "Superstition and Enthusiasm" (1742), *The Philo-
      sophical Works of David Hume,* ed. T. H. Green and T. H. Grose
      (London, 1878), 3 : 149.

17    Henry Gunning, *Reminiscences of the University, Town, and
      County of Cambridge from the year 1780,* ed. M. Beart (London:
      George Bell, 1854), 2 : 29–30, as cited in the entry on Wrangham
      in *The Dictionary of National Biography.*

18    For a listing of Wordsworth's presentation copy, see *Transactions
      of the Wordsworth Society,* no. 6, Rydal Mount Catalogue, as
      cited in Schneider, *Wordsworth's Cambridge Education,* pp. 150,
      280. He praised Dyer's book in 1799; see Edith J. Morley, ed.,
      *Henry Crabb Robinson on Books and their Writers* (London:
      J. M. Dent & Sons, 1938), 1 : 4. For a firsthand account of Robin-
      son's reputation as a preacher, see George Dyer, *Memoires of the
      Life and Writings of Robert Robinson* (London: G.G. and I.
      Robinson, 1796), pp. 198–250. As an undergraduate, Coleridge at-
      tended Robinson's church from time to time and praised Robert
      Hall, his successor in that pulpit, as "the master" of the best style
      of English; his praise of Hall is cited in Davies, *Worship and
      Theology in England,* p. 232 n.

19    Smyth, *Simeon and Church Order,* p. 104.

20    Vice-chancellor Durell expelled James Matthews, Thomas Jones,
      Joseph Shipman, Benjamin Kay, Erasmus Middleton, and Thomas
      Grove; see S. L. Ollard, *The Six Students of St Edmund Hall ex-
      pelled from the University of Oxford in 1768* (Oxford: A. R.
      Mowbray and Co., 1911).

21    Richard Polwhele, ed., *The Enthusiasm of Methodists and Papists
      Compared,* George Lavington, Bishop of Exeter (London, 1820),
      p. cclxxxviii.

22    By 1786 Magdalene had become "the general resort of young men
      seriously impressed with a sense of religion"; see John King,

*Memoires of the Rev. Thomas Dykes* (London, 1849), p. 6. For subsequent developments at the other colleges, see Smyth, *Simeon and Church Order*, pp. 108–10.

23  Canon Smyth has the fullest account of Berridge's ministry (pp. 149–201).

24  Robert Southey, *The Life of Wesley; and Rise and Progress of Methodism*, ed. Maurice H. Fitzgerald (London: Humphrey Milford, 1925), 2 : 170.

25  Dyer, *Memoires*, p. 55.

26  Edwin Sidney, *The Life of Rowland Hill*, 2d ed. (London: Baldwin & Cradock, 1834), pp. 21–22.

27  For Simeon's influence on undergraduates, see Smyth, *Simeon and Church Order*, p. 140.

28  Christopher Wordsworth, *Social Life at the English Universities in the Eighteenth Century* (Cambridge: Deighton, Bell, and Co., 1874), p. 599.

29  For Canon Smyth's thorough discussion of the issue, see *Simeon and Church Order*, pp. 255–312. Simeon was also instrumental in resolving the Calvinist-Arminian controversy, which flared up between Wesley and Whitefield in 1739 and continued for several decades in the pages of Wesley's *Arminian Magazine* and the Calvinist *Gospel Magazine*. Simeon, commanding the respect of the Calvinist Berridge as well as the Arminian Christopher Atkinson, was able, as H. C. G. Moule observes, "to reduce to order, and largely to pacify and harmonize, the predestinarian controversy of the previous generation; pointing out how much . . . of the conflict was over the two sides of one shield"; see Moule's *The Evangelical School in the Church of England* (London: J. Nisbet, 1901), p. 12.

30  The words are those of Henry Venn (19 January 1784), as cited in John Audley, *Memoires of Mr Coxe Feary, first Pastor of the Baptist Church at Bluntisham in Huntingdonshire* (Cambridge: Wright, Johnson & Co., 1823), p. 8.

31  Sidney, *The Life of Rowland Hill*, pp. 161–62.

32  MS recollections of Miss Paramore (daughter of Wesley's printer), as quoted in *Wesleyan Methodist Magazine*, 137 (May 1914) : 323.

33  In the Fenwick note to his "Epistle to Sir George Howland Beaumont," Wordsworth asserts the sufficiency of Anglican forms of worship for spiritual nourishment and gives an amusing portrait of Rowlandson: "Two vices in him used to struggle for mastery, avarice and the love of strong drink: but avarice, as is common in like cases, always got the better of its opponent; for, though he was often intoxicated, it was never, I believe, at his own expense. . . . As a Pastor the curate did little or nothing for [the parishioners]; but what could more strikingly set forth the efficacy of the

Church of England through its Ordinances and Liturgy than that, in spite of the unworthiness of the Minister, his church was regularly attended; and, though there was not much appearance in his flock of what might be called animated piety, intoxication was rare, and dissolute morals unknown?" (*PW*, 4 : 434–35).

34  Walker of Truro, for example, was known for his scripture readings; see the discussion in Davies, *Worship and Theology in England*, pp. 217–22.

35  Sidney, *The Life of Rowland Hill*, p. 45. David Simpson, a member of Hill's Society, made the complaint.

36  *The Satirist, or Monthly Meteor* 2 (May 1808) : 248–49, as cited in Smyth, *Simeon and Church Order*, p. 128.

37  Christopher Wordsworth, *Memoires of William Wordsworth* (London, 1851), 1 : 47.

38  For a study of Wilberforce and the Clapham Sect, see, for example, Edwards, *After Wesley*, pp. 124 ff.

39  Dorothy called Wilberforce "one of the best of men" (*EY*, p. 26). When Jane wondered if marriage between them were possible, Dorothy hastened to reply: "Your way of accounting for my apparent absence of mind diverted me exceedingly. I will set forward with assuring you that my heart is perfectly disengaged and then endeavour to shew you how very improbable it is that Mr. W. would think of me. . . . Mr. W. would, were he ever to marry, look for a lady possessed with many more accomplishments than I can boast. . . . But perhaps all the time I am endeavouring to clear myself, you are laughing at me for treating as a serious matter, what might be said merely in jest; however as I was not certain of this I was determined to give you such an answer as might relieve all your doubts" (*EY*, p. 28). Her detailed protests may not have satisfied the "doubts" of her friend. Wilberforce ranked high in her esteem, and if she did not harbor some romantic feeling, it was perhaps because she thought him too far above her.

40  A journal entry headed "Reasons for delaying the publication of 'Practical Christianity,' &c" and subheaded "Forncett, Dec. 6, 1789" reveals Wilberforce's conclusion that the time had not yet come ("Were I to express all I think I should be deemed an enthusiast"), but the entry also discloses his conscientious decision to pursue an alternate course for the present, as a foretaste of the good that would "be done by the work": "Meanwhile let me remember to clear my way more with due regard to preserving of influence, and to speak to friends of all sorts as plainly as I can safely; distribute proper books, &c." For information about the preparation, publication, and enthusiastic reception of *A Practical View*, see Robert Isaac and Samuel Wilberforce, *The Life of William Wilberforce* (London: Bungay, 1838), 2 : 81, 96–97, 199–200, 205, 399–400.

41  On 30 April 1790 Dorothy wrote to Jane: "I am at present reading . . . a little Treatise on Re-generation; which with Mrs. Trimmers Oeconomy of Charity Mr. Wilberforce gave me. I am going to read the New testament with Doddridge's exposition" (*EY*, pp. 30–31). The "little Treatise" was *A Practical Treatise on Regeneration* (1764) by John Witherspoon, President of the College of New Jersey (now Princeton University); this American Presbyterian was admired in Britain not only by the Evangelical Anglican Wilberforce, who reprinted the treatise in 1824, but also by the Nonconformist Evangelical Rowland Hill, who praised Witherspoon for his "fierce moderation" (see Hill, *Journey through the North of England*, p. 27). Sarah Trimmer's volume (1787), subtitled "An Address to Ladies concerning Sunday-schools," reflects the Evangelical interest in education and charitable activity. Perhaps Wilberforce gave Dorothy "Doddridge's exposition" (*The Family Expositor* [1739]); Doddridge's *Rise and Progress of Religion in the Soul*, an instrument of Wilberforce's conversion in 1784 (see Robert and Samuel Wilberforce, *The Life of William Wilberforce*, 2 : 165–66), may also have come to her attention during the Forncett visit.

42  Hoxie Neale Fairchild, *Religious Trends in English Poetry* (New York: Columbia University Press, 1939–57), 3 : 160.

43  Dorothy recalled that their conversations took place on daily walks in the garden between dinner and tea (*EY*, p. 96). On 16 June 1793 Dorothy wrote that there was "no pleasure he would not give up with joy for half an hour's conversation with me" (*EY*, p. 96).

44  Francis Wrangham, *Thirteen Practical Sermons, founded on Doddridge's Rise and Progress of Religion in the Soul* (London, 1800), p. 3.

45  James Russell Lowell, *Among My Books*, 2d ser. (Boston: Houghton Mifflin and Co., 1892), pp. 201–02.

46  For the Dissenters' opinion of *A Practical View*, see Robert and Samuel Wilberforce, *The Life of William Wilberforce*, 2 : 399–400.

47  In 1793, for example, Newton preached at St. Mary Woolnoth, near Wordsworth's living quarters; see Moorman, *William Wordsworth*, 1 : 219–20. Wordsworth could have felt the "various power" of Evangelical orators then or during his London visit of 1791, after the Forncett reunion with Dorothy.

48  For the background on latitudinarian style, see, for example, W. Fraser Mitchell, *English Pulpit Oratory from Andrewes to Tillotson* (London: S.P.C.K., 1932) and Davies, *Worship and Theology in England*, pp. 65–67. The quotation is from Bishop Warburton's praise of Tillotson's preaching, in *Letters from a late Eminent Prelate to one of his friends*, Letter L, p. 127, as cited in Davies, pp. 72–73.

49 Oliver Goldsmith, "Some Remarks on the modern manner of Preaching" (*Lady's Magazine* [December 1760]), *Collected Works of Oliver Goldsmith,* ed. Arthur Friedman (Oxford: Clarendon Press, 1966), 3 : 151, 153–54.

50 H. S. Milford, ed., *The Poetical Works of William Cowper,* 4th ed. (London: Oxford University Press, 1934), p. 155; subsequent references to this edition will appear in the text. For Cowper's reaction against latitudinarianism, see, for example, Gilbert Thomas, *William Cowper and the Eighteenth Century* (London: Ivor Nicholson and Watson, 1935), pp. 168–76.

51 Tyerman, *The Life and Times of John Wesley,* 2 : 582.

52 Friedman, ed., *Collected Works of Oliver Goldsmith,* 3 : 153–54.

53 Tyerman, *The Life and Times of John Wesley,* 2 : 583.

54 Morley, ed., *Henry Crabb Robinson on Books and their Writers,* 1 : 87.

55 Tyerman, *The Life and Times of John Wesley,* 3 : 627–28.

56 For a discussion of the philosophical foundations of Unitarianism, see Davies, *Worship and Theology in England,* pp. 91 ff.

57 F. D. Maurice traces "the passage of the old Puritans into the modern Unitarians" in chapter 1 of his autobiography (*The Life of Frederick Denison Maurice* [New York: Charles Scribner's Sons, 1884]). For modern studies of this pattern, see Geoffrey F. Nuttall, ed., *Philip Doddridge: His Contribution to English Religion* (London: Independent Press, 1951), pp. 122–30 and Batho, *The Later Wordsworth,* pp. 238 ff.

58 William Wilberforce, *A Practical View of the Religious System of Professed Christians, in the Higher and Middle Classes in this Country, Contrasted with Real Christianity,* ed. Daniel Wilson (1798; rpt. Philadelphia: Key and Biddle, 1835), p. 309.

59 Crabb Robinson to Thomas Robinson (17 January 1847), as cited in Batho, *The Later Wordsworth,* p. 238 n.

60 Robert Bloomfield, *The Farmer's Boy, A Rural Poem* (London: Vernon and Hood, 1800), p. ix.

61 For the Evangelical participation in the fight, see Reginald Coupland, *The British Anti-Slavery Movement* (1933; rpt. London: Frank Cass & Co., 1964), pp. 86–111; Audrey Lawson and Herbert Lawson, *The Man Who Freed the Slaves: The Story of William Wilberforce* (London: Faber and Faber, 1962), pp. 58–91.

62 Thomas Clarkson, *History of the Rise, Progress, and Accomplishment of the Abolition of the African Slave Trade by the British Parliament* (London: Longman, Hurst, Rees, and Orme, 1808), 2 : 585–86.

63 Paul Sangster, *Pity My Simplicity: The Evangelical Revival and the Religious Education of Children 1738–1800* (London: Epworth Press, 1964), pp. 110–11.

64  Whiteley, *Wesley's England*, p. 331.
65  In his review of *The Excursion*, Montgomery was somewhat dis-
    turbed that Wordsworth did not more clearly make Christ the
    "chief cornerstone," but in general he was pleased with the poem's
    "evangelical notions," which reminded him of the subjects of
    Cowper's poems. Montgomery concluded that "Mr. W. *could* so
    sing of Christ's kingdom . . . as would for ever set the question at
    rest," and he lavished high praise on *The Excursion:* "The poem
    in my opinion . . . is incomparably the greatest and most beauti-
    ful work of the present age of poetry, and sets Mr. W. beyond
    controversy above all the living and almost all the dead of his
    fraternity. I assure you that, the spirit of that Book . . . so
    possessed me that I have scarcely yet recovered my relish for any
    other modern verse." See Montgomery's untitled review in *The
    Eclectic Review* 3 (January 1815), pp. 19–21, and Dorothy Words-
    worth's lengthy quotations from it in her letter (16 March 1815)
    to Catherine Clarkson (*MY*, 2 : 652). In the same letter Dorothy
    reported "holy Hannah" More's admiration for *The Excursion*
    and expressed pleasure, and some surprise, that "William has made
    a conquest even of *her*" (*MY*, 2 : 655).
66  Robert P. Graves, "Recollections of Wordsworth and the Lake
    Country," *The Afternoon Lectures on Literature and Art* (Dublin:
    W. McGee, 1869), pp. 319–20, as cited in Markham L. Peacock,
    *The Critical Opinions of William Wordsworth* (Baltimore: The
    Johns Hopkins Press, 1950), p. 122.
67  Wilberforce, *A Practical View*, pp. 281–82.

*Chapter 2*

1  In *The Romantic Movement and Methodism* (pp. 79–95), F. C.
   Gill recognizes the importance of Bunyan's influence on the
   Methodists and discusses testimonies by George Shadford, Sampson
   Staniforth, Christopher Hopper, Thomas Olivers, Richard Rodda,
   Thomas Hanson, John Pritchard, John Nelson, and Thomas
   Rankin. For the influence of *Grace Abounding* on the Methodist
   autobiographies, and a demonstration of their continued popularity
   in the nineteenth century, see, for example, T. B. Shepherd,
   *Methodism and the Literature of the Eighteenth Century*, pp.
   143–44.
2  Robert Southey, *The Life of Wesley; and the Rise and Progress
   of Methodism*, 2d ed. (London: Longman, Hurst, Rees, Orme, and
   Brown, 1820), 2 : 86.
3  Griggs, ed., *Collected Letters of Samuel Taylor Coleridge*, 1 : 302.
   Subsequent references to this edition, hereafter abbreviated *CL*,
   appear in the text.

4  See G. A. Starr, *Defoe and Spiritual Autobiography* (Princeton: Princeton University Press, 1965), and J. Paul Hunter, *The Reluctant Pilgrim: Defoe's Emblematic Method and Quest for Form in Robinson Crusoe* (Baltimore: The Johns Hopkins Press, 1966). *Robinson Crusoe* was among the books that made a deep impression on Coleridge from an early age (*CL*, 1 : 347).

5  Wesley defined Christian perfection as "a constant communion with God, which fills the heart with humble love"; "to this," he insisted, "every believer might attain" (see Southey, *The Life of Wesley*, 2 : 183–85). According to this definition, the exhilarating Arminian belief in each man's capacity for a vital spiritual life coexists with Christian humility (chapter 3 examines the implications of the doctrine of perfection for Wordsworth's poetry).

6  William Angus Knight, ed., *The Poetical Works of William Wordsworth* (Edinburgh: W. Paterson, 1889), 2 (vol. 3 of *The Life of William Wordsworth*) : 356–57.

7  Ernest de Selincourt, ed., *Journals of Dorothy Wordsworth* (London: Macmillan, 1941), 1 : 105.

8  For a discussion of the sequence of spiritual events, not just in the lives of the preachers but among many converts to Methodism, see S. G. Dimond, *The Psychology of Methodism* (London: Epworth Press, 1932) and Wilfred Lawson Jones, *A Psychological Study of Religious Conversion* (London: Epworth Press, 1937).

9  At Oxford, before his conversion experience in 1738, Wesley was troubled by the fact that his childhood had seemed a joyless period (he even brought the matter to the attention of his parents, who gave differing responses). In his spiritual experience, joy came only during and after conversion; true joy was impossible for the unconverted (see the discussion in Sangster, *Pity My Simplicity*, pp. 158–68). The argument above employs Wesley's view that childhood is the proper period for the development of humility.

10 For a recent comprehensive study of psychological development in the persona of *The Prelude*, see Richard J. Onorato, *The Character of the Poet: Wordsworth in The Prelude* (Princeton: Princeton University Press, 1971). Jonathan Bishop, in "Wordsworth and the 'Spots of Time,'" *ELH* 26 (1959) : 45–65, sees a chastening of the persona's pride and guilt, but he emphasizes the psychological aspects of this pattern. Herbert Lindenberger's emphasis is primarily structural (see *On Wordsworth's Prelude* [Princeton: Princeton University Press, 1963]), and Hartman stresses Hebraic elements in the spots of time (see *Wordsworth's Poetry*, p. 225). See also Alan Grob, "Wordsworth's *Nutting*," *Journal of English and Germanic Philology* 61 (1962) : 826–32.

11 The stolen boat episode and the Esthwaite skating scene, both of which appear in Book I of *The Prelude*, were composed in Goslar, Germany, in the winter of 1799.

12  Hyder Edward Rollins, ed., *The Letters of John Keats 1814–1821* (Cambridge, Mass.: Harvard University Press, 1958), 1 : 223, 265, 387. For suggestions that Wordsworth was a representative Romantic solipsist, see, for example, remarks by Owen Barfield and J. H. Van den Berg in *Romanticism and Consciousness: Essays in Criticism,* ed. Harold Bloom (New York: W. W. Norton & Co., 1970), pp. 41–46, 57–65.

13  P. P. Howe, ed., *The Complete Works of William Hazlitt* (London: J. M. Dent & Sons, 1932), 11 : 87.

14  David Perkins, ed., *English Romantic Writers* (New York: Harcourt, Brace, and World, 1967), p. 256 n.

15  For the hymn, see James Montgomery, *The Wanderer of Switzerland, and other poems* (Morristown, Pa.: Johnson, 1811), pp. 110–12; for "The Peak Mountains," see Robert Carruthers, ed., *The Poetical Works of James Montgomery* (Boston: Houghton, Mifflin, and Co., 1858), 2 : 139–41. Subsequent references to the latter edition appear in the text.

16  The titles of Wesley's relevant essays (cited in the text) are as follows: "On the Education of Children," "On Obedience to Parents," and "Of the Nature and Design of our Afflictions and Mortality." G. E. Harrison's *Son to Susanna: The Private Life of John Wesley* and Paul Sangster's *Pity My Simplicity: The Evangelical Revival and the Religious Education of Children 1738–1800* provide delightful studies of the Evangelicals' practice in rearing children.

17  Wordsworth recommended in 1808 that Christians read Law's *A Serious Call to a Devout and Holy Life* (1728); see *MY,* 1 : 225. Newton P. Stallknecht, in *Strange Seas of Thought: Studies in William Wordsworth's Philosophy of Man and Nature,* has suggested that Law was instrumental in transmitting to Wordsworth the mysticism of Jakob Boehme.

18  The phrase is Isaiah's: "But we are all as an unclean thing, and all our righteousnesses are as filthy rags; and we all do fade as a leaf; and our iniquities, like the wind, have taken us away" (64 : 6). The controversy over this and similar texts was troublesome to Wesley. When some of his fellow preachers became antinomian and proclaimed that morality was worthless, he rebuked them for going a bit too far. For his sympathy with antinomianism, see Wesley, 8 : 284–85. For his reservations about it, see Wesley, 8 : 300; 9 : 101–02, 110; 10 : 399–401; 11 : 430–32; 12 : 297. For his animadversions against the antinomianism among Calvinists, see Wesley, 8 : 278, 328, 336–37, 433.

19  Alexander Cruden, *A Complete Concordance to the Holy Scriptures of the Old and New Testament; or, A Dictionary and Alphabetical Index to the Bible,* 3d ed. (New York: Dodd Mead & Co., 1823), p. 219.

20 Henry Stebbing, ed., *The Works of John Bunyan* (London: J. S. Virtue, 1859; rpt. New York: Johnson Reprint Corporation, 1970), 1 : 5. Bunyan's recollection appears in *Grace Abounding*.

21 John Woolman, *A Journal of the Life, Gospel Labours, and Christian Experiences of that Faithful Minister of Jesus Christ, John Woolman* (1776; rpt. Philadelphia: T. E. Chapman, 1837), pp. 13–14. This citation documents subsequent references and quotations.

22 For philosophically oriented discussions, see, for example, Colin Clarke, *Romantic Paradox: An Essay on the Poetry of Wordsworth* (New York: Barnes & Noble, 1963); E. D. Hirsch, Jr., *Wordsworth and Schelling: A Typological Study of Romanticism* (New Haven: Yale University Press, 1960); M. H. Abrams, "Structure and Style in the Greater Romantic Lyric," in *From Sensibility to Romanticism,* ed. Hilles and Bloom; Robert Langbaum, *The Poetry of Experience: The Dramatic Monologue in Modern Literary Tradition* (London: Chatto & Windus, 1957); and Alan Grob, *The Philosophic Mind: A Study of Wordsworth's Poetry and Thought, 1797–1805* (Columbus: Ohio State University Press, 1973). In "The Rhetoric of Temporality," appearing in Charles Singleton, ed., *Interpretation: Theory and Practice* (Baltimore: The Johns Hopkins University Press, 1969), pp. 173–208, Paul de Man has taken issue with the subject/object, epistemological emphasis of recent criticism of the Romantics; the creative transcendence of the subject-object dualism, along with the concomitant transcendence of time, is not the authentic moment in Wordsworth but, according to de Man, precisely the reverse: man's authentic destiny is temporal. Wordsworth, I believe, combined the epistemological and Evangelical idioms to delineate man's spiritual destiny (see especially my chapter 3).

23 Potts, *Wordsworth's Prelude,* pp. 226–27.

24 In *Innocence and Experience: An Introduction to Blake* (New Haven: Yale University Press, 1964), for example, E. D. Hirsch, Jr. has suggested that "Spring," from *The Songs of Innocence,* effects a "fusion of the natural with the prophetic or visionary landscape" and prophesies in its opening words—"Sound the Flute! / Now it's mute"—"the last trumpet" (p. 39). For similar suggestions concerning aural imagery and apocalyptic landscape in Romantic poetry, see Harold Bloom's discussion of Keats's "To Autumn" in *The Visionary Company: A Reading of English Romantic Poetry* (New York: Doubleday, 1961), pp. 422–25. Geoffrey Hartman, devoting considerable attention to the passage on the boy of Winander, argues that his "tumultuous mimicry" is interrupted by a pause "gently foretelling" "a later state of mind": "the consciousness of nature's separate life"; see *Wordsworth's Poetry,* p. 19.

25 James Blanton Wharey, ed., *The Pilgrim's Progress from this World to That which is to Come* (Oxford: Clarendon Press, 1928), p. 169. Subsequent references to this edition appear in the text.
26 Cited in Sangster, *Pity My Simplicity*, p. 56.
27 Stebbing, ed., *The Complete Works of John Bunyan*, 1 : 25.
28 For a skillful analysis of this tradition as employed by Pope, see Aubrey L. Williams, "The 'Fall' of China and *The Rape of the Lock*," *Philological Quarterly* 41 (1962) : 412–25.
29 The early version differs markedly only in the concluding lines:

> And it was proved indeed that not in vain
> I had been taught to reverence a Power
> That is the very quality and shape
> And image of right reason, that matures
> Her processes by steadfast laws, gives birth
> To no impatient or fallacious hopes,
> No heat of passion, or excessive zeal,
> No vain conceits, provokes to no quick turns
> Of self-applauding intellect, but lifts
> The Being into magnanimity . . . .
>
> [XII.21–32]

Wordsworth's designation of the Power as "the very quality and shape / And image of right reason," in terms of the epistemological language of empiricist philosophy, linguistically establishes both the internal and the external reality of an apparently traditional *ratio recta*. "The very quality" is a phrase suggesting the thing in itself, apart from any perception of it; and the words *shape* and *image*, of course, refer to truth as visibly perceived and perhaps therefore wholly internalized. Simultaneously, then, the poet sustains the dual *loci* of reality and, by means of the unifying coordinate conjunction, avoids the problem of dualism; and the phrase in the later version, "the visible quality," suggests in three words that the Power is both autonomous and mind-dependent without being delimited or dichotomized.

30 The phrase is Wordsworth's and occurs in his famous recollection in the Fenwick note to "Ode: Intimations of Immortality from Recollections of Early Childhood," a recollection that shows how he wrestled in his boyhood with solipsistic tendencies: "I was often unable to think of external things as having external existence, and I communed with all that I saw as something not apart from, but inherent in, my own immaterial nature. Many times while going to school have I grasped at a wall or tree to recall myself from this abyss of idealism to the reality. At that time I was afraid of such processes" (*PW*, 4 : 463).

We have seen that, according to his testimony in *The Prelude*, Wordsworth's early struggle with self was more moral and spiritual than philosophic in nature, and indeed it is difficult to imagine a youth, however precocious, with the perceptual and epistemological sophistication of a Thomas Hobbes or a David Hume. Compare Coleridge's similarly pejorative use of the word *idealism* in his own comments on the solipsistic problem: "It is the table itself, which the man of common sense believes himself to see, not the phantom of a table, from which he may argumentatively deduce the reality of a table, which he does not see. If to destroy the reality of all, that we actually behold, be idealism, what can be more egregiously so, than the system of modern metaphysics, which banishes us to a land of shadows, surrounds us with apparitions, and distinguishes truth from illusion only by the majority of those who dream the same dream? '*I* asserted that the world was mad,' exclaimed poor Lee, 'and the world said, that I was mad, and confound them, they outvoted me.' " See S. T. Coleridge, *Biographia Literaria,* ed. John Shawcross (London: Humphrey Milford, 1907), 1 : 179.

Geoffrey Hartman, in his extensive discussion of the passage on crossing the Alps, sees religious implications in the poet's sudden change (though he does not stress, as I do, the moral and spiritual function of Wordsworth's imagination): "Wordsworth's experience, like Petrarch's or Augustine's, is a conversion: a turning about of the mind as from one belief to its opposite, and a turning *ad se ipsum*" (*Wordsworth's Poetry,* p. 49). As contrasted with a philosophical self-sufficiency, a spiritual self-possession seems to me to characterize the persona of *The Prelude* (see the discussion throughout chapter 3).

*Chapter 3*

1   Taylor's *Natural History of Enthusiasm* (London: Holdsworth & Ball, 1830) and *Fanaticism* (London: Holdsworth, 1833) were among Wordsworth's books; see *Transactions of the Wordsworth Society,* 6 (10 May 1884) : 226.
2   Isaac Taylor, *Four Lectures on Spiritual Christianity* (London: H. Bohn, 1841), p. 107.
3   John Fletcher, *The Works of the Rev. John Fletcher, Late Vicar of Madeley* (London, 1826), 6 : 190–92. Subsequent references to this edition appear in the text.
4   In his sermon "The Christian Temper," Wrangham urged men to establish "secret contact" with God's Spirit; see his *Thirteen Practical Sermons,* p. 106. Clarkson wrote at length about the contemporary Quaker emphasis on God's gift of the Spirit; without this "principle," he observed, Quaker religion would become "no more Christianity, than the dead carcass of a man, when the

spirit is departed." He added that the "excellent," "worthy," and "desirable" characteristics of the entire Christian faith should be ascribed to the effects of the Spirit's witness; see his *A Portraiture of Quakerism* (New York: Samuel Stansbury, 1806), 2 : 154, 159, 208, 276, 279. For Wilberforce's discussion of the contemporary "operations of the Holy Spirit," see, for example, *A Practical View*, pp. 104–29.

5 Southey, *The Life of Wesley*, 2 : 127.

6 For a discussion of Wesley's views on conversion—as expressed in his sermons "The New Birth" and "The Marks of the New Birth" (nos. 39 and 14, respectively, in Sugden's edition of the "standard" sermons)—and Whitefield's views on conversion—as expressed in the sermons "Marks of Having Received the Holy Ghost" and "Of Regeneration" (nos. 42 and 49, respectively, in John Gillies, ed., *The Works of the Reverend George Whitefield*, 6 vols. [London: E. and C. Dilly, 1771–72)—see Davies, *Worship and Theology in England*, pp. 153–60.

7 Henry's *Baptismal Covenant* is included in the anonymous Presbyterian manual, *The Celebration of Infant-Baptism among Protestant Dissenters* (London, 1747), p. 13.

8 I follow the Evangelicals' occasional practice of capitalizing the terms *Ordinary* and *Extraordinary;* I do so in discussing Wordsworth's poetry only when his spiritual idiom seems especially precise.

9 Taylor, *Four Lectures on Spiritual Christianity*, p. 101.

10 For the origins of covenant church organization, see, for example, Davies, *Worship and Theology in England*, pp. 25, 94–113, 128–39.

11 Robert Browne, *A Booke which sheweth the Life and Manners of all True Christians* (Middelburgh, Belgium: Richarde Painter, 1582), p. 2.

12 As quoted in *The Baptist Quarterly* 3 (1926–27) : 28.

13 For Robinson's views on the Spirit's daily guidance, see *A History of Baptism* (London: Thomas Knott, 1790), pp. 536–37.

14 John Wesley, *Directions for Renewing our Covenant with God*, 5th ed. (London: G. Whitfield, 1794), pp. 13–14.

15 Newton Flew, *The Idea of Perfection in Christian Theology* (1934; rpt. New York: Humanities Press, 1968), p. 405.

16 Frederick Maurice, ed., *The Life of Frederick Denison Maurice* (New York: Macmillan, 1884), 2 : 59. The passage has been quoted by Lindenberger (*On Wordsworth's Prelude*, p. 276) and Abrams (*Natural Supernaturalism*, pp. 122–23).

17 In 1798, for example, when Coleridge preached at the Unitarian chapel in Shrewsbury, he reflected the spiritual themes of the Evangelical ministry. Hazlitt, in "My First Acquaintance with Poets," describes the effect: "A poet and a philosopher getting up

into a Unitarian pulpit to preach the Gospel, was a romance in these degenerate days, *a sort of revival of the primitive spirit of Christianity,* which was not to be resisted" (my italics). See Carl R. Woodring, ed., *Prose of the Romantic Period* (Boston: Houghton Mifflin, 1961), p. 280.

18  Alan Grob, in "Wordsworth and Godwin: A Reassessment," *Studies in Romanticism* 6 (1967) : 98–119, argues that Wordsworth was Godwinian whenever he responded to rationality rather than feelings and experience and anti-Godwinian whenever he responded to an ethics based on self-interest; Grob, like R. D. Havens (in *The Mind of a Poet*), thus takes a middle position between Legouis (who in *La Jeunesse de William Wordsworth* argues that the poet rejected Godwinianism as early as *The Borderers* [1797]) and H. W. Garrod (who in *Wordsworth* views even *The Borderers* as Godwinian). Helen Darbishire, in "Wordsworth's Belief in the Doctrine of Necessity," *Review of English Studies* 24 (1948) : 121–25, distinguishes between Wordsworth's idea of the perfectibility of man and that of Godwin; Wordsworth's idea, as I argue above, closely resembles the doctrine of Christian perfection. And his religious response to the Revolution is consistent with what we have learned about his political views. F. M. Todd (*Politics and the Poet*) argues that his early liberalism was not deeply rooted, and Carl Woodring (*Politics in English Romantic Poetry*) suggests that *The Prelude* seriously questions whether a poet can enter the world of action and power without compromising himself.

19  The early version, though somewhat less explicitly religious in tone, differs in only a few details:

> . . . yea I could almost
> Have pray'd that throughout earth upon all souls
> By patient exercise of reason made
> Worthy of liberty, upon every soul
> Matured to live in plainness and in truth
> The gift of tongues might fall, and men arrive
> From the four quarters of the winds to do
> For France what without help she could not do,
> A work of honour; think not that to this
> I added, work of safety; from such thought
> And the least fear about the end of things
> I was as far as Angels are from guilt.
>
>                                                    [X.117–28]

20  Bostetter and Hartman, in *The Romantic Ventriloquists* and *Wordsworth's Poetry,* respectively, see the poem as a flight from vision. J. S. Lyon, in *The Excursion: A Study* (New Haven: Yale University Press, 1950), discusses the reputation, composition, style,

content, and sources; the Christianity of the poem, he argues, "is incomplete and occasionally heterodox" (p. 113).

21 See Hartman, *Wordsworth's Poetry*, p. 292.

22 Albert Gérard, in "Dark Passages: Exploring *Tintern Abbey*," *Studies in Romanticism* 3 (1963) : 10–23, sees a "systolic rhythm" between passages of affirmation and passages in which the diffident speaker recoils from vision. Harold Bloom, in *The Visionary Company*, finds signs of desperation and waning faith toward the end of the poem. See also the discussion of the play of faith and doubt in Eudo C. Mason's *Versdichtung der englischen Romantik*.

23 Jonathan Edwards's *A Treatise Concerning Religious Affections* (Boston: S. Kneeland and T. Green, 1746), included in Wesley's *Christian Library*, identifies human affections with such New Testament graces as hope, love, joy, and gratitude (p. 10).

24 For a discussion of the persona's escape, see Albert Gérard's " 'Resolution and Independence': Wordsworth's Coming of Age," *English Studies in Africa* 3 (1960) : 8–20. See also Anthony E. M. Conran's "The Dialectic of Experience: A Study of Wordsworth's *Resolution and Independence*," *PMLA* 75 (1960) : 66–74. Alan Grob, in "Process and Permanence in *Resolution and Independence*," *ELH* 28 (1961) : 89–100, and Bostetter, in *The Romantic Ventriloquists*, both discuss the waning importance of nature.

25 Jane Worthington, *Wordsworth's Reading of Roman Prose* (New Haven: Yale University Press, 1946), pp. 61–65.

*Chapter 4*

1 The description of God's sublimity in nature is found in Erasmus Warren, *Geologia; or, A Discourse concerning the Earth before the Deluge, Wherein the Form and Properties Ascribed to It, in a Book Intituled The Theory of the Earth, Are Excepted Against, and It Is Made to Appear That the Dissolution of That Earth Was Not the Cause of the Universal Flood* (London, 1690), pp. 121–22, as quoted in Marjorie Hope Nicolson, *Mountain Gloom and Mountain Glory: The Development of the Aesthetics of the Infinite* (1959; rpt. New York: W. W. Norton & Co., 1963), p. 267.

I am indebted to James B. Twitchell for reading and commenting on this chapter.

2 For discussions of the medieval interpretation of the book of nature, see, for example, D. W. Robertson, Jr., *A Preface to Chaucer: Studies in Medieval Perspectives* (Princeton: Princeton University Press, 1962); Rosemund Tuve, *Allegorical Imagery: Some Medieval Books and their Posterity* (Princeton: Princeton University Press, 1966); Beryl Smalley, *The Study of the Bible in the Middle Ages* (Notre Dame, Ind.: University of Notre Dame Press, 1964). For

the survival of this tradition in the eighteenth century, see Victor
Harris, "Allegory to Analogy in the Interpretation of Scriptures,"
*Philological Quarterly* 45 (1966) : 1–23.

3  For indispensable studies of Wordsworth's critical theory, see
M. H. Abrams, *The Mirror and the Lamp: Romantic Theory and
the Critical Tradition* (1953; rpt. New York: W. W. Norton & Co.,
1958) and James A. W. Heffernan, *Wordsworth's Theory of Poetry:
The Transforming Imagination* (Ithaca: Cornell University Press,
1969). For the philosophical implications of his natural imagery,
see, for example, Herbert Lindenberger, *On Wordsworth's Prelude*
and W. K. Wimsatt, "The Structure of Romantic Nature Imagery,"
in his *The Verbal Icon* (Lexington: University of Kentucky Press,
1954).

4  For Luther's view ("All creatures, yea, even the sun and moon,
have as it were put on sackcloth; they were all originally 'good', but
by sin and the curse they have become defiled and noxious"), see
J. M. Lenker, ed., *Critical and Devotional Commentaries on
Genesis* (Minneapolis: The Luther Press, 1904), 1 : 152–53. For
Calvin's view ("On all his works [God] hath inscribed his glory in
characters so clear, unequivocal, and striking, that the most il-
literate and stupid cannot exculpate themselves from the plea of
ignorance"), see John Calvin, *Institutes of the Christian Religion*
(1536; New Haven, 1816), 1 : 61. For Burnet's commentary on the
Alps, see Thomas Burnet, *The Sacred Theory of the Earth: Con-
taining an Account of the Original of the Earth and of All the
General Changes Which It Hath Already Undergone or Is to
Undergo, till the Consummation of All Things*, 6th ed. (London:
J. Hooke, 1726), 1 : 173–74. The natural theologies represented by
Calvin and Luther, as well as Burnet's eclectic view of nature, are
discussed in Nicolson, *Mountain Gloom and Mountain Glory*,
pp. 96–104, 184–270.

5  James Hervey, *Meditations and Contemplations*, 28th ed. (Lon-
don: A. Law, W. Miller, & T. Martin, 1794), 1 : 208–09, 246–47.

6  John Newton, *Letters and Sermons, With a Review of Ecclesiasti-
cal History, and Hymns*, ed. T. Haweis (London, 1787), 1 : 210–11.
Subsequent references to this edition appear in the text.

7  The quotation appears in Coleridge's *Statesman's Manual* (appen-
dix B); see his *Lay Sermons*, 3d ed. (London: Moxon, 1852), pp.
74–75.

8  William Powell Jones, *The Rhetoric of Sciences: A Study of Scien-
tific Ideas and Imagery in Eighteenth-century English Poetry* (Berke-
ley: University of California Press, 1966), pp. 8–9, 233–35, and
passim.

9  L. N. Broughton, ed., *Wordsworth and Reed* (Ithaca: Cornell
University Press, 1933), p. 144.

10  Francis Quarles, *Emblems, Divine and Moral; together with*

*Hieroglyphics of the Life of Man,* ed. Augustus Toplady (London, 1823), p. ix. Subsequent references to this edition appear in the text.

11 The phrase is used in Hunter's *The Reluctant Pilgrim: Defoe's Emblematic Method and Quest for Form in Robinson Crusoe* (Baltimore: The Johns Hopkins Press, 1966). For a discussion of Bunyan's emblems, see David J. Alpaugh, "Emblem and Interpretation in *The Pilgrim's Progress*," *ELH* 33 (1966) : 299–314. For pioneering discussions of Wordsworth's emblems, see James R. Baird's "Wordsworth's 'Inscrutable Workmanship' and the Emblems of Reality," *PMLA* 68 (1953) : 444–57, Enid Welsford's *Salisbury Plain: A Study in the Development of Wordsworth's Mind and Art,* and James Heffernan's *Wordsworth's Theory of Poetry* (Heffernan's discussion concentrates on *The White Doe of Rylstone*). For the quotation from *Pilgrim's Progress,* see John Bunyan, *The Pilgrim's Progress from this World to That Which is to Come,* ed. James Blanton Wharey (Oxford: Clarendon Press, 1928), pp. 212, 216; subsequent references to this edition, hereafter abbreviated "Wharey," appear in the text.

12 See Emblems ii, viii, and xiii of Book IV, in the following widely available nineteenth-century edition: Charles Bennett and W. Harry Rogers, eds., *Quarles' Emblems* (London: James Nisbet and Co., 1861), pp. 200, 224, 244.

13 In one notable formulation of this doctrine, the famous nineteenth-century Evangelical minister, the Reverend Henry Melvill, seems to associate the doctrine with the reading of the book of nature: "The Bible is as actually a divine communication as though its words came to us in the voice of Almighty, mysteriously syllabled, and breathed from the firmament" ("The Advantages Resulting from Possession of the Scriptures" [New York, 1854], 1 : 159, as cited in George Landow, *The Aesthetic and Critical Theories of John Ruskin* [Princeton: Princeton University Press, 1971], p. 354). Professor Landow traces the increasing emphasis on this doctrine during the nineteenth century, an emphasis understandable in terms of the Evangelicals' intellectual responses to philosophical empiricism, natural science, biblical criticism, and comparative philology (see pp. 352–56); he also has an excellent discussion of the allegorizing of nature among the Evangelicals (pp. 321–427).

14 Clarkson's Evangelicalism can be seen, for example, in his participation with Wilberforce in the fight against the slave trade (see pp. 33–34). See also Reginald Coupland, *The British Anti-Slavery Movement* (1933; rpt. London: Frank Cass & Co., 1964), pp. 86–111; Audrey Lawson and Herbert Lawson, *The Man Who Freed the Slaves: The Story of William Wilberforce* (London: Faber and Faber, 1962), pp. 58–91.

15 Deism was anathema to the Evangelicals. Wordsworth's friend the

Reverend Francis Wrangham, in his edition of Philip Doddridge's *The Evidences of Christianity,* stresses the Deists' response to Doddridge's book, an early work (1758) of the Great Awakening (see pp. 17–18); Wrangham cites Job Orton's testimony that "these sermons convinced two Deists that Christianity was true and divine" (p. 3). For the relationship between Deism and Evangelicalism, see, for example, Davies, *Worship and Theology in England,* pp. 143, 159, 167, 173, 179, 202.

16  John Wilson, *Essays Critical and Imaginative* (Edinburgh: W. Blackwood & Sons, 1867), 5 : 397.

17  Thomas Clarkson, *A Portraiture of Quakerism, as taken from a view of the moral education, discipline, peculiar customs, religious principles, political and civil oeconomy, and character, of the Society of Friends* (New York: Samuel Stansbury, 1806), 2 : 128–29. Subsequent references to this edition appear in the text.

18  On 23 July 1806, Dorothy informed Catherine Clarkson that "Wm has read most of Mr. Clarkson's book and has been much pleased" (*MY,* 1 : 47–48). In her letters to Catherine, Dorothy referred to the book twelve times from February of 1805 to June of 1808 (*MY,* 1 : 16–17, 34, 38–39, 42, 47–48, 118, 154–56, 184, 229).

19  See Potts, *Wordsworth's Prelude,* p. 203.

20  George Landow (*The Aesthetic and Critical Theories of John Ruskin,* p. 344) cites Henry Melvill's commentary on Exodus 11 : 6: "The circumstances of the rock yielding no water, until smitten by the rod of Moses, represented the important truth, that the Mediator must receive the blows of the law before he could be the source of salvation to a parched and perishing world" (*Sermons* [London, 1836], pp. 163–64).

21  Bennett and Rogers, eds., *Quarles' Emblems,* pp. 58, 60. William Wordsworth, *The Prose Works of William Wordsworth,* ed. Alexander B. Grosart (London: Moxon, 1876), 1 : 319.

22  C. R. Leslie, *Memoirs of the Life of John Constable,* ed. Jonathan Mayne (London: Phaidon Press, 1951), p. 73, as cited in Russell Noyes, *Wordsworth and the Art of Landscape,* p. 79.

23  This passage, with its explicit Christian content, is a late interpolation and does not appear in the highly regarded 1799 version ("MS. D"), which has recently been transcribed by Jonathan Wordsworth in *The Music of Humanity: A Critical Study of Wordsworth's "Ruined Cottage"* (London: Nelson, 1969). We now tend to think that Margaret's story as told in Book I "is attenuated in style, and attempts to mitigate the impact of Margaret's sufferings . . . by attributing to her a Christian piety which is conventional rather than deeply realized" (see M. H. Abrams's commentary in Abrams et al., ed., *The Norton Anthology of English Literature: Revised,* Major Authors Edition [New York:

W. W. Norton & Co., 1968, pp. 1285–86]). We admire the early version because, as Abrams puts it, Wordsworth makes us "feel what it is to be able to look upon and master the fact of human suffering, unsupported by any consoling creed of a beneficent power, whether in or out of nature."

I do not question the effectiveness of "MS. D," nor do I suggest that *Excursion* I is without flaw. Above, however, I stress the continuity of Wordsworth's thought and indicate my growing conviction, based on the consistency of his symbology, that when he revised he did not so much introduce his religious point of view as he further brought it out; the "Christian piety" in *The Excursion* might have been intended to make explicit the implicit religious character of Margaret's hope as it repeatedly surfaces in the early version. It is true, Wordsworth does not often mention a "beneficent power" in "The Ruined Cottage" (though God is praised near the beginning [l. 132]), but he does imply a "consoling creed": Margaret finds the strength to hope (ll. 132, 277, 359). She finds such strength even at the end, where, though sick and dying, she continues to wait for her husband and hope for his return:

> She loved this wretched spot, nor would for worlds
> Have parted hence; and still that length of road,
> And this rude bench, one torturing hope endeared,
> Fast rooted at the heart.
>
> [ll. 487–90]

Thus she exemplifies faithful endurance. In Book I the Wanderer takes a similar view of her, and his "conventional" piety is poetically functional: it adds thematic justification for a hope hitherto warranted for reasons only partially expressed.

24 H. W. Piper, *The Active Universe: Pantheism and the Concept of Imagination in the English Romantic Poets* (London: The Athlone Press, 1962), pp. 16–19 and passim.

25 Denis Diderot, *Oeuvres complètes*, ed. J. Assézat (Paris, 1875–77), 2 : 47–48, as cited and translated by Piper, *The Active Universe*, p. 20. Diderot's observation was made in response to a scientific treatise by Pierre-Louis Moreau de Maupertuis, entitled *Essai sur la formation des corps organisés* (Berlin, 1754).

26 Donald Greene, *The Age of Exuberance: Backgrounds to Eighteenth-Century English Literature* (New York: Random House, 1970), p. 4.

27 For British influence on German Pietism, see, for example, August Lang, *Puritanismus und Pietismus: Studien zu ihrer Entwicklung von M. Butzer bis zum Methodismus* (Neukirchen: Kreis Moers, 1941); and Auguste Sann, *Bunyan in Deutschland: Studien zur*

*literarischen Wechselbeziehung zwischen England und dem deut-*
*schen Pietismus* (Giessen: W. Schmitz, 1951). Sann (pp.
62–86) indicates the presence of a once-removed Puritanism and Evangeli-
calism in the work of poets such as Klopstock, to whom Words-
worth was introduced in 1799. For a discussion of Puritan typology
in America, see Charles Feidelson, Jr., *Symbolism and American
Literature* (Chicago: University of Chicago Press, 1953), p. 90.

28   Bostetter, for example, has argued that Wordsworth's myth of
interchange between man and nature is largely confined to his
periods of subjective happiness (e.g. 1797–1800); see *The Roman-
tic Ventriloquists.* And David Ferry, in *The Limits of Mortality:
An Essay on Wordsworth's Major Poems* (Middletown, Conn.:
Wesleyan University Press, 1959), discerns times when Wordsworth's
attitude toward nature was ambivalent because of a tension be-
tween his sacramentalist and mystical concepts.

# INDEX

Abrams, M. H., 9, 172, 192, 194–95
Alford, Henry, 9–10, 36
Anglicanism: and Dissent, 5; and Evangelicalism, 6; and spiritual aspiration, 10–11; and church order, 21–22; its homiletical tradition, 26, 119
Annesley, Samuel, 5
*Arminian Magazine, The*, 34, 38, 173, 179
Arminianism, 30, 38, 39. *See also* Calvinist/Arminian controversy
Assurance, doctrine of, 120, 133–34
Atkinson, Christopher, 179
Augustine, Saint, of Hippo, 6, 11–12

Balleine, G. R., 4
Baptists, 5, 75, 98. *See also* Bunyan, John; Robinson, Robert
Barker, John, 6–7
Barrow, Isaac, 26
Batho, Edith C., 14–15
Beatty, Arthur, ix
Beaumont, Sir George, 13, 28, 29, 37–38
Beaupuy, Michel, 104–06
Bell, Andrew, 34
Bellow, Saul, 2
Bentley, Richard, 146
Benziger, James, 175
Berkeley, Bishop George, 165
Berridge, John, 20–21, 27, 99, 179
Bett, Henry, 6

Bible: New Testament, 11; John, 12; Isaiah 9 : 2, 17; John 8 : 32, 19; Luke 10 : 25–37, 31; Matthew 25 : 35–36, 32; Matthew 6 : 19–20, 32; John 8 : 32–33, 33; Ephesians 4 : 22–24, 38, 95, 137; Luke 15 : 11–32, 41; Hebrews 12 : 5–9, 46; I Corinthians 13 : 4, 48; Matthew 25 : 33–34, 49; Zechariah 13 : 1, 49; Revelation 21 : 1, 52; I Corinthians 15 : 52, 58; Ephesians 5 : 22–24, 59; I Peter 3 : 7, 60; Ephesians 4 : 14, 60; Matthew 7 : 14, 64; Revelation 1 : 8, 65; Ephesians 5 : 9, 70; Ephesians 5 : 19–20, 70, 96; Acts 2 : 33, 70; 2 Timothy 1 : 7, 70; Galatians 5 : 22–23, 70; Romans 5 : 4, 70; I Peter 1 : 8, 71; Romans 5 : 5, 71; John 14, 73; James 1 : 4, 76; James 2 : 22, 76; Hebrews 13 : 20–21, 76; John 17 : 19, 76; I John 5 : 17, 77; John 17 : 22–23, 77; I Corinthians 2 : 1–6, 83; Ephesians 5 : 18–19, 97; Mark 13 : 26–35, 97; Matthew 20 : 1–16, 99; Hebrews 12 : 23, 120, 138; Matthew 6 : 28, 120; Exodus 11 : 6, 121, 157; Ezekiel 9 : 19–20, 122; Matthew 6 : 26–30, 127; Psalms 33 : 18, 132; Hebrews 12 : 23, 138; Psalms 19 : 1–6, 139; Isaiah 40 : 6, 148; John 11 : 25, 159; Isaiah 64 :6, 185
Birrell, Augustine, 7